LOVE IN A COOL CLIMATE

Love in a Cool Climate

The letters of
Mark Pattison and Meta Bradley,
1879–1884

VIVIAN GREEN
Rector of Lincoln College, Oxford

CLARENDON PRESS · OXFORD
1985

Oxford University Press, Walton Street, Oxford OX2 6DP

Oxford New York Toronto
Delhi Bombay Calcutta Madras Karachi
Kuala Lumpur Singapore Hong Kong Tokyo
Nairobi Dar es Salaam Cape Town
Melbourne Auckland

and associated companies in
Beirut Berlin Ibadan Nicosia

Oxford is a trade mark of Oxford University Press

Published in the United States
by Oxford University Press, New York

© Vivian Green 1985

British Library Cataloguing in Publication Data

Pattison, Mark
Love in a cool climate: the letters of Mark
Pattison and Meta Bradley, 1879-1884.
1. Oxford (Oxfordshire)–Social life and customs
I. Title   II. Bradley, Meta   III. Green, Vivian
942.5′74081   DA690.09
ISBN 0-19-820080-3

Library of Congress Cataloging in Publication Data

Pattison, Mark, 1813-1884.
Love in a cool climate.
Bibliography: p.
Includes index.
1. Pattison, Mark, 1813-1884.   2. Bradley, Meta,
1853-1923.   3. Oxford University. Lincoln College–
Presidents–Biography.   4. College presidents–
England-Correspondence.   I. Bradley, Meta, 1853-1923.
II. Green, Vivian Hubert Howard.   III. Title.
LF624.P3P37 1985   378′.111 [B]   85-13883
ISBN 0-19-820080-3

Typeset by Joshua Associates Limited, Oxford
Printed and bound in Great Britain by
Biddles Limited, Guildford and King's Lynn

For

W. S. S.

who understands the reason

Acknowledgements

My thanks are due to the Curators of the Bodleian Library, Oxford, and to the Keeper of the Western Manuscripts for access to the Pattison manuscripts which have made this book possible; to Sir John Winnifrith and Mrs Mary Bennett for the loan of letters; and for illustrations the National Portrait Gallery, London (Mrs Pattison and Sir Charles Dilke), John Sparrow Esq. (Rector Pattison), Sir John Winnifrith (Meta Bradley and the Revd Charles Bradley), and Thomas Photos, Oxford. I am also grateful to Mr John Sparrow for his careful reading of the manuscript.

Contents

Illustrations

between pp. 142 and 143

Dramatis Personae

Meta Bradley, their daughter (1853-1923).

Lettice, later Mrs H. A. L. Fisher, and Olive, later Mrs Heseltine, daughters of Jessie and Courtenay Ilbert.

OXFORD PERSONALITIES

Thomas Fowler, fellow and sub-rector of Lincoln College (1855-82), later President of Corpus Christi College (d. 1904).

Donald Crawford (1837-1919), fellow of Lincoln College (1861-82), lawyer and liberal politician, married to Virginia, daughter of Mrs Eustace Smith (d. 1948).

Ingram Bywater (1840-1914), classical scholar, fellow of Exeter College.

Henry Smith (1826-83), mathematician, fellow of Corpus Christi College.

Ellen, his sister, correspondent of Mr and Mrs Pattison.

Rhoda Broughton (1840-1920), novelist, living in Oxford.

Mrs Percival, née Louise Holland, wife of John Percival, President of Trinity College, Oxford (1879-87).

Benjamin Jowett (1817-93), Master of Balliol College, Oxford.

ACQUAINTANCES AND FRIENDS

Sir Andrew Clark, medical specialist, physician to Mark Pattison and Charles Bradley.

Dr Tuckwell, Pattison's Oxford physician, related by marriage to Mrs Pattison.

May Laffan, Irish novelist, friend of Pattison.

Mrs Hertz and Mrs Pfeiffer, poetess and authoress, friends of Pattison.

Mrs Thursfield, wife of J. R. Thursfield, fellow of Jesus College, Oxford, friend of Pattison.

Fanny Kensington, friend of Pattison and Meta Bradley.

Grace Toynbee, later Mrs Percy Frankland, sister of Arnold and Mary Toynbee, friend of Meta Bradley and Pattison.

Helen Colvill, novelist (Katherine Wylde), friend of Meta Bradley.

Gertrude Tuckwell, niece of Mrs Pattison, often stayed at the Rector's Lodgings in Oxford.

Alfred Milner (1854-1925), fellow of New College, journalist, later statesman (Viscount Milner), pupil of Jowett, friend of Meta Bradley.

The Revd R. M. Tabor, Headmaster of Cheam School, friend of Meta Bradley.

Lewis Campbell (1830-1908), Professor of Greek at St. Andrews, pupil and future biographer of Jowett, friend of Meta Bradley.

Henry Hart, headmaster of Sedbergh School, friend of Meta Bradley

Mr and Mrs Tomkinson, friends of Meta Bradley.

Mrs Hilton, née Christina Sanders, married to the Revd Musgrave Hilton the vicar of West Lavington, Sussex (1878-85), friend of Meta Bradley.

Introduction

THE principal source for this study is the collection of 450 or so
letters which passed between the Oxford scholar, Mark Pattison,
the Rector of Lincoln College, and Miss Meta Bradley, a young
woman some forty years his junior, between 1879 and 1884, the year
of Pattison's death. 'I have now', he wrote to Meta on 11 July 1882,
'accumulated a pile of your letters, too good to be lost ... They are
quite a diary of a life.' The letters were, however, more than the
story of a single life. They formed a dialogue of two lives, his and
hers. 'What incomplete ideas one gets of people when only the
letters written to them are read', Meta herself commented, on
9 December 1883. 'Really and truly our correspondence would give a
much truer representation of you from aet. 70 than other folks'
letters to you. How unreal most lives are! I always have a strong
suspicion as I glance through them that the episodes which would
give one real insight into the man's character are suppressed or even
unknown to the compiler.'

'Our letters', Meta told her correspondent, 'would be invaluable
in 1983 as showing the life of this age. I wonder whether they would
be a fair specimen? I shall never bear to destroy them. I wonder
whether they could be kept sealed somewhere. We might be quite
celebrated!' Rector Pattison, with sure historical insight, realized
that his letters and diaries would some day provide the social
historian with invaluable fodder. He left all his papers to the
Bodleian Library at Oxford, with instructions that they should not
be opened until thirty years after his death. 'Are you going to do as
you intended long ago', Meta enquired of him, 'about your correspondence i.e. put it in the Bodleian and let Mr Bywater and me
have access to it?' Although Pattison intended Meta to be his
literary executor, she had no real part in the disposal of his papers.
But she had his letters to her as well as her letters to him, for she had
insisted on their return, and she kept and treasured them until her
death in 1923 when she bequeathed them to Pattison's admirer and

pupil, T. F. Althaus, from whom they came to the Bodleian Library
to join the many other volumes of the Pattison archive in 1927.

'One can recreate the past', another indefatigable letter writer,
H. H. Asquith, wrote to his confidante, Venetia Stanley, 'from letters
better than in any other way, and how different the perspective often
is, when, after years, one reads them again.' A century has now
elapsed since Pattison's death. He was one of the outstanding
scholars of his generation. His views on the nature of University education were well ahead of his time. His *Memoirs*, published post-
humously in 1885, if now read only by connoisseurs, remains a minor
literary classic. His personality, and the personal relationships which
sprang from it, fascinated his contemporaries. His letters to Meta
Bradley, if void of sensationalism, would, if published in his own day,
have created a stir. 'Really, I see nothing in any of your letters', he
told Meta Bradley, 'which I could not read out to the whole College
if they desired to listen, as I am sure you might read mine, to all your
visitors ... Nobody could possibly have any curiosity about the
things we say to each other if ever anyone dropped upon them. He
could only wonder how we could think such worth writing.' If there
was a grain of truth in this statement, yet the fellows of the College
no less than Mrs Pattison would have listened with scandalized
interest.

The letters, however, deserve consideration less because of their
basic, if often trivial, content, than because they reflect some aspects
of Victorian middle-class society and unfold a human relationship,
tragic in some of its features, which is of enduring interest. When the
letters first came to the Bodleian Library, they were read by the
future novelist, Robert Liddell, then on the staff of the library, and
they were used by him in a work of imaginative fiction, *The Almond
Tree*, published by Jonathan Cape in 1938. The novel was very
plainly based on the letters, though the setting was changed from an
Oxford college to a public school, Pattison reappearing as a headmaster, Dr Paul Ramus. Mr John Sparrow briefly discussed Meta
Bradley's *rôle* in Pattison's life in his elegant and informative study,
Mark Pattison and the Idea of a University, published by the Cambridge
University Press in 1967. In her biography of Lady Dilke, published
by Chatto and Windus in 1969, to which I am indebted for some
detail, Betty Askwith treated the scenario with sympathy and

insight. I too have made some use of this material in two books, *Oxford Common Room*, published by Edward Arnold in 1957, and the *Commonwealth of Lincoln College*, published by Oxford University Press in 1979. Now that we approach the centenary year of the publication of Pattison's *Memoirs*, it seems very fitting that some attention should be focused on the correspondence which, historically interesting and personally moving, surely forms a significant if minor contribution to our understanding of Victorian society.

I

Prologue

ON a late autumn day in 1879 Miss Meta Bradley, expectant, earnest and eager for knowledge, arrived at Oxford station. She was to stay with her cousin, Margaret Woods, at her house in picturesque Holywell. Daisy, as Meta always called Margaret, was the wife of a Trinity don, the Reverend Henry Woods, later Master of the Temple. Her father was Granville Bradley, the Master of University College. The Bradleys were a numerous, philoprogenitive clan. Meta's and Daisy's grandfather, Charles Bradley, had been a well-known Evangelical clergyman, curate of High Wycombe and eventually incumbent of St James's Chapel, Clapham. He was also the vicar of Glasbury-on-Wye in Brecknockshire from 1825 until his death in 1871. But Clapham was the centre of his life. His handsome presence and resonant oratory drew large congregations, more especially of fashionable women. 'As a great treat', one of his congregation later commented, 'and on very rare occasions we were taken to St James's to hear the Revd Charles Bradley . . . I remember perfectly his manner and appearance; the pleasant kindly face, with the iron-grey hair and whiskers, the attractive style, the clear voice, the loving earnest way of analysing his subject.' He was twice married. His first wife, Catherine Shepherd, who bore him thirteen children, died in 1831. Eight years later he married Emma Linton, the daughter of a stockbroker living in Clapham, by whom he had eight more; no male descendant in the direct line now survives.

Meta Bradley's father, another Charles, was the eldest of his seven sons. Educated at University College, Oxford, he had won a fellowship at Worcester College. He too was ordained and adhered to his father's evangelical principles. He became the proprietor of a highly successful school at Southgate, near London, which his pupil Augustus Hare described graphically in his *Story of My Life*. Hare paid tribute to Bradley's qualities as a tutor: 'I felt I owed everything to Mr Bradley . . . He had a natural enthusiasm for knowledge himself and imparted it to his pupils.'[1]

Hare's personal relations with Bradley fluctuated, in part as a consequence of what he described as his 'extraordinary peculiarities'. 'I could never', he wrote to his mother on 9 February 1851, shortly after his admission to the school, 'like him as a man.' 'He is much too familiar with his pupils, pulls their hair or hits them on the toes with the poker when they make mistakes.' Pupils who did not perform well were detained on their half-holidays, or received 'three severe boxes on the ear'. For writing after prayers on Sunday, a culprit might be deprived of his fire for a month. While the food was ample, no one was permitted to leave anything on his plate, not even fat.

Hare was struck by Bradley's parsimony. 'The tradespeople are allowed to put in their bills, Pane of Glass broken by Portman or Brooke, &c. When I asked him to lend me a pen, he said, "Oh, I don't provide my pupils with pens". The first thing he said to me after I entered the house was, pointing to the sideboard, "Mind you never take either of those two candles; those are Mrs Bradley's and mine".' 'We', Hare added, 'have sickly-smelling farthing dips in dirty japanned candlesticks.' At first he reconciled himself to Bradley's tiresome ways, so much so that he could write that he felt happier at Southgate than he had ever been before. 'Southgate is absolute paradise, the meals are so merry and the little congregation round the fire afterwards, and work is carried on with such zest and made so interesting.'

But Bradley's methods ultimately sapped his pupil's goodwill. A strict disciplinarian, he endeavoured to remedy repeated errors in Latin grammar by humiliating the miscreants, nor would he ever tolerate any difference of opinion. When, in October 1851, Hare stood up for himself, Bradley told him that he would have to leave the school. 'I am so sorry', he told his mother, 'you should be troubled by this ... and even now I think Bradley will not be so *infatuated* as to send away the only one of his pupils who likes him much.' So Bradley relented, and his wife gave Hare 'a beautiful myrtle branch from the nursery garden, as a sign that all was right'.

Even so, Hare, who was then a boy of nearly 19 years of age, was increasingly alienated by the punishments that Bradley sought to impose on him for trivial grammatical faults, 'such as wearing his coat inside out running with a tin kettle tied to his coat-tail through the village'. The climax came, in 1853, when after Hare had made a mistake in his Latin prose, Bradley 'decreed publicly, that, for each of my commonest blunders, one of my companions should kiss me!' Naturally Hare refused to comply with this order, so that when three weeks later, he made another similar mistake and Bradley ordered a 'big Scotchman named Buchan' to kiss him, Hare saw red. 'Immediately the whole room was in motion, and Buchan in hot pursuit. I barricaded the way with chairs, jumped on the table, splashing right and left from all the inkstands, but eventually I was caught and kissed. In a blind fury scarcely knowing what I did, I knocked Buchan's head against the sharp edge of the bookcase, and seizing a great Liddell and Scott lexicon, rushed upon Bradley who was seated unsuspecting in a low chair by the fire, and taking him unawares, banged him on the bald scalp with the lexicon until I could bang no longer.' After the fracas, Bradley ordered him to leave the school immediately, and Hare took refuge at Harrow with Dr C. J. Vaughan, a clerical academic whose amorous indiscretions were later to cost him his job.[2] Vaughan persuaded Bradley to take Hare (who needed coaching for admission to Oxford) back into the school. 'This he consented to do only on condition that he was never expected to speak to me out of work-time, and he never did.'

Hare's encounter with Bradley throws some light on the schoolmaster's complex character. The Reverend Charles Bradley was a man of great mental vigour and high spirits and, like his father, dominant and dictatorial in disposition. In 1844 he had married Anne George, from a large family in Herefordshire, a sensitive and somewhat reserved girl who was often embarrassed by her husband's eccentricities. On one occasion he had a donkey carriage constructed out of a clothes basket in which he insisted that his wife should drive to church.

Anne Bradley seems to have been a vivacious and kind-hearted woman. Augustus Hare found her good-natured. Her children clearly adored her. In a letter from Southgate, dated June 1860, she

[2] Vaughan resigned from the headmastership as a result of his infatuation with a boy, Alfred Pretor, in 1858; Pretor's friend, J. A. Symonds, told his father of the affair, and Vaughan resigned (see *The Memoirs of John Addington Symonds*, ed. Phyllis Grosskurth, London, 1984, 97, 111-14). The scandal was hushed up and Vaughan became vicar of Doncaster (1860-9), Master of the Temple (1869-94) and Dean of Llandaff (1879-97), making his house a centre for training ordination candidates, known as Vaughan's doves.

told Meta, her youngest: 'I have often longed to be with you, and shall welcome you home more thankfully than ever. But we must both be patient and try to get strong and well, or we shall not be ready for our journey.'[2] Enclosed with the letter there was a special hymn for Meta:

> I meant to be an angel
> And with the Angels stand
> A crown upon my forehead,
> A harp within my hand;
> There right before my Saviour,
> So glorious and so bright
> I'd make the sweetest music
> And praise him day and night.
>
> I know I'm weak and sinful
> But Jesus will forgive
> For many little children
> Have gone to Heaven to live.
> Dear Saviour when I languish
> And lay me down to die
> Oh send a shining angel
> To bear me to the sky!

Anne Bradley had a short time to live. One other letter to Meta survives, written from Llandrindod. She told her young daughter 'It is not a pleasant place for us [she was there with her sister] and you would be quite lost here. There are two little girls of eight and nine years here and their only amusement is going on the top of a coach for a drive and when it rains they are popped inside and then they vomit!' Llandrindod lacked charm. Her room was so tiny that she could only write on her bed, and every meal was half an hour late.[3]

The letter was undated. Perhaps it was her last trip, for she died at her uncle Offley's home in the late summer of 1866. '"God knows"', a friend, Mrs Laseron, wrote to Meta's sister Jessie, '"what is for the best". These were almost the last words which she uttered to me the day before she left for Wales. . . . The last thing your dear departed mother did, before she left for Wales, was to supply our dear Orphans with Cabbages and Rhubarb. There was crying among our dear children when I told them that she had gone to be with Jesus.'[4]

Meta never got over her mother's death. With the passing of the years the ache became, if anything, the more agonizing.

Meta had an elder brother, Charles, who evidently reacted against the rigid environment of school and family. He was, according to his sister Jessie, 'extremely clever, amusing, good-looking and very mischievous'. Like his father he was sent to school at Rugby but he broke his leg skating on the ice and through a misunderstanding (Rugby understood that he was not to return for six *months* instead of six *weeks*) his place there was filled. He was packed off to Marlborough where his uncle, Granville, was then headmaster. He disliked the school, his mischievous nature got him deeply into trouble and he was asked to leave. Various alternatives faced his father. He could send Charles to a crammer to equip himself for an entry into college or he could go into the army. He spent three months in Dresden to learn German, but gadded about, for he fell easily for feminine charm. He lodged with a family called Foss. One of the girls was to marry Professor Althaus, the father of T. F. Althaus, one of Mark Pattison's few favoured pupils.[b] 'I've told you often, dear Sir!', Meta Bradley told Mark Pattison in March 1882 when he expressed surprise at Mrs Althaus's visit to her London home, 'that my brother used to board in Dresden with Mrs Althaus's people'. Fraülein Foss was apparently discovered on board the ship which was to take Charley to Australia, but his parents peremptorily sent her back home.[c]

The colonies were the natural alternative to a commission in the army. Through the good offices of Charley's uncle, Offley Crewe Reid, the Moretons, sons of Lord Ducie, agreed to take him as a pupil in Queensland to teach him stock rearing.[d] He sailed for Australia on 27 May 1864. His mother was grief stricken at her son's departure. 'Poor Charlie', Mrs Laseron wrote after her death two years later, 'Let us pray for him. Your dearly beloved Mother and I agreed to pray daily for him at a certain hour and so I did for the last 3 years and I believe God will answer her prayer.'

[b] After a walk with T. F. Althaus (25 April 1879), Pattison described him as 'sensible and well-behaved'.

[c] Jessie Ilbert doubted the truth of this canard which she attributed to her sister, Meta.

[d] Berkeley, the 4th Earl of Ducie (1834–1924) was Minister of Public Instruction in Queensland 1885–8. This account of Charles Bradley comes from a written statement dictated by Lady Ilbert to Joyce Bradley.

Mrs Laseron's faith seemed hardly to be justified by the turn of events. The Moretons entertained a young Irish girl; she was only 17, a Mrs Brance, married to an actor. On the second night of her stay she came into Charley's bedroom in a state of great agitation. 'Mr Bradley', she declared, 'you must drive me as hard as you can and as fast as you can, my husband has left me and left me this note, he has left me to Mr Moreton to pay a gambling debt.' The young farmer drove her to a neighbouring town and soon set up house with her; the Moretons, irritated by the departure of their pledge, broke with Charley. A child was born, though its paternity seems to have been a matter of some doubt. In the remote outback, where Charley's mistress once had to repel an attack by aborigines singlehanded, Charley's farming ventures hardly prospered. Jessie, who had idolized her brother in her girl-hood, learned of the situation and remonstrated with him. He feared that news of his liaison would threaten the small annuity which he was receiving from his father. At the last an anonymous letter alerted the Reverend Charles Bradley. He took the news somewhat better than might have been expected. He was indeed by that time ailing in health as was his son. Meta hardly knew Charley but she tried, though for the most part vainly, to get the articles which he wrote accepted by London journals, writing to John Morley to get them inserted in the *Pall Mall Gazette*. 'I sent on the Queensland MS to Morley', Pattison commented, 'but the writer should hold his hand, as the *Pall Mall Gazette* will begin to make difficulties.' 'He will be dreadfully disappointed, poor fellow,' Meta wrote, 'we are shortly sending him a box of clothes, new and old, which he hopes will contain some *Pall Mall Gazette* money.'

His sister Jessica, Jessie, was very different in character from either Charley or Meta. She resembled her father in physique, for she was large of bosom, as in personality. Endowed with a peerless skin, large blue eyes and chestnut hair, Jessie was an attractive girl of high spirits. Although so clearly her father's favourite, she managed to escape from his direct surveillance by entering the field of social work under Octavia Hill. She trained as a nurse, met Courtenay Ilbert, one of her uncle Granville's promising pupils, future distinguished civil servant and administrator, and married him in 1874 when she was twenty-four years old.

Meta was physically and mentally very different from Jessie. She was introspective, fragile (though at one stage she confessed to weighing eight and a half stone), and in some ways a distinctly silly girl. To her father she seemed an ugly duckling whose wayward opinions had to be countered. After his first wife's death, Charles had married again, another Annie, the daughter of a Mr Hathaway, surgeon and private secretary to Lord Lawrence; she was a kindly but feather-pated woman whose incessant chattering frayed Meta's nerves. She was, however, devoted to her husband. He seems a caricature of the Victorian paterfamilias, stern, demanding and unable to understand why Meta seemed to give him so little affection. His evangelical faith appeared bleak and negative, his piety too little softened by tolerance. He forbade his daughters to go to dances or theatres.ᵉ Although Jessie was a bad sailor and habitually sick, he expected her to accompany him on long voyages on his yacht, the *Swift*. His granddaughter, Olive Heseltine, recalled the atmosphere of the Bradley ménage at 25 Orsett Terrace in her novel *The Three Daughters*, published in 1930 under the pseudonym Jane Dashwood.

A dreary day Sunday had been. Blinds down; all the books, except *Pilgrim's Progress*, Foxe's *Book of Martyrs* and Blair's *Tomb*,ᶠ put away. Church three times. And dear Papa increasingly Evangelical and more difficult to live with. His mania for small economies! How she remembered that evening, when coming home late after a party (not a dance: Papa wouldn't hear of dances and, of course, strictly forbade the theatre) at which she had worn her pink tarlatan with a gold locket on black velvet . . . She found Papa sitting up in the drawing room with a face white with fury.

'Oh, Papa why did you sit up?'

'*Look* at this!' And with trembling fingers he had pointed to an envelope on which was written:

'Don't wait up for me: Emma Fanshaw is seeing me home.'

ᵉ Augustus Hare throws a curious light on the ways in which he sought to instruct his children. 'All the moral lessons to his little daughter Jesse (*sic*) are taken from reminiscences of his "poor dear first wife" who never existed. I am used to it now, but was amazed when I first heard little Jesse ask something about "your poor dear first wife, papa" and he took out a handkerchief and covered both their heads that no one might see them cry, which the little girl did abundantly at the touching story told her. Little Charlie's education was carried on a similar way, only the model held up to him was a son of Mrs Bradley's by an imaginary first husband, who "died and is buried in Oxfordshire".'

ᶠ i.e. Robert Blair's *The Grave, a poem* (1808).

'You should not have used an *envelope*' (in a voice of thunder),
'You should have used a *HALF-SHEET*!'
Naturally it was necessary to conceal a good many things from Papa; unlike Minnie [Meta] who blurted everything out (and how Minnie had irritated him!) ... And Papa's second marriage ... what a perfect fool! After this it became extremely desirable to leave home.'[6]

Jessie's training and marriage had brought this about, but Meta, unmarried, remained, depending for her livelihood on a father whom she came to loathe while for his part he resented any assertion of independence.[g]

Meta's uncle, Granville Bradley, was the fourth son. He was a large-minded scholarly man who had had a brilliantly successful career, mounting the academic *cursus honorum* with ease, first as Headmaster of Marlborough College and then from 1870 somewhat less happily as Master of University College, Oxford, whence he was to move in 1881 to the deanery of Westminster in succession to his friend and fellow liberal, A. P. Stanley. 'Presently', A. C. Benson recalled, seeing him in old age at Gladstone's funeral in May 1898, 'the Dean came out ... His pale sharp features — long silken hair very picturesque, to say nothing of his thin voice and little sharp glances.'[8] He died shortly after his retirement at the age of 82 in 1903. His wife Marian was a woman of rigid views, the daughter of Benjamin Philpot, Archdeacon of Sodor and Man, whom Granville had married in 1849. 'Why, oh why, is he so pleasant and she so disagreeable?' Meta Bradley commented after they had taken tea at her home in Orsett Terrace. They had two sons and five daughters, among them, Meta's hostess, Margaret Woods, Mabel (later Lady Birchenough), Nem (later Mrs Murray Smith), and Posy (later Mrs Rose Bradley). The future Shakespearian scholar, Andrew Cecil Bradley, and the philosopher F. H. Bradley, were his half-brothers.

In 1879 Meta was twenty-six years old. She was impulsive, naïve, and enthusiastic. She lacked tact and could be irritating, as her nieces later asserted. 'Their Aunt Minnie's presence', Olive Heseltine, one of them, wrote in her novel, 'affected the inmates of Conyngham Place with that faint uneasiness which is roused by the humming of a

---

[g] 'I hope', Meta was to write on 25 May 1882, 'there will be some good actors left when my father removes his embargo on my going to see a play by removing himself from the earthly stage. I feel that by that time I shall be too old to care for theatres.'[7]

mosquito. With none but benevolent intentions towards the whole human race, she nevertheless contrived to vex and depress every member of the family to whose interests she was unselfishly devoted.' Not blessed particularly with good looks, grey strands in her hair made her look even in 1879 older than her years. In some respects she appeared prim and even puritanical, but in others her views were radical and unconventional. She once said that if she were a politician, she would devote her policies to 'pulling down and rebuilding workmen's houses, altering marriage laws and opening public places on Sunday.' Already, she was finding an outlet for her energies in the good works which were to take up more and more of her time. 'A tiny piping cry'—Olive Heseltine again—'"Cooee! Cooee!" and a vague scratching on the door preceded the entrance of a small figure clad in a check coat and skirt, with a heavy velvet toque placed at a rakish angle on her short grey hair, and a propitiatory smile on her face ... Well, ducky—I thought I must have a peep at you before I go off for the meeting of the S.R.O.B.H.'[9] This was Aunt Meta of later years. In 1879, lacking a formal education, she possessed intellectual aspirations. Eager to escape from the grinding dullness of 25 Orsett Terrace, she looked forward to the zest of informed conversation and the sociabilities of academic society.

On an earlier visit she had made the acquaintance of Mark Pattison, the Rector of Lincoln College. It took place, she thought, the year of his sister Dora's death, as she recalled from the wide black-edged paper on which the Rector's invitation to her had been written; but her memory seems to have been at fault for Dora Pattison died in December 1878, and Meta had first met Mark Pattison the previous March. It can have meant little to her at the time and nothing to him, though he noted in his diary for 14 March that 'at 4 Daisy and her Bradley cousin came to tea'.[h] 'How dreadfully frightened I was!' she recalled six years later, 'and we wound up (after a walk) with tea, which was still more alarming. I clearly recollect asking you a question which you were so long answering (your eyes shut) that in the twilight I thought you had fallen asleep from sheer boredom. I can't think now how I ever so completely got

---

[h] Meta thought that they met first on 10 March, 1878. Daisy, described by Pattison on 24 January 1877, as a 'most interesting child', married H. G. Woods in 1879. She was the author of many novels and other literary works and died, at the age of 89, in 1945.

over that awe of you.'[10] Awesome was an adjective appropriate
enough to apply to this enigmatic scholar, reputed internationally
for his learning but angular and unpopular. He had published only
one major work, a study of the Renaissance scholar, Isaac Casaubon,
in 1875, but he was working, in somewhat desultory fashion, on a
sequel, a life and study of Scaliger.[i] His reputation as a critic was
enhanced by a native taciturnity and a caustic tongue. While an
instinctive if misguided sense of duty made him invite undergraduates of his College to accompany him on walks and to breakfast in
the Rector's Lodgings, his silence made the experience a dreaded
ordeal. Occasionally a solitary young intellectual, a T. F. Althaus,
would break through the oyster and find, if not pearls of wisdom, at
least keen reflection and crisp judgement. The Rector, egocentric
and over-sensitive, purred when such youthful curiosity pierced his
native crust.

His relations with his fellow dons in the University and College
were rarely more congenial. He had a few close friends, J. M. Wilson
the President of Corpus, Henry Smith, the mathematician, Ingram
Bywater, the classical scholar of Exeter; 'Bywater and Smith dined',
he noted on Sunday 23 February 1880, 'and scattered their wit over a
wide field of subjects.' He had, however, no real intimates and many
critics. His defection from the Tractarian party with which he had
been aligned until 1845 had been followed first by a broad churchmanship, outwardly manifest in his contribution to *Essays and
Reviews*, with the inception of which he had been closely associated,
and then by the slow erosion of his faith.[11] Ultimately an agnostic, he
managed to combine a lack of belief with the retention of his Orders
and participation in religious services. He was regarded with suspicion and distrust by the conservative clericals in Oxford. Even the
University liberals, whose cause he had once espoused, looked ask-
ance at the critical attitudes which he had subsequently adopted towards the reform commissioners that the goverment had appointed
recently to investigate the state of the University.

[i] Pattison had intended originally to work on Scaliger, but the publication of Abbé
Bernay's study in 1855 led him to divert his attention to Casaubon. In later life he took
up the work again, but never got very far with it. 'I am like the dying gladiator summon-
ing life's ebbing energies', he wrote in 1882, 'to write the life of J. Scaliger, which I have
had in hand for 30 years, and have such a mass of materials for that I don't know how to
reduce them to shape. It will kill me!'

He had been Rector of Lincoln College since 1861, but the high hopes which his supporters had had of his governance there had been acutely disappointed. The College basked in the glow of his reputation as a scholar, but it remained a comparatively undistinguished backwater in the university world. The Rector's interests in the College with which he had been closely associated since his election to a fellowship in 1839 seemed narrow and introspective. He cared little for the undergraduates, was appallingly ineffective as a chairman and left most of the business to the Sub-rector, the philosopher Tommy Fowler, whom he greatly disliked. Although he had a few close friends among the younger fellows, none closer to him than the admirable classical scholar and ornithologist Warde Fowler, 'interesting and superior', for the most part he regarded Lincoln's dons with contempt akin to dislike, regarding them as time servers of limited intellectual capacity incapable of creative or original scholarly work. When he was elected to the rectorship in 1861, he had been for ten years in the wilderness, defeated at a previous rectorial election in ways which he regarded as underhand and devious.[12] The grievous disappointment which he had undergone in 1851 had been a traumatic blow to a personality made frustrated and bitter by his earlier life.

The anfractuosities of Pattison's character only appear explicable in terms of inheritance and environment. Born in 1813 the elder son of a Yorkshire clergyman, an older Mark Pattison, he had been brought up in the quietude of the countryside of the North Riding. The freedom and fruition of the rushing river Ure and the wind-strewn moors of Wensleydale provided the growing boy with physical recreation and a sense of spiritual harmony which he was never entirely to lose. But the atmosphere of the rectory in the small village of Hauxwell created by contrast a prison for the spirit as well as the mind. Even by comparison with the Brontës's home at Haworth only a few miles away, Hauxwell rectory can only be described as 'doom-laden'. The elder Pattison was an Oxford graduate, of Brasenose, a relatively well-read man who took it upon himself to instruct the son in whose future he placed great hopes. Yet he was by nature introspective and domineering; in his small parish he had little to do and that little he tended to neglect or leave to curates. In theology he could be described as a high and dry Evangelical; the onset of

Tractarianism made him first suspicious and then, when the infection tarnished his family circle, almost hysterically hostile. His wife, Jane Wynn, a banker's daughter from the neighbouring town of Richmond, nourished by a rigid biblicism, rarely opposed her husband's whims; his demands as a husband must have been heavy. Between 1813 and 1834 eleven children were born, all girls except for the eldest, Mark, and the youngest, Frank. They were birds in a cage, for as they grew older, their father peremptorily discouraged them either from following a career or even from marriage. It was not until 1853 that Eleanor, then aged 36, broke the chains that bound her and her sisters to the rectory by marrying the Reverend Frederick Mann. Her father tried to prevent the marriage by hinting that there was insanity in the family. There was, in himself, for he had suffered an acute nervous breakdown from which he never effectually recovered; though he was to remain in office, at least nominally, until his death at the age of 77 in 1865.

The elder Pattison's breakdown coincided with Mark's undergraduate career. His home education and gauche manners[j] made him ill-fitted for the sophistication of Oriel College in the 1830s, a society which was then in the vanguard of intellectual progress and soon to be the nest of religious agitation in the shape of the Tractarian movement. Although Pattison failed to win a first-class in the Schools, in the still fossilized learning of the University he had glimpsed a vision of scholarship which in its integrity and depth was the one enchantment that never deserted him. By dint of persistence he was elected in 1839 to a fellowship at one of the least distinguished of the Oxford colleges, Lincoln, still labouring in the heavy fumes of conservatism and reaction. Simultaneously he became associated with the religious revival which was creating a ferment in Oxford senior common rooms. Newman was a fellow and tutor of Oriel College but as an undergraduate Pattison had only come across him in a proctorial capacity. Momentarily fresh insights, the sympathetic doctoring of the rigidities of Protestantism by Catholic tradition, the warm friendships to which the movement gave rise, absorbed him totally.

---

[j] Cf. the description of his first 'wine' party, 'Oh, the icy coldness, the dreary Egyptian blankness of that "wine"; the guests slipped away one by one under pretext of engagements, and I was left alone with an almost untouched dessert, to be carried off as perquisite by the college scout.'[13]

He played only a subordinate part in it but his adherence seemed so unquestioning that he sincerely considered whether or not he should, like Newman, cross the frontier Romewards. In remote Wensleydale his sisters caught his enthusiasm, drawing their father's flailing wrath upon themselves, so precipitating a break between father and son which would never be healed. Yet, underneath the emotional and spiritual enthusiasm which adhesion to the movement evoked, a strong rational current still flowed in his mind, leading to an eventual atrophy of the religious beliefs which had sustained him for more than a decade.[14] He developed a deep distaste for the Tractarianism which he had once regarded with such fervour. 'I was then', he wrote later, '"too étourdi" to be trusted. Newman always doubted where I would go.' Moreover the experience had seared him spiritually, leaving in its wake less a sense of liberation than a feeling of frustration and disgust. His father remained unforgiving, for liberal churchmanship had no more appeal than catholicism. His mother was full of cold sympathy but misunderstanding. His sisters, who had endured so many disagreeable scenes and so many persecuting pinpricks, were dismayed by his change of front. The syrup of their love continued to lap him, but he found it increasingly unpalatable, doubting indeed whether, apart from his favourite Rachel, who, to his great grief, had died in 1874, any of his family ever had a capacity for genuine affection.[k]

His election to the rectorship in 1861 made possible a marriage which as a celibate fellow he could not by statute have envisaged. He was now forty-eight years old. His earlier emotional life is screened from us. He had had strong male friendships and had been regarded by some of his Lincoln pupils with deep affection, but there is nothing to suggest on his part any genuine committal, certainly no committal with sexual undertones. Similarly no evidence linked him with a woman's name. It was obvious that he was well liked by women, by women more than men. He thawed more easily in their presence, enjoyed taking part in their play-reading circles and cackled with high-pitched laughter at their tea-parties and soirées. Even at forty-eight he was in appearance prematurely aged, withered

---

[k] Compare the entry in his diary for 9 November 1874: 'A horrible vacuum in my life! What is loss of friends! I never knew what till now ... O bitter! bitter! ... O what a blank is that! My world is half-perished in her loss.'

in countenance, with straggling reddish whiskers streaked with wisps of grey, the face gaunt and pallid, the back stooped, but the eyes were exceptionally bright and lively. It is, however, useless to speculate about what might have happened in the stresses of his sexual life, during the first forty years of his life; it is only evident that he was an emotionally castrated man.

Mark was elected Rector of Lincoln College on 25 January 1861. He married Emily Francis Strong at Iffley Church on the 10 September following. When he first met her is unclear, but on any grounds it was an extraordinary union, explicable as it has seemed to many only in terms of the marriage of Dorothea Brooke to Dr Casaubon in *Middlemarch*, whether or not the novelist, with whom both Mark and his wife were friendly, founded her story on their broken romance.[15] Francis Strong (it was only after her marriage to Sir Charles Dilke that she reverted to her first name Emily or Emilia) was twenty-seven years younger than her husband, a radiant, energetic and intelligent girl.[16] She was the third daughter of Henry Strong, a retired captain in the Indian army—who had since 1841 been manager of the London and County Bank at Iffley near Oxford, where his family occupied an early Victorian house, the Elms. Francis had studied art at the new School of Art in South Kensington, where the future Sir Charles Dilke must have been a fellow student. Here she acquired the foundations of her lifelong interest in art history as well as an element of sophistication in clothes and manners. She came home to Iffley, met Mark, became engaged to him in June and was married in September. From one point it was the marriage of summer and autumn, perhaps of spring and winter. It is impossible to do more than surmise about what drew them together. In spite of appearance Mark was a warm-blooded man, attracted by clever, beautiful young women. He craved affection. 'My heart', he confided to his diary on New Year's Day 1877, 'is sick from starvation! I have much kindness from many, but love is what I live for, and have not got.' Self-centred and introspective, he wished to be loved, even though he found it difficult to give love in return. There can be no doubt that he was momentarily delighted with this elegant and intelligent young woman, in so many ways different from the sedate and dull daughters of the Oxford bourgeoisie. She had *élan*, a distaste for convention, a capacity for being educated, even moulded, to ideal companionship—ideal, that is, as the Rector construed it.

If it is relatively easy to see why Mark fell in love with Francis, it is more difficult to understand why Francis accepted the prospect of a lifelong relationship with a man who, on outward appearance, was so evidently lacking in physical attraction. Was it, as with Dorothea Brooke and Dr Casaubon, a marriage of minds? Francis was still very young and impressionable. She must have been immensely flattered by the attention which was being paid to her by a scholar of international reputation. She was relatively impecunious. How attractive must have been the notion of security, within the confines of the Rector's spacious lodgings. Heads of houses, as the masters of Oxford colleges were called, were at this date virtually still the only married dons. Their wives were the social leaders in the provincial society of the city and University. She may have seen herself as the centre of an intellectual and civilized salon.

But Francis Strong's motives cannot have been solely materialistic. She was always an idealist. At this stage she was deeply imbued with the Tractarian views which her husband had already abandoned; later she embraced positivism. She certainly found between herself and Mark a concert of interest. Limited in her experience, she was impressed by Mark's intellectual mastery. He was a teacher who would instruct, train her, introduce to her the world of ideas, unfold the sublime realities of existence. She would bring enthusiasm and the warmth which would melt the cool carapace in which he seemed ensheathed. Mark accepted the challenge, and at first Francis proved a very ready, even amenable, pupil. 'When I began', she later told her favourite niece, Gertrude Tuckwell, 'it was put before me that if I wished to make *a position* to command *respect* I must make myself THE authority on some one subject which interested me.'[17]

In time she would become an internationally recognized authority on the history of French art, the author of *The Renaissance of Art in France* (1879), *Claude Lorrain, Sa vie et ses œuvres* (1884), and of four authoritative volumes on the history of French art in the eighteenth century. If such works were the product of later life, the foundations were laid in the early years of her married life. She became an accomplished linguist, completely at home in French, Latin, German, and Italian, with an adequate reading acquaintance with Greek, Spanish, Portuguese, Dutch and Provençal; shortly before her death she was learning Swedish and had begun Welsh. Mark had an apt and responsive pupil, so much so that she outgrew the limitations of pedantic contemporary Oxford scholarship. The Lodgings which once seemed so attractive became at the last frowsty and old-fashioned.

Their original attraction to a young and penniless girl must have been enormous, in alliance with a brilliant and affectionate older husband. She would not merely enjoy freedom from domestic chores and a secure income, but the opportunity to mix with some of the best minds in Europe. Her husband's liberalism, his identification with the reform party in the University, his sympathetic understanding of what at the time seemed to be radical causes, scientific research, the higher education of women, endowed him with some degree of personal magnetism. She admired and liked him to the extent that she believed that she was in love with him. Later she admitted that this was a great deceit to which she clung desperately in the belief that she might to able to make it come true. When he was ill she was at first moved by genuine pity and concern. 'I see you do not know what trouble we are in', she told her sister on 11 January 1870, 'Mark has been seriously ill, for two days there was the gravest anxiety and for the last ten days we have not been able to leave him night or day . . . It has been a sad new year, but yet I feel so thankful to see him coming back to us as it were.'[18] Yet she soon began to suspect that his illnesses were often hysterical ploys designed to engage her affection or at least to underline her obligations to her husband.[1] More and more she resented the curb which marriage placed on her independence. In her heart of hearts she knew she no longer loved her husband, had indeed never loved him. The feeling induced in her a sense of guilt, the more pronounced as after 1875 she became increasingly attracted to the Liberal politician, Sir Charles Dilke. Although she never or very rarely gave way to self-pity, her frustration contributed to the nervous prostration from which she periodically suffered.

[1] Compare Mrs Pattison's letter to Ellen Smith: 'The "fainting" is always exaggerated like everything else which can excite commiseration. I have seen him throw himself down on the landing with great care in similar attacks . . .'[19]

In practice married life may have been less than harmonious from the very start. She relished Mark's scholarly conversation, the evening readings, the savage criticism of illiberal clericals; but Mark had been a bachelor too long to adapt himself to the exigencies of marriage.[m] He was unused to giving much consideration to others, and was self-regarding so far as his own needs went. Liberal-minded in attitude to public causes, in private life he held firmly to the *mores* of the Victorian paterfamilias which he had so loathed in his father. He was cantankerous, egocentric, and parsimonious. He obliged his wife to list the most petty of her purchases; and Mrs Pattison was by nature, if not spendthrift, at least attracted to beautiful and costly clothes which would set off her beauty and golden hair. He demanded his conjugal rights, an experience which his young wife found from the start physically embarrassing and which eventually became completely abhorrent to her. It was a relief to leave Oxford, to stay, for instance, in the lost magnificence of Bamburgh Castle on its windswept heights (in the 1860s the Rector of Lincoln, as one of Lord Crewe's trustees, had a right to stay there for some weeks each year) or to accompany her husband on continental tours where his knowledge and interest would revive the dying bond between them.[21]

More and more she wished to breathe a more rarified, sophisticated, civilized, even in some senses more worldly, air than could be found in the still provincial, clerical society of contemporary Oxford. She hankered after London, reluctantly persuading Mark that on grounds of health it would be better for her to live part of her time there rather than in Oxford. She began to play a *rôle* in London society. Her interest in art history brought her into contact with European scholars with whom she carried on a close and, particularly, in the case of Eugene Müntz, an affectionate correspondence. She became review editor of *The Academy*. Her

[m] As a young girl, Miss Mary Arnold (later Mrs Humphry Ward) remembered a visit to the Lodgings at Lincoln: 'My first sight of a college garden lying cool and shaded between grey college walls, and on the grass a figure that held me fascinated—a lady in a green brocade dress, with a belt and chatelaine of Russian silver, who was playing croquet, then a novelty in Oxford, and seemed to me, as I watched her, a perfect model of grace and vivacity.' 'With her gaiety, picturesqueness, her impatience of Oxford solemnities and decorums, her sharp restless wit, her determination *not* to be academic, to hold on to the greater world outside', she greatly impressed the seventeen-year-old girl, who was 'much scandalized . . . by the speculative freedom of the talk.'[20]

deteriorating health, taking the form of nervous prostration and gouty arthritis, gave her an increasing justification for staying away from Oxford, more especially during the damp winter months. If Francis believed her husband's illnesses to have a psychological root, her own, though undoubtedly real, may have been partly psychosomatic in origin.

The Rector resented his wife's absences. They seemed to him a dereliction of duty. They involved him in unnecessary expense. 'I tried to make him look forward to my coming back', she wrote to her Oxford friend, Ellen Smith, 'well enough to go into harness again, Bodley, croquet, ten lines of Greek in the evening. But I am really at a loss as to how to deal with him . . . It *is* very trying . . . but it does get worse, and I *do* think the more blame one takes to oneself (which is what I've been always doing for the sake of peace) the worse he gets.'[22] Ellen Smith was the sister of Henry Smith, the mathematician; she was an intelligent and compassionate woman who managed to retain the friendship of both Mark and his wife. They both treated her as their confidante.

In July 1875, Francis Pattison went to the German spa at Wildbad in search of health. She was ill with arthritic gout and some painful abscesses. The Rector was not placated by his wife's outwardly affectionate letters. 'Dear Mark,' she wrote, not wholly sincerely, 'we *must* look foward to the time we shall be hard at work again, you in your room, and I in mine, it distresses me to find that you get so depressed, and grieves me to think of you all alone. I always feel myself responsible for the state of mind you are in.'[23] The doctors at Wildbad advised her that she should winter abroad rather than risk the English climate. Her husband reacted strongly. 'His letters', she commented, 'almost drive me out of my mind, and I feel so helpless to combat . . . I'm at the end of my resources. I've tried affectionately comforting, I've tried reasoning, and I've tried taking no notice, all in vain . . . He pretends to think (I can't believe *he really thinks*) that I suggested to Hewitt to say I must winter out of Oxford.'[24]

Momentarily, if inwardly groaning, Mark joined his wife. Together with her and her French maid Madame Moreau, henceforth her inseparable companion, he travelled to Nice. When Mark returned to Oxford, his wife moved to a small apartment in the higher part of Nice from which she wrote mollifying letters to her husband, and complaining ones to Ellen Smith. 'The only things I miss downright', she confessed to Ellen, 'are you and the Bodleian'; but she could hardly be so honest in her avowals to the Rector, in which she reiterated her real desire to return to Oxford as soon as possible. Her general health, however, made this unlikely at least until the Spring. 'I can never go out if it's *cold* or *wet*; never get up in an underwarmed room, or *sit* at a low temperature.'[25]

She did, however, feel that the moment had arrived to tell the Rector that there must be henceforth some limitation of his conjugal rights. 'Oxford', she mentioned almost casually in a letter of 21 January 1876, 'knows certainly (which Nice does not) a type of life (of which type *you* always seem to me the most perfect and complete expression) with which I deeply sympathize. So deeply indeed that there is but one side of the life with you into which I do not enter and that is so distasteful to me that the fear of its renewal has often preoccupied me to the exclusion of all other considerations. It is a physical aversion which always existed, though I strove hard to overcome it, and which is now wholly beyond control. But with your "intellectual life" it has and always will be a pleasure and a pride to enter, to be allowed in any degree to share.'[26] Francis can hardly have realized what a deep wound she was inflicting on her husband, arousing as it did all the latent bitterness and frustration to which the marriage had given rise.

Mark was outraged, his masculine vanity incurably hurt. Although his response does not survive, there can be little doubt that he felt bitterly humiliated. 'I will not attempt', his wife wrote in a further letter, 'to defend myself against the accusations either stated or implied which you bring against me. But you cannot forget that from the first I expressed the strongest aversion to that side of the common life, during '73–4 this became almost insufferable but I tried to conceal it hoping that it might settle itself. You had told me constantly all along that it would soon cease and when I thought it had by Acland's direction [Henry Acland was the Regius Professor of Medicine at Oxford] I rejoiced because I felt saved from any charge of wounding you or distressing you. I almost wish now that I had not told you since I see how I have grieved you—anyway anything of the sort in my state of health must be impossible for a long time to come. All I meant when I said "that fear preoccupied me" was that when you were with me I often refrained from showing you the affection that I feel on that account. I cannot but think I am differently constituted to most, and the excessive nervous irritability which is always generated by the malady which I suffer is the reason for the distress I laboured under throughout '74. You know you were greatly annoyed with me at Le Locle, at Geneva and in Paris, and I was trying hard for self-control.'[27] Francis Pattison's attempts at self-justification did little to soften the Rector's rancour, and added to his inbuilt melancholy.

Her own growing and intimate friendship with the radical Liberal politician, Sir Charles Dilke, made her position the more difficult. Dilke's wife had died in childbirth in September 1874. In the following winter he had revived an affair with a former mistress, Mrs Eustace Smith, the wife of the MP for Tynemouth, only breaking it off after meeting Mrs Pattison—though it seems most improbable that his relationship with her had as yet an actual physical aspect. The consequences of Dilke's breach with Mrs Smith were to prove ultimately disastrous. In March 1876, Maye, Mrs Eustace Smith's eldest daughter, had married Dilke's younger brother, Ashton, while Maye's sister, Virginia, later became engaged to a fellow of Lincoln, Donald Crawford, a practising barrister and Liberal politician. Whatever Francis's relations with Dilke, and she was a fastidious woman, they were seeing each other regularly (Dilke had a villa near Toulon) and corresponding often. Dilke's position in society, his radical politics, the rumoured supposition that he might even succeed Gladstone as leader of the Liberal party, the wide range of his interests and his worldliness, all appealed to Mrs Pattison. 'The man who is shooting ahead', the novelist Henry James commented in 1878, 'much faster than anyone else is Sir Charles Dilke. His ability is not at all rare, but he is very skilful and very ambitious, and though he is only thirty-five years old, he would almost certainly, if the Liberals should come into power tomorrow, be a cabinet minister.'[n] His robust personality contrasted strikingly with her hypo-

[n] Another of his comments was less favourable to Dilke: 'Dilke is a very good fellow, and a specimen of a fortunate Englishman born, without exceptional talents, to a big property, a place in the world, and a political ambition which—resolute industry and force of social circumstances aiding—he is steadily *en train* to realize. And withal, not a grain of genius or inspiration. But he is only now emerging—much less radical than he began—from his early cloud—his having attacked the Queen and *cremated* his deceased wife.'[28]

chondriacal dried-up husband. The friendship represented an opening into a wider world, confirming her release from the pettiness of
the Lodgings at Lincoln where Mark refused to answer her letters
and complained bitterly of her neglect of him. He knew of her
friendship with Dilke but seems to have expressed no disapproval.
Relations between Mark and his wife were thus under strain. 'I am
very grieved to hear what you say of the Rector', she wrote to Ellen
Smith on 9 November 1876, 'If he says that he "hears nothing from
me", he has very likely induced himself to think so. In spite of his
persistently not answering and not even taking *any notice* of my
long letters I have steadily continued to write since I left. From him
I have only heard three times—two notes and 1 scrap of five lines
from Liverpool ... It *is* heartbreaking to think of your picture of
his increasing *moroseness* and all that I too well know it includes and
threatens ... The attitude of mind which it implies can only be
quieted by the ruthless sacrifice of everyone about him. With all his
fine qualities he is incapable of recognizing as lawful any other
wants than those he himself can and does feel. The more *I look on*
instead of *living* the more I feel that open war, or be ground under
his heel, is the only choice.'[29] On Mark's side their relationship had
developed into a sort of cold war. 'My heart', he confided to his
diary on 1 January 1877 'is sick from starvation.' He returned to the
Lodgings after walking round the Parks with her on a fine June day
to describe the expedition as a 'dreary loveless walk'. Their evenings
together were 'unprofitable and unhappy'.

In the winter of 1877–8 Francis Pattison had moved from Grasse
to a pleasant house owned by the faithful Madame Moreau at the Île
des Rosiers near Draguignan in Provence. Next winter she visited
Rome and expressed the hope that Mark would join her there. She
may not have relished his company, but he would provide much-
needed financial support. But as it happened in the autumn of 1879
the Rector's thoughts veered away from his wife's hopes and fears
towards an interest very much nearer home.

II

1879-1880

DAISY WOODS took Meta to a gathering at which the Rector of
Lincoln was another guest. They talked. The ageing scholar, forty
years older than Meta, was flattered by her wide-eyed curiosity and
on his return to the Lodgings sent a brief note to Holywell. 'Is there
any chance of my getting a little talk with you? To refresh our
acquaintance so pleasantly begun?' He would not call at Daisy's
house, 'having a bad cold, am afraid of being out after sunset'.[1] But
would she come to tea the following Friday? It was, however, not on
the Friday but on the following Sunday, 26 October 1879, that Meta
sipped her tea in the dark panelled drawing-room of the Lodgings in
the awesome company of the oriental scholar, Max Müller[2] and his
wife and a young classical scholar, a fellow of Lincoln, Nathan
Bodington, whom Pattison rather liked.[a] As Meta gazed at the grey
wall of the neighbouring college Brasenose, and beyond it to the
rounded dome of the Radcliffe Camera, the Rector's interest was
aroused. Perhaps she would walk with him up Shotover Hill? It was
All Saints' Day when they strolled softly, the gold of autumn turned
into wintry grey. But the Rector was exhilarated by his walk. All
Saints' was a College Gaudy, a festal day, which the Rector normally
detested, his digestion disturbed by the rich food, his mind battered
by the bore of prolonged conversation; sustained by the afternoon's
excursion he 'got through it somehow but lamely and absently.'[3]
Before Meta returned to London he drank tea with her and Daisy at
Holywell (at 6.30 p.m.), having a 'cosy chat' disconsolately inter-
rupted by the unexpected return of Daisy's husband, Henry Woods.

[a] Nathan Bodington (1848–1911), fellow of Lincoln College 1875–85; first Professor
of Greek, Mason College, Birmingham 1881; Professor of Greek and Principal of Yorkshire College, Leeds, 1882; Vice-Chancellor of Victoria University, Manchester 1896–
1900; promoted the independent university of Leeds which was founded with
Bodington as Vice-Chancellor 1904. After a walk with him (5 November 1878), Pattison
described him as 'very sensible', and 'taking a serious interest in the college which no
other fellow does'.

From time to time letters arrived from Draguignan where his wife was spending the winter; but he was less unmoved than irritated, for these epistles formed only an unwelcome reminder of a partnership which he preferred to forget. 'Another letter from Francis', he noted on 17 November 1879, 'who perseveres in writing, making it difficult for me to be silent any longer. I had hoped that when she saw I did not respond, she would cease.'⁴ But if she had stopped writing, he would have been the first to complain.

Mrs Pattison still held up the prospect of meeting him in Rome, nor did he reject the idea out of hand. 'I continue', she was to write to Ellen Smith early the next year, 'to write every ten days or so. Looking at the situation from a worldly point of view I know I have everything to gain by keeping on outwardly decent terms with him, but if no other interests than my own were involved I should be inclined to take a much more decided line. He is a creature forever intellectually greedy of satisfaction which he has never (I guess) had the physical or moral power to enjoy, and money being recognized as *the* ruling force in affairs he cannot understand that some things are only to be bought by other coin. This, I think, has shortened his arm among men, he can neither excite nor feel a truly generous impulse, calculation destroys the first germ. If he were to agree to be in Rome he would probably compromise me by his eccentric conduct.' The 'other interest' was probably Sir Charles Dilke whom she regarded already with deep affection.⁵

He was immersed in the trivial round of existence. College business indeed occupied little of his time, and what time he so spent he considered to be time lost, 'time lost to the soul, mind and heart' as he noted of the College Chapter Day meeting on 6 November 1879. Ingram Bywater and other friends came in to talk and to smoke;ᵇ the novelist Rhoda Broughton read German novels to him, though he confided to his diary that her 'restless vanity which requires to be constantly ministered to' was an irritant.ᶜ Walter Pater's sister, Clara, came to tea, bringing the young Edmund Gosse. Yet all this afforded him only minimal satisfaction.

ᵇ Ingram Bywater (1840–1914), fellow of Exeter College, Oxford, 1863–84; Regius Professor of Greek 1893–1908.⁶

ᶜ Rhoda Broughton (1840–1920), popular novelist; author of *Cometh Up as a Flower*, *Not Wisely but Too Well* (1867), *Good-bye, Sweetheart* (1872), *Nancy* (1873), *Joan* (1876), *Belinda* (1883), etc.⁷

The one bright spot was the presence in his Lodgings of his young niece, Mary Stirke, the elder daughter of his favourite sister Rachel. Rachel had wed a gentleman farmer who after Rachel died had married again; the Stirkes lived at a farmstead, Grazing Nook, in Wensleydale. In his wife's absence the Rector was allowed to have young girls to help to supervise the Lodgings, and more especially to read to him during the long lamp-lit evenings. Mark enjoyed Mary's company, at least that winter. He pottered while she skated on the ice of the pond in Worcester College. Together they visited the new Provost at Queen's, Mark disapproving of the furnishings and finding the company dull; 'jaded and dispirited' he returned home at midnight. His only motive for dining out, he confessed, 'is to take my dear Mary Stirke who looked very well and quite enjoyed her evening'. She was 'just the most amiable and lovable creature in the world', adding characteristically, 'being only 19 and totally ignorant'.[8]

But Mary could only go so far to stir her uncle's sluggish feelings. The College's annual audit day on 22 December, which entailed a long meeting during which the fellows discussed the accounts of the previous year, was 'consumed in vanity and nothingness'. Ever morbidly and unnecessarily worried about his own financial situation, the Rector's mind turned darkly to the impact of the current agricultural depression on his stipend; he felt 'a dull sense of pain for loss of income and uncertainty of how much it is to be.'[9] Even in those things dearest to him he suffered irritating pinpricks. He had recently published a short life of John Milton for a series of which John Morley, the Liberal politician and an old member of Lincoln College, was the editor. Like many other authors, his esteem was hurt by critical reviews in *The Academy* and *The Athenaeum*, 'envious, spiteful and conceited, yet, though I know that this review was only prompted by envy, I had not philosophy enough to despise it.[10] It plagued me all night and next morning.'[d] He approached Morley.

---

[d] Gardiner's review was generally appreciative and only mildly critical. 'When he deals with Milton as a poet the reader who loves his Milton feels that his only becoming attitude is that of a listening disciple at the feet of a master. Every page gives us something new to learn, or something old put in such a way as to be almost disappointing in its dealing with Milton's appearance in the world of politics. Mr Pattison entertains too strong a contempt to allow him to speak of Milton as he speaks of his literary work.'[11] Pattison says in his diary: 'After supper Mary Stirke read aloud *Spectator*, and the

Would Macmillan's allow him to make corrections for a second edition? The answer was a depressing negative.

In this narrow world, outwardly so comfortable and secure,
everything combined to torment and fatigue him. 'It seems as if
everything I touch is doomed to disappoint me ... I walk alone,
spiritless and desponding about everything.'[12] In the limited frontiers of his jaundiced spirit the most trivial incidents took on
unprecedented significance. As the last night of 1879 sped towards
the New Year, he tossed and turned in his bed, wakeful and
depressed. The pangs of hunger sent him downstairs in search of
food, but in the candle-lit gloom even the kitchen cupboard was
bare. 'I could not get a piece of bread'. What was there of hope for so
introspective a mind, atomized by self-pity, void of love, in the
promise of the coming year? Even when the College tenants were
entertained, they 'came to dine but not to pay'. The University
reform commissioners insisted on new statutes for the College, so
involving him as its head in a series of lengthy and tedious meetings
which left him so 'thoroughly knocked up' that 'he could hardly sit
in my chair'. 'Et haec dies tota periit.'[13]

He recollected Meta's eager curiosity and admiring glances, and
in late January 1880, tentatively suggested that she might, perhaps,
like to take part in the reading of a Shakespearian play, a pastime
which he often enjoyed himself. How she responded we do not
know, but in mid-January he took Mary Stirke on a visit to
London—and almost certainly called on Meta. It was bitterly cold,
inducing 'great intellectual stagnation'. 'Late hours in London, parties every night have rather jacked me.' But the 'dear Miss Bradley'
of the letter of 26 January had become the 'Dearest Meta' of February 14 when he suggested a 'turn in the Park together if it is fine
and the streets clean' and the possibility of a visit to Oxford, with
Mary acting as a chaperon. The weather proved to be 'too dirty and
windy' for the projected excursion. Mary, however, was persuaded

review of my Milton in *Academy* and *Athenaeum*. S. R. Gardiner revenging in the
Academy his private grievance about Bedford College.' Compare entry in his diary for 9
December 1879: 'Much put out in these days by the undeserved treatment which I have
met with from *The Athenaeum*. I suspect the writer of the page to be Edward Dowden a
sad tongued and unscrupulous Irish man, but though the malignity of the article pro-
ceeds from its author, the insertion of it, in the paper, is a distinct act of ill-will on the
part either of editor or subeditor.'

to postpone her departure to Yorkshire to enable Meta to make a visit to Oxford at the end of February. 'It is perhaps not absolutely necessary', the Rector told Meta, referring to Mary's presence in the Lodgings, 'but it is perhaps better, that she should be there during your visit. You being young and doubtless flighty, I might not be held by public opinion capable of satisfactorily looking after you.'[14]

Given the social climate of Oxford and its capacity for gossip, the precaution may have been wise. The Rector's propensity for the company of young girls was well known, though supposed at least by his wife to be harmless. Walter Pater observed that Mark's favourite pastime was romping with great girls among the gooseberry bushes, which would surely have afforded the least comfortable cover for a clandestine affair.[c] Mary Stirke was his young niece; she afforded an unimpeachable alibi which even his wife might accept. He was continuing to ignore her letters. 'I have written, at length, now three times since hearing from him on January 5th', she told Ellen Smith on 10 February, 'and he makes no sign'.[16] 'It is clear', she added, 'that it is his settled purpose if he cannot cast me off to make me at any rate as uncomfortable as possible.' Since he would not contribute towards her expenses, she must give up the idea of visiting Rome. 'It is clear that he will not (I think) incur the expense of taking me to Italy with him. I have done *all* that could be done, and have even entered into his views about his "mucous membrane" requiring "milk at fixed hours" ... What he wants is that *I*, *alone*, should go to pack, and wait on him.' Disappointed as she was by the outcome, she felt that she could 'not face all the discomforts which his habits bring on all those who travel under his escort.'[17]

Meanwhile, escorted by Mark and in Mary's company, Meta travelled to Oxford on Thursday, 27 February. Superficially the short visit did not seem to fulfil all his expectations. Much as he deplored the tedious nature of his existence, he was always exasperated by changes in his daily routine, disturbing the studious quiet, the early supper, the evening readings, the early bed. For Meta and Mary had to be taken to parties, to an evening party at Mrs Newcome's, Rhoda Broughton's sister, which 'quite knocked' him up. It

[c] It is said that this remark resulted from a tea-time conversation with Pater, who had brought Edmund Gosse with him, during which Pattison would only talk of 'petticoats and croquet!'[15]

was especially disconcerting to find that Meta was less intellectual than he had first supposed. The evening readings from books of a more or less serious character, though on occasions the novels of Ouida might be considered suitable for guests of less scholarly tastes, were for Mark the highlight of his day. He had a good reading voice himself. He delighted in Mary's soft tones. But Meta proved a disappointment: 'a quiet evening—Meta Bradley not worth reading to.'[18] What called forth this remark? Did she fidget or yawn? Perhaps make some naïve comment, betraying her ignorance? But the Rector was an educator. Meta might be malleable material, a mind to be made, wafted into a higher sphere. She was eager, almost too eager, to be educated. 'I think, darling', she was to tell him on 27 February 1881, 'that you should try to improve me. Surely you could say a great deal out of your 67 years' experience which my 27 would enable me to understand and use? Don't you feel a responsibility about me as you would about your daughter? You're the one person in the world whom I venerate and love deeply, and to whom I could say anything.' She asked him what to read. He made criticisms, sometimes cold and almost cruel, about her intellectual capacity. Occasionally she would rebel against the master's judgement, but in the end she would sigh and accept. His function would be tutorial as well as avuncular.

All told, her short visit could be adjudged a success. If Meta was young, she was definitely not flighty. She listened sympathetically to the sorrows of his existence. The frigidities of life, seemingly encapsulated in the isolation of academic life, melted away in her compassionate interest. He travelled back with her to London and in the course of a few days stay, during which he lunched with Charlotte Montefiore[f] and dined with Albert Dicey,[g] he called at 25

[f] Montefiores, a well-known Jewish family, with financial and literary interests; Claude Montefiore (1858-1938) took a first at Balliol in 1881, became a well-known biblical and philosophical scholar, and supporter of liberal judaism.

[g] Albert Venn Dicey (1835-1922), fellow of Trinity College Oxford 1860-72; Vinerian Professor of English Law and fellow of All Souls, Oxford 1822-1909. 'What a queer, loosely put together creature he is', Meta Bradley wrote after dining with him, 'decidedly interesting in conversation . . . but I can't think how anyone could bring himself to share his board—one meeting was enough for me.'[19]

Compare Henry James's comment after dinner with the Diceys, 'good but decidedly too ugly, useful—informationish, grotesque—Oxfordish, poor dinnerish etc., too surrounded with emulous types of the same not to make one feel that one can do better.[20]

Orsett Terrace to meet Meta's father and stepmother. When next he
visited London, he suggested a walk together, 'anywhere—Zoo or
where we can be out of the noise of cabs' followed by 'lunch at a
People's cafe'. It all sounded rather unexciting, pedestrian and parsimonious, certainly not romantic.

But the bond between them opened new vistas. In Meta he found
something more, if intangible, that his other young friends, Mary
and her sister Jeannie Stirke, Fanny Kensington,[h] Nancy Paul[i] and
Gertrude Tuckwell[j] lacked. 'It gives me new life', he wrote to Meta
on 3 March 1880, 'to mix with these young and eager souls, full as
they are of fresh aspirations, set off with grace and refinement.
There is now nothing left to me in life, out of which I can get such
nutriment for heart and interest, as out of this kind of paternal
relation—it is the one compensation for growing old.'[24]

In the spring of 1880 he went on a trip to southern Italy in search
of the sun. 'This is Calabria', he told Meta, 'I was Sunday at Taranto

[h] Fanny Kensington was related to Pattison's Oriel contemporary Arthur Kensington (d.1876), matriculated Oriel College 1832, scholar of Trinity 1833–8; fellow 1838–
42: admitted Lincoln's Inn 1837. She was a frequent visitor to the Lodgings.

[i] Nancy Paul was the daughter of Pattison's friend, Kegan Paul (1828–1902), who was
chaplain Eton (1853), became vegetarian and positivist (1854), joined Free Christian
Union (Unitarian) (1870); resigned from C. of E. living (1874). Founder of publishing
firm. Became R.C. After receiving a letter from Nancy Paul (9 December 1879) he had
written in his diary, 'I was quite right in feeling a magnetic attraction to that girl who
repelled everyone else. Compare his letter of 17.7.83, 'I rather pride myself on my
acquaintance with Nancy just because she is, as you say, so difficult to get on with. She
has a nature sensitively alive at every pore and which requires touching with extreme
tact, and above all, sympathy.'

[j] Gertrude Tuckwell ws the daughter of the Revd William Tuckwell and his wife,
Rosa, Mrs Pattison's sister. She was born on 25 April 1861. Her father who matriculated at
New College in 1848, taught at New College School from 1857 to 1864, and he was subsequently headmaster of the Collegiate School at Taunton (1864–78) and Rector of Stock-
ton, Warwick. He was a clergyman of radical views and the author of a readable but a not
wholly reliable book on contemporary Oxford, Reminiscences, in which he gave a forth-
right portrait of Mark Pattison (who disliked him).[21] Miss Tuckwell, Mrs Pattison's
favourite niece, ultimately became a socialist and a member of the Labour party. In 1885
she taught under the London School Board until in 1893 her aunt, now Lady Dilke,
appointed her her secretary. She devoted her strength and energy to vindicating Sir
Charles Dilke whom she regarded as a victim of a miscarriage of justice. She was his literary executor and with Stephen Gwynn wrote his biography.[22]

She was a beautiful and cultured woman, dedicated to philanthropy and good causes,
and a critic of low wage rates, bad sanitation and poor industrial conditions. She died
aged 90 in August 1951.[23]

and coming to this passed over the sites of two other Greek cities—
Sybaris and Metapontum, places in which 2000 years ago all the arts
and appliances of civilized life flourished or abounded—now the
country is one vast desert, the population, even in the towns, only
one degree above savages ... There are inns, such inns! In the
remotest corner of Germany or Bohemia I have never seen such
holes of filth and baseness as the dirty habits of the people. I sadly
want, in my walks, some one to carry my heavy coat, but dare not
put it into the hands of one of these *ragazzi* as he swarms with various vermin. In the towns, and only in them, is meat procurable—
and fish with which the gulf of Taranto abounds—bread and wine
and dried figs are everywhere—good ... But the face of the country
is piteous. Within miles from Cotrone, there is not a stick to be seen,
they have cut down everything that would cut.' But in such bleakness, after London's fogs and Oxford's raw mists, there was sun, 'the
glorious sun from six to six making all the world happy and cheerful
and gilding all the dirt and brutality of man. The sun and the sea—
these only have not changed since Greek days'.

He wrote in similar fashion to another of his female friends, Mrs
Thursfield: 'Here I have at last got the sun for which I was pining,
and such a sun! Think of me at 8 a.m. sitting out on the balcony,
drinking my coffee (out of a tumbler) I who cannot stand the least
draught or open window, and feeling my old bones warmed to the
marrow by the already blazing sun.' The history of these ancient
shores stirred his imagination. 'On Saturday I was at Taranto and
saw where Hannibal dragged the boats across into the river harbour.
Altogether the campaign of Hannibal in Calabria has become much
more intelligible to me and full of interest.' But how could he invoke
for Meta the classical past awash with sparkling seas, burning sun
and grained marble? Unlike Fanny Kensington she could not be
expected to have read what Herodotus wrote about Cotrone where
he was staying. He sighed. He could not hope that she could give
more than a 'fleeting moment to my adventures'. Yet her eager face
peered through that harsh, sunlit landscape. 'Of you I often think in
my solitary wanderings.'[25]

Meta was anxious about this traveller in a distant land, imagining
him ill on a bare bed in an inhospitable inn, nor were her fears unjustified. 'I was', he told Mrs Thursfield, '6 hours struggling against

it, the 2 last of which I really thought was a struggle for life. Violent cramps accompanied the discharge, beginning in the feet, and gradually ascending. I knew if they reached the stomach that it was all up with me. I got so faint at last that I had to be lifted out of bed, and in again every time by a nurse who sat up with me all night. Well, I got through with it, and am only now waiting to recover a little strength for the voyage towards home.'[26] With good reason Meta stressed her gladness at his return from the 'land of your dreams' to the inhospitable climate of an English Spring.

While he had been away Mary Stirke had been staying with Uncle Frank and Aunt Margaret Pattison at 7 Burwood Place not far from the Bradley residence which Mary visited frequently. She was a welcome guest, even winning the approval of Meta's father, who invited her to join his yacht in the Clyde for a holiday in the summer.

Freed from the rural austerities of Wensleydale and the routine of the Rector's Lodgings, Mary plunged into a round of parties. The news caused disquiet to her uncle. It was, he said, a 'very bad sort of life' for her. His puritanical instincts, rooted in the inexorable *régime* of Hauxwell, never lay far below the surface. They were not stilled by learning that Meta and Mary had gone to attend the Hibbert lectures which were being given by the French humanist, Ernest Renan.[k] 'I have been to all', Meta proudly told her mentor, 'and understood a great deal. Renan speaks slowly and we had capital seats so Mary understood more than she expected.'[27]

The Rector was not persuaded. Mary knew no French. She 'could not understand a word of the language, let alone the matter'.[28] What was worse, Mary was tumbling from the pedestal on which he had placed her early in the winter. He had been unwell. But had she offered to come to Oxford? 'If Mary had been the girl she ought to be, she would have at once come down to nurse me. As it is she has not even thought it worth while to write me a line of sympathy in answer to the piteous letters I sent her telling her of my forlorn condition.'[29] Perhaps Mary had learned enough from her winter's stay in Oxford to realize her uncle's dominating nature. She continued to stay in London. Even Meta was roused to Mary's defence. 'What do you mean, dearest Meta', Mark responded, 'by saying Mary is very

[k] The lectures were a series of historical sketches of the influence of Rome on Christianity and the developments of the Christian Church.

penitent? Has she expressed herself to you at all aware of her improper behaviour in his business?' 'All those weeks', he commented censoriously, 'without a duty or an occupation', mingling 'with people who live without any moral ideal.'[30]

The charge was monstrously unfair and wounding. Hurt by Mark's disapproval, Mary decided to refuse Meta's father's invitation to cruise on his yacht and sped trainwards to the quiet green dales of home. 'She knew', Meta told Mark, 'you were quite right and that she ought to have gone home; but I could not guess how awfully she liked being in London (I do trust that does not refer to any man).' The letter was intended to propitiate; its reference to a young man prim and puritanical. It showed that Meta still feared Mark's disapproval. He was not wholly persuaded of Mary's 'consciousness of error'. She was, he admitted, if a trifle grudgingly, 'solidly good' with a 'heart so fresh', but 'she was being made too much of, while her good qualities were due to her not having been flattered and admired'. Mary's relations with her uncle were never to be so close or harmonious again; and his attitude demonstrated the limitations of his sympathy where his own interests were at stake.

The trivial saga of Mary's extended stay in London carried on to early summer. Mark had returned to face the Trinity term in Oxford with a heavy cold and low spirits. 'You must be very lonely', Meta wrote; unerringly this time she had touched a raw nerve.[31] This was exactly what he felt. 'I am very wretched, shut up alone with my cold, and no one coming to see me. I have my books to which I come back fresh, but the eyes and head are not equal to living 14 hours on books—and weariness, if not satiety, comes before the afternoon is over.'[32]

Her own dejection created a sympathetic bond between them. She visualized a 'most unpleasant summer', her stepmother absent in America, though that was no great loss, and herself forced into her father's company on his yacht. 'The prospect makes me feel wretched already.' But could anything be done, Mark enquired, 'to help you out of the fix?' Momentarily he toyed with the idea of inviting her to Oxford, then recollected how his wife would react, and regretfully for the nonce dismissed it. To meet abroad 'without a chaperon' was an impossibility. Meta must console herself with the notion that she was fulfilling a filial duty. She must, even in Mark's

liberal view, submit herself to the self-destructive pressure of paren-
tal demand by making an act of self-sacrifice; 'You will have the sense
of duty to support you through the discomforts and trials which
inevitably await you.'[33] It might reasonably be thought that to spend
the summer cruising in the Scottish isles, even in the company of an
unloved parent, was an act neither of martyrdom nor of self-sacrifice.
But Mark and Meta tended to dramatize the trivial discomforts of
their existence. The letter was in any case a sign of his deepening
affection. 'Confide', he begged, 'your troubles to me.'

    She had troubles. Relations with her father had become strained to
breaking-point. She admitted that he had good points, nobility and,
in certain situations, a measure of generosity. 'As a curate he lived on
next to nothing, wore the shabbiest clothes, did without a horse for a
large straggling parish, etc. that he might send Granville and the
other brothers to Rugby and Oxford.' But he was rigid, intolerant,
and opinionated, with a 'passion for keeping people in order and cor-
recting their faults, always sees faults before good points'.[34] Meta
could not forget her mother. 'She was the friend and confidante of
everyone who came across her, even for an hour.'[35] 'When I lost my
mother, I lost the one person whom I almost worshipped, and
though I was only twelve I don't think I feel much less wretched than
I did at first.'[36] Nor could she forgive her father his second marriage.
The second Mrs Charles Bradley was an interloper. 'Can't you
imagine how I almost hated Mrs Bradley and my father though I
never said so to a soul.'[37] That unfortunate well-disposed woman,
who showed so much more understanding of Meta's relationship
with Mark than her husband, was a 'perfect fool', a chatterbox with
no intellectual interests whatsoever. 'I'm sure the White Queen in
Alice was succinct in comparison.'[38][m] 'Mrs Bradley', she remarked,
'rambled on without a pause from soup to the middle of pudding
today! Did you ever live with a garulous [sic—Meta's spelling was not
impeccable] fool? If I were cook I should put some poison into the
family food.' However much Mrs Bradley wished to be kind to Meta,
she would not have dared to oppose her husband.

[1] 'allowing him [C. Bradley] to think that you are looking forward to the expedition
with delight is a pitch of virtue beyond the limits of martyrdom, and which even the
most stoical novelist could not exact.'

[m] Mark did not share Meta's harsh view of her stepmother, 'I wish you were nice to
Mrs Bradley. No doubt she is trying but she has spoken so well about you.'

In such a household she found herself, or believed herself, to be a square peg in a round hole, 'as I can't give Mrs Bradley any, or my father much, affection... You can't, I hope, imagine what it is to live with people who rub you up the wrong way every moment you are with them.'[39] 'It requires', she told Mark six months later, 'such a heavenly temper to put up with perpetual complaints about trifles! You can have no idea of the sort of life I lead at home. As far as conversation goes we might be living in the middle ages. The weather and people we have met are our only topics.'[40] Perhaps Meta's comment was somewhat unfair to medieval society.

If Meta could be provoking, as even Mark discovered, all the fault was not on her side. She was certainly prickly and impulsive, lacking in tact and diplomacy. 'I can't pretend to care for people when I prefer their absence to their presence.'[41] 'I am very unlike most people', perhaps she prided herself unduly on her individuality.[42] She pictured herself as 'very impulsive, uncomfortably frank, absurdly sentimental, romantic and dreamy and absent, dreadfully excitable, irritable, always bent on having my own way, though affectionate'.[43] 'That you are irritable', Mark agreed, 'I know full well enough, but hesitate to subscribe to your being "sentimental and romantic". Images and emotions do not abide in you long [enough] to generate a sentiment. Your mind is swept by a constant succession of images each effacing the one before it without giving it time to impress itself.'[44]

She saw herself in contemporary terms as a high-minded, serious, idealistic young woman. Her religious beliefs had evaporated into a near-agnosticism. Characteristically her father expected her to attend church. Her lack of religious conviction was an open cause of friction with her father and a secret bond with Mark.

Although Mark fulfilled his rectorial duties at Oxford by attending chapel and even on occasions celebrating the Communion service[n] as well as assisting his brother-in-law, Canon Roberts, the Rector of Richmond, when he was holidaying in Yorkshire, his faith had attenuated itself to some sort of instinctive belief in a Platonic or Hegelian world-consciousness. 'What a resource prayer

---

[n] e.g. entries in his diary 3.3.79; 5.2.82; 26.5.82; ('It being Merry's Communion Sunday read the whole service, for which he never said thank you'); 13.5.82 ('Communion, officiated and read morning service, not omitting the Athanasian Creed').

is to those who can pray', he once wrote to Meta, '... for those who have no supernatural aid at hand, there is an appeal to moral energy, to the power of the will.'[45] He had come to regard orthodoxy theology as little better than superstition and had a rancorous destestation of clericalism in any shape or form. 'Priests', he once wrote to Gertrude Tuckwell, 'are generally professional quacks trading in beliefs they don't share.'[46] No wonder that Meta's Oxford relatives feared for the pernicious influence that he might have over Meta's soul. But if Meta had liberated herself from religious creeds, unlike Mark, she was wedded to the notion of social improvement. She believed in and practised redemption by good works. 'Indifferent to her own comfort', Meta's niece Olive Heseltine wrote of her, 'a zealous and indefatigable social worker, her protégés were as numerous as they were ungrateful, and few good causes lacked her support.'[47] 'Your aunt', commented Sir Cradoc Pomfret in Olive's novel *The Three Daughters*, 'has been pestering me to sign some petition for rest houses for overworked bus horses.'[48] But her immersion in social work was as yet something in the future.

It was by and large expected of Victorian young women that they would find fulfilment in marriage. It was probably what Charles Bradley expected of Meta. But although Meta from time to time alluded to possible suitors, none seemed in sight. She did not designedly make herself attractive to men. As Mark himself somewhat petulantly told her, for a woman she was curiously neglectful of and indifferent to what she wore. 'I so hate the trouble of choosing clothes, that I shall struggle on in rags until I have a spare day.'[49] When Meta told Mark that she wanted to buy him a racket-press, he replied spiritedly, 'If you have such a superfluity of cash, lay it out on a dress, and make yourself more tidy.'[50] He offered to buy her a new jacket at Marshall and Snelgrove's ('what fun we will have choosing it') but at this point she showed some independence.[51] 'Don't be too sure about the jacket; I must consult my dress-maker. I don't think I could get what I want ready-made, and it is too important a thing to take only one man to help to choose it.'[52] Eventually Mark agreed that Meta should select the jacket on her own and he would pay for it, adding penuriously and characteristically, 'I need not pay till July'.[53] 'Why', she said aggressively, 'should I dress well? I don't care to be noticed or to make myself look more than just tidy.'[54] However much the Rector might suggest marriage as a serious solution to her problems, even at twenty-six she seemed ordained to join the band of frustrated spinsters.

Meta was in the familiar position of many a Victorian unmarried daughter. She lacked any professional skill which would enable her to earn a living, or at any rate to find a job which would have been thought suitable for a woman of genteel birth. She was financially dependent on her father, so that whenever he pulled the strings she was obliged to obey. Without effective education and yet desirous of self-improvement she found her lot lonely as well as unhappy. 'Can't you imagine', she remarked to the Rector, 'how often I've gone out for a solitary walk when in the country and rolled on the grass in an agony of tears which no one ever dreamed of.'[55] Loneliness and the craving for affection constituted a bond which drew them together in spite of the yawning gap of age. Perhaps because she realized her loneliness, Meta reacted strongly to Mark's suggestion that she lacked friends. 'I must be very lucky', she told him, 'in girls I know. I never meet the idiots one perpetually comes across in books, and I find it rather difficult to believe in the existence of utterly frivolous creatures without a thought but their own amusement.'[56] If she had female friends, they were not such that she could treat them as confidantes in the way that she came to treat Mark.

She had never met anyone like him before. She was fascinated, even enchanted, by his learning. He could be confessor, father, friend, though whatever his own secret sexual needs, it was doubtful how far he could take on effectively the *rôle* of an actual lover. He would provide sympathy, guidance, and direction. When Meta and her companion, Fanny Kensington, left to join her father's yacht, he readily provided a reading list. 'For books you should have *two* going at once—one poetry for your higher moods—one a novel for ordinary wear, say *Aurora Leigh* or *Childe Harold* for poetry, and for novel any well-written one—*The Pirate* or *The Princess of Thule* would be appropriate in point of subject.'[57] The advice was almost Gladstonian in its pedantry and seriousness. If she was awed by his scholarship and condescension, he glowed in the heat of her genuine interest, admiration, and compassion. However odd such a friendship might appear to the outside world, they had a need of each other. The need generated affection, though how far into the deeper recesses of love we shall never know.

The spring and early summer of 1880 brought them closer together. Mark tried to find a regular meeting-place, such as the National Gallery where Meta went to study drawing. 'Dear Meta, if there is a fine morning, we will arrange for a walk somewhere to lunch.'[58] 'I waited', he wrote a little regretfully, 'at the gate of the National Gallery ten minutes this morning, from 11.5 to 11.15, as I saw nothing of you I conclude you were punctual in arriving and had got into the building during the first five minutes of its being open! It being a Students' day I was not allowed to enter.'[59] A further vain attempt at meeting led him to comment that Meta had become 'tired of your painting'. 'I could meet you in Trafalgar Square.'[60] For where Mark was punctilious to the point of pedantry, Meta was often vague about times and places. Courtenay Ilbert told his wife in January 1880 that he had found a young lady at Orsett Terrace whom Meta had invited to lunch while Meta had gone to lunch at the Toynbees. 'It was a characteristic performance of Meta's.' None the less they managed to get together. Meta introduced Mark to one of her friends, Grace Toynbee, whom she persuaded the Rector to invite to Oxford.[61] 'Certainly', Mark confessed, 'I like new acquisitions', adding 'that does not make me waver in my fidelity to the old ones when I have once found one with whom I can have a feeling about the heart.'[o] She wanted him to meet another friend, Helen Colvill, who had recently written a novel, *A Dreamer*, under the pen-name of Katherine Wylde which *The Times* and *Spectator* had praised but the *Saturday Review* had criticized harshly.[p] She is rather younger than I am, lives in the country with an invalid mother, and evangelical father, knows no men and hardly any girls, is ugly and minds it.'[q] It seemed a prescription that would be unlikely to win Mark's patronage. Mark replied cautiously. There could be only limited conversation in the National Gallery and Helen was so shy. For the moment the suggestion was shelved.

[o] Grace Toynbee (1858–1946), sister of Arnold and Mary Toynbee, educated Bedford College, author and journalist, researched into bacteriology, wrote life of Pasteur.[62]

[p] The story 'is not that easy to follow or to describe, for it is full of complications. Moreover it is so very dull that it is almost impossible to summon up sufficient patience to master the plot.'[63]

[q] 'Colonel Colvill is icy and forbidding, not obnoxious.'[64]

Between Mark and Meta there was a deepening bond of intimacy
which the gentle walks—'how immensely I enjoyed my stroll with
you'—the meetings at the National Gallery and the Grosvenor, the
conversations at the College for men and women in Queen Square
and University College in Gordon Square, all helped to promote.[65]
When they could not meet, they felt wounded; some indispensable
element was missing. 'I used to flatter myself', Meta told Mark, 'that I
had grown too old to be disappointed much, but whenever I am
unlucky to miss you I feel horribly cross for days.'[66] Too old at 26!
Mark, only four years short of seventy, found Meta's letters a source
of new life: 'practical yet full of another interest, which practical
peoples' letters seldom are'. 'Has knowing me "made" a difference to
your life? To be able to be of use to any soul, is my one interest in living now, and if I would think that I could afford you the sympathy
you require, it would be a source of the greatest satisfaction to me. I
am unable yet to decide which is the greater pleasure, to give, or to
receive sympathy.'[67] It would surely be wrong to dismiss, as most of
his critics have done, Mark's interest in Meta as purely self-centred.
She had opened, if fleetingly, ducts of warmth long closed through
which genuine affection circulated. 'Good-bye! dearest Meta', he
wrote as she left to join her father's yacht, the *Swift*, at Rothesay,
'and may I live to see you return safe and sound from your expedition . . . I shall look for your letters, with anxious expectation.'[68]

Naturally taciturn, often finding conversation an effort, he found
that correspondence was an especially satisfactory medium for
strengthening their relationship. In his presence Meta was still a trifle
embarrassed, even tongue-tied. She found it much easier to talk to
Daisy Woods than to Mark. 'When I am with you I feel so self-
conscious, such an utter idiot, that I can't talk to you comfortably.
You are the only man of whom I have ever felt the least afraid, and
though I am getting over that, I still feel queer when I am with you.
Writing is different.'[69] Writing *was* different. Meta was no stylist.
Her words poured out in indiscriminate profusion; the paragraphs
were loose; the sentences often ponderous; the judgements frequently jejune; the content trivial. 'There is no art in her writing',
Mark confided to his diary, 'but without art she will reproduce most
vividly what has passed in her presence.'[70] In her letters Meta could
explore her thoughts and express her personality.

During the summer expedition to Scotland nothing gave her greater pleasure than to retire to her cabin and in the dim low light write her long scrawls to Mark. 'One thing', he observed, 'your yachting cruise has brought about, distasteful as it is to you in many respects, that it has opened your consciousness and your heart in my view, in a way which it has never so displayed yet, one which has been an equal surprise and delight to me.'[71] Yet she was not visually observant. 'Do you feel a "deep peacefulness" when surrounded by beautiful scenery? I hardly ever am affected by it in that way.'[72] Her descriptions were platitudinous to the point of mediocrity. She compared Scotland with Switzerland, the latter so 'clear and distinct . . . little feeling of mystery though much of awe. Here everything is restless and changing, one moment dazzlingly bright and the next hidden by mist, with a good deal more cloud than sunshine, like one's life.'[73] 'I think', as Mark told her later, 'you can be enthusiastic about some things, but not about nature. The truth is you don't know enough about it, and only take that superficial view which would be equally gratified by the drop curtain in the Haymarket.'[74]

Her comments on literature, which she was at pains to insert since she believed that these might impress Mark, were as unsophisticated as her pen portraits of the landscape. Deeply aware of her ignorance, she had, it will be remembered, sought the Rector's guidance as to what books to read on the voyage. She kept him informed of her progress. 'I've been reading *Adonais* . . . How wonderfully beautiful Shelley is . . . Reading in bed is extra tempting on board, as one has a candleholder swinging just over one's head. I've been reading 'Marmion', 'The Lay' and 'Lord of the Isles.'[75] She thought Scott 'spiritual and stirring' but deficient in the human element. The Rector was pleased at her growing interest in literature. 'A person who is broad enough to feel both Shelley and Scott has made progress pretty far.'[76] To spur on her efforts he sent her journals, *Truth, The Athenaeum*, as well as the newspapers. She had still some way to go to touch an answering chord in his literary guarded mind. He was surprised when she told him that a poem had brought tears to her eyes. 'You always seem to me so indifferent. You would sit and listen patiently to anything I would read, or read it to me, but it would be all the same to you whatever it was.'[77]

Letter-writing helped Meta to forget the depression which had gripped her at the thought of the voyage. Her mood had been so black when she embarked that she had retired immediately to her cabin, tormented by a 'huge blue devil'. 'I wonder whether it is one of the advantages of age to feel a calm not altogether unpleasant sort of melancholy, or whether you still know what intense, overpowering wretchedness is, for which tears are no relief.' In London there were at least diversions, but in Campbeltown there was only a sense of hopelessness. 'What a wonderful thing death is. It causes one such hopeless misery when it carries away one's dearest, while one can often look forward to one's own death with something of longing and perfect peacefulness.'[78] The mood was made darker by fond memories of a past holiday spent with her mother in Cantire (Kintore). But Mark, obsessively aware of the passage of time which old age highlights, saw death as an enemy rather than as a neutral arbiter.

Actually the cruise round the western isles turned out to be a good deal better than Meta thought it would be. She had two congenial girls as companions, Helen Ilbert and Fanny Kensington. Mark had himself once picked out Fanny as a possible ideal companion, only to find in her a 'deficiency of sentiment ... the want [of which] made itself felt in the long run'. Meta was herself not wholly happy about Fanny. Although she had 'quite lost that simper ... She has aged a good deal and does not seem all that strong ... All the little life she had has been quite knocked out of her.'[79] Since both girls knew the Rector, Meta was delighted with the opportunity to talk about him. 'We don't exactly talk about you, having done that long ago, but are often referring to you, wishing you could see this view, read that remark, or even exclaiming, "That is just what the Rector would have said!!!" '[80] And so slowly from Campbeltown to Tignabruiach, Inverary to Rothesay. They panted up Goat Fell and paddled in the cool highland burns. They sketched and read to each other, Fanny selecting appropriately enough Boswell's *Tour to the Hebrides* which Meta found 'very entertaining'. Even Charles Bradley relaxed in a plethora of feminine company—Meta thought some of the girls not 'particularly attractive'—finding Helen Ilbert especially pleasant since she behaved more like he hoped his daughter would behave.[r]

---

[r] Helen Ilbert was the sister of Courtenay Ilbert. She was a woman of some character and determination.

Sustained by regular correspondence, the intimacy between Mark and Meta ripened. The Rector planned that Meta should visit Oxford in the autumn. 'I intend to be "very nice" to you when Daisy [Woods] is away.' Sitting in the solitude of his study or pacing up and down the narrow book-room it was the image of Meta which became imprinted firmly on his mind. 'You don't know how much you count in my poor life.'[81] 'Do I really "count for something in your life"', Meta responded, 'it seems much too good and improbable to be true, and yet I can't think that you would say it if you didn't mean it.' 'I think of you so much oftener than of any living being . . . Of course I shan't forget your invitation for October and I'll stay as long as ever you like! . . . I'm afraid that I shall never understand how you can possibly take the least interest in me. I must be content to add another to the many mysteries of my life.'[82] 'Are you really', Mark replied, 'what your two last letters seem to imply you are? If you are, dearest Meta, you are the very person I have been looking for, but despaired of finding! . . . Now I am deeply interested in you and am already off on a voyage of discovery over your mind and nature. I almost long for it to be October, that I may prosecute my researches. No, you never expanded in conversation like this, but I am aware,' he added in an unusual self-revelatory note, 'that I am myself in fault there, for though I know that I am of a tenderly sympathetic nature, I am aware of a certain chilliness of manner which hinders those I should most willingly approach from doing so. Now the ice is broken with you, and after what you have revealed to me in your yachting meditations, I take you to my heart in an inner sense.'[83]

The summer had been placid. He could retire to imbibe long draughts of reading in the cool of the book-room, redolent with the scent of old leather, 'all the economy alone to roam about my books, a family which has multiplied of late so fast that I have come not to know them by sight even.'[84] One visit cast some shadows over the future, for Mrs Eustace Smith spent a day at the Lodgings 'and we had a most pleasant ramble down the meadows in search of fritil-laries': Donald Crawford and his wife, Mrs Smith's daughter, Virginia, came to dinner that evening. His wife's niece, Gertrude Tuckwell, 'a very dear girl but a child', was there to cheer him up; she was, he thought, 'wonderfully intelligent, but deficient in interest, [she] has the air of a girl who is blasé by having had a wide surface presented to her view, and not habituated to penetrate to the inside of anything.'[s]

If Oxford was peaceful, it was also humid. He felt suffocated by college walls and yearned to savour the country air, fresh and free, and to enjoy the wide open spaces of moor and dale. Unlike Meta, he remained at heart a countryman. 'There comes over me', he exclaimed after reading Meta's account of her Scottish trip, 'the wish at times that I were with you there among the "nodding promontories and blue isles, and cloud like mountains and dividuous waves"—the deep peacefulness which such surroundings never fail to bring me.' 'For want of oxygen' he was 'dropping below par'. His wife's presence added to his want of ease. 'Had to sit with F[rancis] now from 7 to 9 for civility's sake which is very fretting', he wrote on 12 June, 'at 9 made my escape under the pretence of smoking and read Mrs Pfeiffer's *Glen Alarch*.'[86] In early August he travelled up to Yorkshire. Richmond—'no town in England equals Richmond in picturesquesness of situation'—was his immediate destination, but he moved north in the foreknowledge that Meta was herself going to join her sister Jessie at Grasmere after she left the yacht. So the desire for country air may well have been strengthened by the expectation that he would see and talk with Meta. The 'magnetic attraction you will exercise will tell more at a shorter distance. If I come will you promise to read Wordsworth to me?'[87]

Mark's roots were deep in the North Riding. 'My mother was a native of Richmond, and my father had, first a curacy [at Hornsby] then a living [Hauxwell] at little distance from the town. When I have "Heimweh" which happens to me every spring, it is for Wensleydale and Swaledale. I am not happy unless I have had a breath of this air at least once every two years.'[88] Outside Wensleydale in some sense his heart was in exile. He had spent his formative years walking and fishing there before he went to Oxford. Some of his sisters lived still in the neighbourhood—Mary, the wife of Canon Roberts, the Rector of Richmond, Sarah Bowes, the wife of the local doctor, and Fanny, still

---

[s] Pattison corresponded with Gertrude Tuckwell. Most of his letters to her deal with intellectual or semi-academic questions and are generally impersonal in tone e.g. 'My dear G, I like you to write to me . . . Surely I never said you wanted "information" . . . If I were to say anything about you, I should say what you wanted was (not information but) interests.' (l. 9.80): 'To begin with these supreme problems . . . is to begin at the wrong end.[85] You should begin with the grammar of philosophy and work up.' (15.4.81.)

unmarried.[t] The children of his favourite sister, Rachel, Mary and
Jeannie Stirke, as we have seen, lived with their stepmother at Grazing Nook. Yet Mark had no deep affection for his relatives: 'None of
the Pattisons have any heart.'[89]

But he had not returned to the North Riding for human companionship. He sought solace for his spirit in the natural wildness of
grass and heather, wind, water and sunlight. 'I came down here', he
told Meta, 'on Tuesday, suffering much from 14 hours' train, and
dawdle in stations, branch lines, late arrivings, and all the miseries,
but, dear Meta, I was compensated on Wednesday for all I had gone
through on the previous day. I had a most glorious day up Swaledale
5 or 6 hours by the riverside in a wild glen—absolutely alone—no
sight or sound of human being, wood, water, hill, cloud, birds, fishes,
such splendid company—no London salon was to be compared to it.
It sank into me, and I was thirsting for it. ... One can have one such
day in a season—not many such in a life-time. O, to arrive each
Monday morning from London, to land each Tuesday from the rich
Levant! But Keats did not consider that if the sensation were to be
repeated each week, it would lose its savour. How preposterous is
the Paterian notion of a life made up of agreeable sensations—if you
want to repeat them, the sensation is there but the pleasure is wanting?' With such auspices his spirit soared, shedding if but temporarily the natural melancholy that clouded his life at Oxford. 'O! I
had such a delicious day yesterday up the dale. My sister has got me a
fishing leave on Mr. Hutton's water ... I spend 6 to 7 hours each
morning on the banks of one of the most lovely streams of the
North, without seeing one single human being. Absolute solitude,
yet this is not a wild moor bleak and waste, but is a smiling grassy
dale with just enough cliff to be romantic without being savage. I
have a trap to take me up about 4 miles, and to meet me again in the
afternoon in time to dress for 4 o'clock tea.'[90] It would have been so
pleasant if Meta and her sister could have joined him at Richmond,
for the omens for his own visit to Grasmere were not wholly propi-
tious. Meta had sprained her ankle and was confined to the sofa, so
making it impossible for her to take the pleasant strolls to which he
so looked forward. Moreover the coincidence of his visit with the

[t] Fanny Pattison (1821–92) eventually became Mother Superior of the Holy Rood at
Middlesbrough.

Grasmere sports had made the finding of accommodation no easy matter. At the minimum he required a bedroom with a private sitting-room. 'Fortune', he growled, 'has been so against me, that I feel somehow as if my visit to Grasmere was one of the things that are not to be.' But his 'first hunger' for his native streams and walks had abated, so he packed his bags and on a Friday, in late August, joined Meta and her sister Jessie at Grasmere.

Victorian Grasmere, steeped in memories of Wordsworth (Mark had brought with him *Selections* of his poetry and looked forward to their reading *The Prelude* together), verdant, wooded, hill-strewn, its minute lake diamond-paned, had still an idyllic quality, even if Mark was later to compare it unfavourably with Wensleydale. There were already too many tourists and too much litter. Although Meta's sprain made walking impossible, the visit passed agreeably. Jessie, though later critical of Mark's relationship with her younger sister, went out of her way to make herself pleasant. Jessie was temperamentally a woman of 'decisive temper and positive opinions' who frequently criticized Meta for her argumentativeness and lack of taste in what she wore. But she behaved very graciously to Mark at their first meeting, even going so far as to make chicken sandwiches for him to eat on the journey home. 'I assure you', Meta told him, 'that my sister's niceness to you was quite unsuggested by me . . . She has never been pleasant to any friend of mine, as such, so you really must make up your mind that her action was caused by regard for you, not me!'[91]

Refreshed and stimulated by Meta's evident affection, Mark returned to college. 'Dear Meta', he wrote on his arrival, 'There is now no one from whom I get the special form of attachment which you have found it in your heart to bestow upon me. I am now building upon it for my old age, as I used to do on Mary, who has failed me. Can you wonder if, having been so often deceived, I have misgivings about everybody, yes about you, who have unsolicited, taken me into your goodwill.'[92] 'No, dear Rector', she reassured him, 'I neither wonder nor feel hurt at your misgivings about the durability of my affection for you. I know perfectly well that it will last as long as I do, but I can't expect you to have the same confidence, after your experience. No, you can't do anything for me except let me care as much for you as ever I like, and love me a little in return. When you were here [i.e. Grasmere] I felt so happy merely in being with you that I didn't care very much about anything else. I don't think I've ever been so happy since I was a child.'[93]

The exhilaration which he had felt immediately on his return soon faded. Deprived of Meta's companionship, he sank inevitably into a mood of dejection. 'It is melancholy work, so petted as I have been lately, to come back here where no one cares if I am alive or dead.'[94] The summer heat, which had, as he put it, caused some 'relaxation of his nervous membrane' at Grasmere, left the atmosphere dry and brittle; there were cracks in the tennis courts on which he played. His plans for a trip abroad were foiled by lack of congenial companions to go with him. Since the Lodgings were about to be painted and cleaned, he had to find alternative accommodation.

As he approached the dreaded anniversary of his wedding day on 10 September, his spirits sank to an even lower ebb. 'Do you know the 10 September is an anniversary which depresses me to the lowest depths of misery. The heart pain which it brings with it lasts for days and is still vivid.'[95] The remainder of the letter was deliberately cut out, but the intensity of his feeling was plain enough. Aware of how he felt, Meta tried to be reassuring.

I wish I could once for all make you understand my feelings about you. . . . Do try and imagine yourself a girl who could not care very much for her nearest relations, and was always being told by them she had no heart. She didn't agree with them, but was obliged to confess to herself that she didn't love any living being very much . . . This young woman meets someone of whom she has always heard as a mine of learning etc., and to her great surprise he actually takes a friendly interest in her. At first she is only grateful and alarmed, but she soon feels that this kind friend somewhere feels as lonely and wretched very often as she does; and then by degrees she thinks much oftener of him than of anyone and gets to feel for him what she feared she never should feel for anyone, what other people say they feel for several of their relatives. Can't you imagine, dear Rector, what I feel for the person who has shown me that I still have a heart, and how glad I am that my deep and real affection is some comfort to what you call your old age! You must tear up this sheet which might astonish your servants' weak minds.[96]

Mark disregarded this last request, as he was to do with other similar ones. The letter was too precious, an epistle to be read and re-read, not to be relegated to the waste-paper basket.

Indeed its arrival, more or less coinciding with the fateful anniversary, touched Mark deeply. '... I feel deeply thankful for the assurance it brings me that I have, in my last moments, been fortunate enough to obtain such friendship as that which you are ready to bestow upon me. I am still amazed at the accident of our "rapprochement" for there does not seem "prima facie" any ground of sympathy, while the difference of ages opposes a barrier to begin with, which ought to have made it doubly difficult to bring heart into play. Oh! that your good will towards me may only last my life, that is all my prayer now, what a consolation it will be to me in my time of decay.'[97]

Meta promised him enduring sympathy and affection. 'I can't think', she wrote, 'how you can have lived through those dreadfully painful years with only a tiny ray of hope to keep you up ... The thought of then and now must be almost maddening. Nothing can deprive you of the long years of such loving companionship as I imagine few people are capable of, but those years only make their successors the darker by contrast. Separation by death would have been far less agonizing. Perhaps some day you'll tell me what built up such a wall of ice between you ... To meet must be most painful and I don't wonder that you could stay at Oxford no longer. That such love as yours should be rejected is indeed a strange and cruel fate. Of course no one can in the least be to you what she was. I have never so much regretted my mental inferiority as I do now, but I can't doubt that my deep affection is much to you ... I do wish I had some right to be with you in Lincoln whenever you feel extra lonely and wretched ... I thought of your loneliness last night for hours ... I should be proud to give my life to alter things for you.'[98]

Mark's account of his married life, so uncritically accepted by Meta, was one-sided and partisan. Meta's letter helped to confirm him in his belief that he was the injured party, whereas it was painfully apparent that he had to bear some responsibility for the gradual collapse of his marriage. 'At least one person in the world', he responded, 'knows what a heavy cross I have to carry about, and can at least see something of the difficult path I have to act in my behaviour to my wife. You say that some day I may tell you *how* such a wall of ice came to be built between us. If I do not do so now, it is not because your words of intelligent sympathy are not

sufficient encouragement for me to do so, but partly on account of
the difficulty of putting such a history on paper; partly because to
have said as much as I have done has been such a wrench to my
reserve, that I have not the force to make a second effort.'[99]

Feeling as he did, he was not pleased to learn that his wife
intended to make a brief visit to Oxford, presumably to check the
arrangements for the re-decoration of the Lodgings. She had come to
London much concerned about the state of Sir Charles Dilke's
health. 'I have had a great deal of anxiety, and *now* have for that
matter', she told Ellen Smith at the end of August. 'The discharge of
which I had told you causing so much suffering to our friend [Dilke]
was stopped by strong remedies which seem to have caused frightful
congestion and piles. The torture was so great from that that on the
15th at York House he was creeping about white to the lips with
anguish. He then took to his bed and now it is found there is an
internal abcess which, if not burst by tomorrow, is to be lanced.'[100]

The Rector reacted to his wife's arrival by telling Meta not to write
to him at Oxford; 'she opens my letters and though she would not
read one from you, you might prefer sending yours to me direct. So
wait till I can send you an address.'[101] Mark had in fact under-
estimated his wife's curiosity. She opened Meta's heart-felt letter of
10 September whilst the Rector was away, and forwarded it to him
with a note on the back beginning 'I was delighted to get a line from
you dear Mark this morning, and guess you were not feeling ill.' 'I
have', she told Ellen Smith, 'been doing my best to fit in with the
Rector in vain, as usual, or worse than in vain! He told me he would
be absent September, so I made arrangements to the Grant Duffs, my
sisters, with Mrs Earle for the whole of September. He has now been
absent for the whole of *this* month [August], but has never let us
know whether he was staying away for a day or a week or a month,
so one has been on the "fidgets" the whole time. Having been absent
so long I *suspect* that the September visit to Germany is off, and that
he will be here all that month. If so I shall curtail my visits but I shall
not abandon them as I now believe he takes a crooked pleasure in
throwing me out in this way, and that the more I yield to it the more
"contrairy" he will be.'[102]

The visit to Germany was certainly off, but he was disinclined to
stay at the Lodgings where the workmen were taking over. As the

weather had broken, he abandoned the idea of returning to York-shire.

He visited his friends, the Taylors, at Aston Rowant, to play tennis, finding the younger Taylor girl, then a student at Girton, quite attractive company, 'yet even she has a taint of the emulation system, and wants true interest, in *what* she is learning, though full of zeal for the process'. Then he went to London to consult his doctor, Andrew Clark, but as Clark was out of town he only saw his locum, Dr Cayley, who was 'not very helpful'. He lunched at Putney with the writer Emily Pfeiffer,[u] 'very sensible in spite of her feathers, and her head on one side—two things which the women cannot for-give'.[103] He called too on his friend Emily Herbert, recently married to a fellow of Jesus College, Oxford, J. R. Thursfield, later a distin-guished naval historian (and knighted in 1920), 'fresh, young, pleasing, good-looking, well-mannered and very anxious to improve herself, but that seems to me all'.

London did not raise his spirits. It impressed him as a 'mean and filthy hole', redeemed only by the fresh green of its parks. 'I felt a sense of loneliness being there by myself.' A touch of rheumatism in his left shoulder made him select a southerly resort, Ventnor in the Isle of Wight. Although there was no tennis (a good ground but no net or 'young ladies to play if there was one'), his hotel, the Royal, proved to be an excellent choice. 'I have a cheerful room looking on to the sea, and a Brobdingnagian beaker of milk, real milk, with the breakfast coffee.' He strolled along the seashore, treading the shingle, towards Steephill and Bonchurch. The sun shone. 'I have not seen, or felt, such a sun since Sicily', and imperceptibly he felt more cheerful.

From Ventnor he went on to visit his Jewish friends, the Monte-fiores, at their house, Cold East, at Waltham. 'I hate staying in people's houses, yet I don't seem to have better to propose to myself just now.' Yet even 'Charlotte [Montefiore] sacrificed herself to what she supposed to be my wishes and entertainment for two days and I

---

[u] Emily Pfeiffer (1827-90), the daughter of an army officer, married Jurgen Edward Pfeiffer, London merchant, in 1853. She was the author of many books of poetry, *Guste-man's Grave* (1879), *Sonnets and Soup* (1880), *Under the Aspen* (1882), *The Rhyme of the Lady of the Rock* (1884), and *Flying Leaves*. A keen feminist and philanthropist, she founded an orphanage, designed the endowment of a school of dramatic art, and left money to promote women's higher education; the residential hall for women students, Aberdare Hall, was opened at Cardiff in 1895 as a result of her benefaction.

was petted and made as much of as I could desire.'[104] By early October he was back in College, preparing for the Salt lecture which he delivered on 7 October.'[v] 'The whole evening was very satisfactory, and the Salt and Byles set just the sort I like, cultivated and ladylike enough, but having other solid interests in life besides those of merely being cultivated and ladylike, yet not busybodies like the Norham Gardens women.'[w]

Meta too had been engaged in a round of visits since leaving Grasmere on 20 September, staying first with Mr H. Nicholls and his wife at Ponsonby Hall, Carnforth. Nicholls was a wealthy Jew but 'quite devoid of Jewish prejudices (as well as beliefs) ... made his money in trade, is very well-informed and interested in most things, draws really well.'[105] Meta became very friendly with his daughter, Rose. Meta and Rose went fishing in the river Calder, but Rose only caught a branch of a tree. They 'drove to a dear little place called Seascale. Its right in front of the sea. There's an excellent cheap hotel where they board you for 5/6 a day, and I saw a tennis-ground. It is just the place to pick one up and I think you'd like it.'[106]

From Ponsonby Hall she moved to the Falks at Liverpool. Rachel Falk was a Toynbee.[x] Meta made a trip by steamer to New Brighton but her general impression of the town was unfavourable. 'Liverpool seems almost as dreary as London, without the nice people who make London bearable.'[107]

Mr Falk was a positivist and he took Meta to a positivist service which greatly intrigued her.[y] 'The faces of some of the men were very striking. One man looked so like a French revolutionist! There were thirty people of whom only five were women. Most of the men looked like schoolboys, and it is hard to believe that they understood

[v] Salt Lecture, the inaugural address to the Salt Schools delivered in the Victorian Hall at the opening of the schools at Saltaire near Bradford.

[w] Norham Gardens was a residential area of north Oxford where many married dons lived. Fellows had for the most part only been allowed to marry since the findings of the Commission of 1877 (A. J. Engel, *From Clergyman to Don* (Oxford, 1983), pp. 106–14, 158–61, 273–4).

[x] John Falk was a Liverpool business man who had married Rachel, the daughter of Joseph Toynbee.

[y] Although Mark was interested in positivism as an intellectual exercise, it made no great appeal to him: 'as soon as a statement has passed into the condition of a dogma it has ceased to have intelligent life, i.e. to have meaning. All of Positivism that has life has been taken up into the general consciousness, and we gladly leave you the husks'.[108]

half they heard.'[109] Although, in reaction to her father's harsh
evangelical faith, Meta's opinions had become increasingly agnostic,
she was still an earnest seeker after truth. 'I gradually had to give up
believing in everything which had been such a comfort to me for
many years. Now for the last year or two I have known that I must
always be content with absolute ignorance on the subject and that it
is impossible I could ever take up any other position.' Did this mean,
she wondered, whether the inability to believe in a personal God
made love more available 'to be given to one's dearest'. 'If so it's
some compensation for one's loss in having no God to whom to pour
out one's gratitude for that dearest and who would understand the
depths of one's love.'[110] 'When people have the ordinary ideas about
God', she commented some months later, 'they can bear troubles
quite differently. Prayer is, I remember, an immense relief, and the
assurance that whatever happens is His will keeps one up.'[111]

Naturally Mark, whose spiritual pilgrimage had brought him to a
not dissimilar position, found her views on religion sympathetic. In
general, however, he was himself temperamentally and intellectually
disinclined to parade his lack of belief, the more inadmissible in view
of the position which he held. But, encouraged by her own openness,
he abandoned his usual reticence, and from the solitude of Wensleydale he made a moving statement of his beliefs or lack of them: 'Yes,
dear, Prayer is a grand resource, and the sense of the special guar-
dianship of the All powerful, the thought that one's pains are sent
one for one's good and that suffering is a blessing! That is a phase of
feeling one passes through. The growth of the mind leaves it behind,
and one cannot have it back. Protestantism took away the saints who
once were invisibly all about us, and now Agnosticism has taken
away Providence as death takes away the mother from the child, and
leaves us forlorn of protection and love. Man is an energy which has a
given time in which to spend itself, and in the spending of that store
of energy is life.'[112]

'Granting', Meta wrote, commenting on the doctrine of the Incar-
nation, 'the Christian account of Christ, I don't see that he was so
wonderfully self-sacrificing after all to spend thirty-three years down
here, very trying years no doubt, but then look at the result, which
he knew all the time. Why, it seems to me that if one could even cure
one human being's anguish one would sacrifice oneself gladly to help

them, and as Christ was supposed to see into everybody's heart I don't see how he could have done a lot less than he did. As for the Christians God I daily realise more what a fiend they have set up for themselves. The whole scheme must be simply revolting to anyone with a spark of justice in their composition.'[113] Mark concurred. 'Yes, that is a very staggering thought, the infinitesimally small effect produced by the intervention of the Almighty 1800 years ago. As I saw it put somewhere, the Devil has (on the Christian scheme) far the best of the struggle, and that without killing his only Son.'[114]

While Meta was finishing her visits and preparing to return to London, Mark was busily engaged in drawing up his list of winter visitors, partly to ensure that at least from time to time there would be a chaperone during Meta's stay at Oxford to still the prying curiosity of the Oxford matrons. 'I must begin', he wrote to Meta on 27 September, 'arranging my relay of visitors, but we must have intervals during which we may be alone.' One of the possible visitors was Helen Colvill whose novel *A Dreamer* Meta had mentioned to Mark some months earlier. Mark had read the book in the train between Oxenholme and London. 'I found it interesting but as a story, it wants art, especially are the conversations feeble. The personages do not speak in character, but all talk alike.' He was curious enough to want to read the second volume—it was a three-tiered novel—and suspected that the authoress might be more interesting than her book. Since Helen was a shy girl, it would be best to have her to stay when Meta was at Oxford, so long as she was not there when Meta celebrated her own birthday on 9 November. 'It will be beautiful having you on your birthday. How I will make much of you! What sort of pudding will you have, and what will you drink to celebrate the anniversary?'[115] 'We won't have dinner', Meta replied, correctly judging Mark's tastes in this matter, 'but high tea, and you must wear those nice grey clothes to which I was introduced at Grasmere! I've never wasted so much time in the whole of my life since Grasmere, just in sitting and thinking about you! You will crop up in the most tiresome way while I'm reading. If I feel this, what must men, who have to work hard mentally, do when they are deeply in love.'[116] 'Do you know', she had written on 19 October 1880, 'that you've made me afraid of something, viz. dying. I used to hope that I should live until I had been quite happy just once. Now that I am that [happy] I've qualms in trains etc lest I should lose it sooner than I need. It's curious that one person can make *all* the difference to one's life.'

Less congenial guests would be Mark's sister and her husband, Canon Roberts, billed for mid-November. The 'orthodox canon of Ripon' was, in his brother-in-law's estimation, an amiable, simple-minded man, but Mary was stiff and formal without 'the smallest spark of humour'. 'Sat 3 hours', he noted of an earlier visit to Richmond in 1878, 'gossiping and retailing news—she knows it all, and takes no interest in anything else. Why is she so repugnant to me?' When, a year later, she visited Oxford, she seemed to her brother as 'frigid and unapproachable as ever.' He cautioned Meta to remember to be 'outwardly civil and deferential'. 'That's what I am, and that is the only manifestation of the human soul which my sister can appreciate. What one *is* she has never attempted to know.'[117] Even when there were other guests in the house, he would keep his study inviolate, 'a sacred recess into which you only shall be admitted'. She was to sleep in a room in the garret, where Mary Stirke had resided, cold but 'a secure retreat from the outer world' where she could read or smoke.

Meta's expectations of the visit were already so high that Mark found it necessary to pour a little cold water. 'It seems to me you are allowing yourself to expect much from your visit to Lincoln in November, which cannot be realised.'[118] 'I'm afraid you'll be so grievously disappointed, no reality can *ever* ever come up to what you are demanding of your imagination. I'll be all to you that it is in my power to be in the way of affection and tenderness, but a craving heart like yours it is impossible to satisfy, and the vacuum becomes a total void as if nothing were being passed in. Do, in mercy to me, dwell on the shady side of the picture a little.' He reminded her that she would find little in the way of entertainment or other diversions. 'The house is dull, and the people who come to it dull and sloppy . . . If I succeed in detaining you a whole fortnight I shall consider it a great triumph.'[119] 'As for your desire to have evenings to ourselves, my only fear is, dear Meta, that you will have too many of them, and before the end of November will be longing for some one to come in, to break the monotony of reading aloud.'[120]

In fact the Rector was looking forward to Meta's visit as much as

she was. 'I shall enjoy petting you so and nursing you upon the sofa',
he had written much earlier, referring to Meta's sprained ankle, 'that
I shall almost wish you may be still hobbling then.'[121] 'You'll never
get rid of me', Meta promised, 'when I am once settled in Mary's
room.'[122] 'I shall', she averred, 'never be able to get on without seeing
you for many months at a time.' 'How shall I love your petting me.
You can never imagine the strange difference you've made in my
life, and I am most deeply thankful that I count for something in
yours.'[123] 'You must', she wrote four days after this letter, 'Surely
understand how very much I care for you, at least more than anyone
else in the world. It's six weeks and a day since I saw you, and in
three weeks and two days, i.e. on November 1st, I shall certainly
turn up at Lincoln.'[124]

Mark's main anxiety arose from the reaction which a prolonged
visit might evoke from her relatives in Oxford as well from others
of his Oxford women friends. Neither Uncle Granville, the Master
of University, nor his wife, Aunt Marian, approved of Pattison,
believing his religious views to be of a dangerously subversive
character. 'Aunt Marian fears that you'll "undermine my religion",
isn't that entertaining! I must speedily endeavour to conciliate her
by talking enthusiastically about Tennyson, Lord Salisbury, Johnnie
Shairp and some of our relations! She doesn't like me, told me
that I was a "thorough Bradley".' On October 21 he saw Meta 'at
her lodgings who was reduced to much distress'. It does not
appear what was the reason for her agitation; but it may have
been connected with the visit which Meta's father and stepmother
went to pay to the Master's Lodgings at University College. For
the next day, 22 October, Pattison thought it politic to pay a
call there only to be made apprehensive by the deep stress which
Charles Bradley placed on his hope that he would not 'keep Meta
too long.'

He decided that it would be a wise measure to write a 'token'
letter to her father, explaining that he had invited Meta to provide
much-needed personal and domestic assistance in the Lodgings, so
playing down any hint of affection. The letter apparently passed
muster, at least for the time being, stilling the doubts which Charles
Bradley had had of the advisability of the visit. But Mark advised
Meta, whose stay, he hoped, would last at least three weeks, to foster

the impression that she was to be in Oxford for only a few days, so allowing the visit to be 'so drawn out silently from week to week, till you are stared at no longer.'

In an ominous and prophetic aside, he reminded her that 'Mrs Grundy ... is a very important personage here.'[125] Whether Meta, brash in attitude, took the warning seriously, may be doubted, but she did reassure him that 'with you to coach me, I shan't be plucked'. She did not really appreciate that Mark, for all his instinctive radicalism, was very wary of challenging the conventions of the society in which he lived. He preferred to put up a screen of respectability. 'What could it matter to anyone in Oxford', Meta pouted, 'if I spend a year with you. However I really will be discreet. I'll even say that I hate staying with you if you like.'[126]

'It is truly wonderful', he exclaimed on the eve of her visit, 'that at my time of life, when I had parted from that one anchor on which I had placed all my trust, I should suddenly have dropped another which holds on the bottom. How long! that is the disturbing thought ... Good-bye dearest! Only five days now.'[127] 'Oh! dearest', Meta replied by return of post, 'I am glad that Monday isn't far off. I feel as if I couldn't hold out much longer—ever·yours very longingly.'[128] 'I have held out', Mark wrote the day before her arrival, 'as long as I can ... but ... I have surrendered myself to the pleasing dream of having found some one to care for me. I have never yet engaged my heart in any quarter, without suffering for it, and it is possible that now I am, in spite of experience, laying up for myself a fresh misery! But the die is cast! I am giving myself away and am yours!'[129] And on the same day Meta told him: 'To-morrow! *ist es möglich*! I feel so insanely happy at the prospect that I'm always being asked what I'm smiling at! These last few days have felt like months, the next three weeks will feel like 3 days, I fear.'[130]z

Meta arrived on the afternoon of the first of November. It was the festival of All Saints, traditionally the day of a College Gaudy or feast which Mark as Rector of the College could not reasonably miss. He sat miserably between Dr Ince, the Regius Professor of Divinity and

---

z Mark sent her a first-class ticket (on 8 October) which Meta at first demurred at using, 'an improper luxury at my age'. She caught the 2.15 p.m. from Paddington, arriving at 4.0 p.m., and was met at the station by a brougham. To draw the driver's attention she arranged to wave her handkerchief out of the carriage window.

Archdeacon Iles, a former fellow who had some twenty years earlier cast his vote against him at the rectorial election because he distrusted Pattison's religious liberalism, implicit in his recent contribution to *Essays and Reviews*.[a] The Rector's thoughts were elsewhere, and at a quarter to nine he made his excuses 'having the happy feeling that Meta was so anxious to have me home as I was to get back.'[131]

So began what for both of them constituted an idyll, the high-water mark in their relationship, from which the tides were slowly and inevitably to recede. The Rector had warned Meta that life with him would be dull, void of entertainment and so by and large it proved to be. His close friends were few; only Ingram Bywater from neighbouring Exeter College came in for a chat and a smoke. The Irish novelist, May Laffan, was an occasional and welcome visitor and a good correspondent.[b] 'I shall show you some of Miss Laffan's letters', he told Meta, 'and you will see what a favoured individual I am to have two such correspondents at the same time.'

Miss Laffan's role in Pattison's life is not very easy to assess, for her surviving letters are limited to a span of eighteen months, between 1882 and 1883. At first sight she might seem to be no more than one of the many women and young girls whom the Rector liked to befriend. Yet Miss Laffan had qualities different from those of his other friends which particularly appealed to Pattison. She wrote fluently and stylishly. 'Miss Laffan's letters are the best I get from any quarters.' 'Meta', he added to his entry in his diary for 6 September 1880, 'is so attentive and has such attaching ways that I can't leave her letters unanswered.' Meta's letters besides those of May Laffan appeared as the compositions of a moderately well-educated school girl. Miss Laffan had written novels largely about Irish life, which were much esteemed at the time. She herself read widely and critically. The contents of her letters to Mark were, by and large, con-

---

[a] William Ince, matriculated Lincoln College 1842, fellow Exeter College 1847; Regius Professor of Divinity 1878–1910; J. H. Iles, fellow Lincoln College 1855–61; Archdeacon of Stafford 1876.

[b] Miss Laffan's letters to Pattison (1882–3) are in Pattison MSS 60. Her novels include: *Hogan, M.P.*, 3 vols. (London, 1876); *The Hon Miss Ferrard*, 3 vols. (London, 1877). In a letter to Ellen Smith, Mrs Pattison had commented, 'Miss Laffan tells me the "doings" which have come to her knowledge were *very bad* but she thinks the Rector *not* in fault, that the girl was wholly to blame which is an opinion which requires modification' (23.3.81); but apparently she became more sympathetic.

cerned with the books she had read, and the political and social problems by which her nation was beset, and on these topics she showed shrewdness and conviction.

On Ireland she found the English naïve, ill-informed and pig-headed, 'forever suggesting schemes, each more silly and impracticable than the others!'. 'Only the pen of Emily Brontë could describe the life of the Irish squire, the utter absence of morality, self-restraint, and contempt for books and all pertaining to them, the wild recklessness and savagery, not one pin about their tenants, just as Miss Edgeworth left them, they are.' 'I want to go to Galway and visit the scene of the late evictions. I am told that *some* hundreds of men women and children are camped on the mountain side without even a furze bush between them and heaven, wretches who have been in receipt of relief for years.'

Her caustic judgement stretched to her fellow men and women, the majority of whom she viewed with some contempt. It was exactly the sort of language which appealed to her scholarly correspondent. 'Have you ever reflected', she asked him 'that at least half of the people you meet are mutually at least, *automata*. An original mind is the rarest product on earth . . . Awfully few women are in the least capable of looking at any subject by *themselves*. Goethe says there are so few voices and so many echoes. These friends of mine are dumb echoes, for one would be well content with, now and again, a secondhand opinion.' Pattison could not have agreed more about the idiocy and illiteracy of the vast majority.

Towards Mark himself she adopted a tone, half-bullying, half-flirtatious. She sometimes addressed him in ways which his other friends would not have dared to use. 'You never wrote in reply to my last. What are you doing, and who has got hold of you? most fickle, inconstant of men. Is it the medievally inclined widow or is there some still newer love?' If she felt at first sympathetically inclined towards his wife [with whom she also corresponded]—'what is wrong with her—she writes in the saddest manner . . . dear, *if you knew the troubles she has*'—her dislike of Sir Charles Dilke made her an invaluable ally. 'How I do hate that fellow! and he hates me too.' 'I have a heap to tell you of *Dilke*, I can't write it.' 'I was amused to see that *Dilke* had called on you. I *hate* that man with all my heart—but jove, what a tale I have for you, I dare not write.' But May Laffan, though she loved coming to London, lived in Dublin. Mark liked her letters, but found her presence in the Lodgings rather overwhelming.

Much nearer home was another novelist, Rhoda Broughton, herself a woman of acute intelligence who lived with her sister, Mrs Newcome, in Oxford. Although Pattison had reservations about her, she was a very welcome visitor because she could read Heine, Kotzebue, and other German authors in their native tongue. She was an observant woman, and, as she read, she noted with a dispassionate eye the Rector's idiosyncrasies which she was later to embody in a malicious, if not positively vindictive, portrait in *Belinda*.

There were occasional dinner parties, games of croquet, and tennis. Sir Charles Dilke, already designated Mrs Pattison's 'fancyman', called. Meta was taken to dine with Jowett at Balliol. The Paters came to dinner in the company of Andrew Lang and his wife.[c] It could not be called exciting, but after the tedium of 25 Orsett Terrace Meta found it positively glamorous.

It was the Michaelmas term, but neither College business nor the undergraduates cast more than a faint shadow on the Rector's existence. Three years earlier he had commented at the start of the Oxford term that he was 'very low spirited at the thought of the weary round of busy, fussed, wasted hours!' He never saw any reason to vary this view. He resented the demands made upon him by College meetings over which he had to preside, and he escaped as hastily as he reasonably could, back to the fastness of the Lodgings. 'This day', he wrote of the College's audit meeting on the 22nd December, 'consumed over the audit which lasted from 10 to 6.30 after which had to dine in C[ommon] R[oom].'[132] He was worried by the activities of the commissioners whom the government had appointed to inquire into the condition of Oxford and Cambridge. Once a leading proponent of University reform, and a warm supporter of the findings of the first commission of inquiry, set up in the 1850s, he had come to believe that reform had taken a wrong direction, leading less to the promotion of scholarship and research, which he held to be the *bene esse* of a University, than to the provi-

[c] Walter Pater (1839–94), fellow of Brasenose College 1864; see M. V. Levey, *The Case of Walter Pater* (1978): Andrew Lang (1844–1912), fellow of Merton 1868; author and essayist.

sion of efficient administrators and educators for the state.[d] 'This day', he wrote, on 11 November, 'lost to me by having to wait on Oxford University Commission. I did all I could to hinder the College from electing me one of the 3 college commissioners, but having been elected, I thought it would be perverse to absent myself contumaciously from the meetings. But I had done much better to have stayed away. I only served to give a decent appearance to the high-handed proceedings of the commission who treated me and our College with supreme contempt, taking at the same time all they could squeeze out of us for their claptrap professors.'[e]

But college affairs were unlikely to make very much impact on Meta's life. Undergraduates came to breakfast, an occasion normally as distasteful to them as to him. It is not clear whether Meta was present, probably not. 'To-day Thompson, a commoner, an utter dolt [to breakfast]—to think that a university, with an apparatus of Professors and libraries should exist for such African savages as these.'[135] Since his relations with the fellows, with a few exceptions, were distant, they were rarely entertained at the Lodgings. So although the death of a young undergraduate, a Mr Walton, from diphtheria contracted in his lodgings at No. 8 the Turl opposite the College caused Mark some disquiet, the institution over which he presided did not mean a great deal to Meta.[136]

Life was amiably domestic, walks round the Parks and up Headington Hill or to Hinksey, tennis, dictation (Meta, for instance, wrote out his review of Richard Christie's book on *Étienne Dolet*), readings in the evenings after supper, sometimes by Mark, sometimes by Meta. 'After lunch read to her out of Ruskin, then walk again, and tried to read Pascal, but head gave way.' 'After supper Meta read to me Miss Laffan's *Game Hen* and I read some Absalom and Achitophel to her.' From Mark's list of books read at this time some would seem to have been pretty heavy going for his young friend: John Nichol's *Byron*, Ruskin's *Arrows of the Chace*,[f]

---

[d] His own concept of a university found expression in his penetrating book, *Suggestions on Academical Organization* (1868).[133]

[e] 'I have not passed a more painful day for a long time, and when I left the room returned home thoroughly despondent and broken.'[134]

[f] *Arrows of the Chace, being a collection of scattered letters, published chiefly in the daily newspapers*, and now edited by an Oxford pupil [A. D. Wedderburn]. (Orpington, 1880);

A. H. Japp's *German Life and Literature*, Dante, Rolleston's *External Aspects*; but he did make occasional concessions to his guest's less sophisticated tastes, John Payn's novel, *Less Black than We'er painted* and also Ouida's recent story, *Moths*.[137] Secretly, as he later admitted, he was a little irritated by Meta's evident lack of interest in what they were reading; but he persevered in the hope of raising her intellectual level and, she, only too aware of her inferiority in this respect, doggedly laboured on at self-improvement. The Roberts' came on 16 November, upsetting, as Mark said, 'our evenings'; they had to have an early supper to allow Canon Roberts to attend a debate at the Oxford Union. No more welcome a visitor, indeed less so, was an old member of the College, the church historian, C. J. Abbey and his wife: 'no talk worth anything—the Abbeys totally in the dark about everything.'[g] His wife's brother-in-law, Gertrude's father, William Tuckwell made an impropitious visit; 'his flighty superficial nature, absolutely destitute of sympathy, rubs against me irritatingly, and made me unhappy all day.'

More welcome to himself and presumably to Meta also was the procession of young ladies. Helen Colvill came the day after Meta's birthday and though Mark was feeling under the weather, 'after supper I read Sonnets and Meta read Besant's French Humourists on Romaunt of the Rose.'[138]

In Helen's honour he gave a dinner for eight and took both girls in the company of Meta's cousin, Mabel, to tea with the Neubauers. There were visits from his wife's niece, Gertrude Tuckwell, Fanny Kensington ('she seems to have lost her mind, and to be quite broken in spirit, which has gone into quiet obstinacy'), and Rose Nicholls. When he had to go to a College meeting, Meta was able to attend 'theatricals' at the Weatherlys.

In part the succession of visitors was intended to allay scandal. Uncle Granville's wife, Marian, who did not attempt to hide her dislike of Meta, registered her disapproval by refusing an invitation to dinner and forbidding her daughter, Mabel, to visit the Lodgings

George Rolleston, *The Modification of the external aspects of organic nature produced by man's interference* a lecture delivered, 12 May 1879.

   [g] C. J. Abbey, matriculated Lincoln College 1852; fellow of University College 1862–6; Rector of Checkendon, 1865; church historian.

whilst Meta was there.[h] When Meta's stay reached the three-week mark, her father, doubtless alerted by his brother's wife, peremptorily, indeed brusquely, told her to come home. Dazed by the letter, Meta put off the evil day by going to stay with her cousin, Mabel, at University College. When the news came, Pattison was in London attending a meeting of the Teachers' Training Society. 'This is a cruel blow. . . . Does Mr Bradley really think it wrong that you should stay in the house with me alone, or is it purely and simply a mode of warfare? Be as it may I see nothing for it but that you must go home, not, however, I suppose till Mrs Thursfield's visit is over. Perhaps your going home may gain you permission to return at least for a week or two in the Spring. But I cannot do without you now. We must therefore make some arrangement for the future of a more permanent kind, one to which your father may be a party.'[140]

This was wishful thinking indeed. But surprisingly the misunderstanding seems to have been patched up and Meta came back to the Lodgings when Fanny Kensington arrived as a guest on 4 December. When Mark went over to the Verneys at Claydon to stay the night, 'pleasant enough, but not so happy as one of our quiet reads up in my studio at home', Meta wrote a passionate avowal of her feelings.[i]

It is so horrid not to have your usual goodnight! I don't suppose you will ever understand the sort of feeling which I have for you, a unique mixture of what people feel for their God, their husband, and their child! Can you make anything out of that I wonder! I really feel wretched without you . . . You'll *have* to adopt me dearest. . . . Before I knew you I never really lived. I was perfectly aware of the fact, but feared that it would always be the case, as I know that I could never care for any ordinary man. That I can make the difference I do in your life, my precious Rector, far exceeds the blessedness of my wildest dreams . . . It is awfully hard that we should not be what we can to each other for the rest of our lives. It's almost harder on me than you, not only because I love you of course 100 times more than you can ever love me, but also because I know that I can never

---

[h] Compare his comment in his diary for 12 November 1877, 'Mabel Bradley came to tea and I walked home with her, very promising'.[139]
[i] 'Wednesday December 8th at 4 over to Claydon to sleep and dine—party Stubbs of Gransborough, Lady Lyttleton, Lord Cottesloe, and Miss Freemantle, Major and Mrs Holmes, Henry Smith, pleasant enough, but not so happy as one of our quiet reads up in my studio at home!'[141]

care half as much for anyone else, and I do think its only fair that everyone should have a few years happiness in this vale of tears. It is hard to have to count by months instead of years. I know that one has no right to expect happiness, but its tantalising to see it within your grasp but unhaveable. How maudlin you'd think me could you see me now, positively crying, though at Lincoln.[142]

Mark had only been away from Oxford for a night.

So Meta stayed on. Rose Nicholls came on Christmas Eve. All three of them walked together on Christmas Day and read Wordsworth aloud. Mark relaxed by playing billiards for two hours with Meta and Dr Childs. In the evening there was more Wordsworth, Bagehot's *Physics and Politics*, and some Ouida. Rose retired early and 'my dear Meta and I remained together till 11.0'. On Boxing Day they walked round the Parks in the morning, had tea with Walter Pater and his sister while Mark made a number of duty calls, on Sidney Owen, Max Müller, Weatherly, Ralli and the Dean's wife, Mrs Liddell. Rose went home on 29 December. Meta's own days in Oxford were now numbered, for the Rector had arranged to visit Paris in the New Year. The 'last quiet evening with my dear Meta!' Mark commented on 4 January 1881.

The visit had certainly established a firm, intimate relationship which survived the egocentric quirks of the Rector's attitudinal neurosis and Meta's occasional fits of irritability and impulsive naïveté. He would give her a ring, not a cheap hoop, nor yet he remarked characteristically, 'at a frightful cost'. 'Something worth wearing, say diamonds and emerald.'[143] He had earlier revoked the codicil to his will leaving £1,000 for Lincoln College, substituting Meta in its place.[144] The language of their letters was one of passionate longing. 'You darling of my life', so Mark addressed Meta.[145] 'I have a sort of perpetual yearning for you, my own precious darling.'[146] 'My dear, if it can be any consolation for your present uncongenial surroundings to know that your entrance within this sphere has entirely changed the life of one human being, you have it. It is not only that you have given me two months of the most perfect sympathy, but the mere thought that you are there now, and live in my life, has given all things a fresh aspect for me. I don't think of you as a vision that came and is gone; I don't even think of your dear image, but I feel your presence always, when unconscious of it in thought.'[147] 'Dear love', Mark was to write on the late evening of 2 February 1881, 'I must have you back again! Seeing does not satisfy me. I must have my arms tightly round that dear waist, with infinite possibilities of kissing.'[148] 'How I wish I were with you this evening to be petted and tucked onto the sofa and read to sleep.'[149]

Meta's letters were as intense, even more so. 'I woke early this morning, and thought of you, and nothing else for a whole hour! Would God it were autumn! ... How you'll miss me, no nice warm coat, and no one to pour out your tea, and, alas, no one to give you a loving hug in the joys of her heart at your return home.'[150] 'Darling pet, this craving to be with you is dreadful. I suppose it will last all my life and won't be gratified. This hungering for you takes so much out of me.'[151] The very next day she admitted, 'I shall cry myself to sleep or to a bad headache just because I can't cuddle into your loving arms for a goodnight benediction ... To know that things can't possibly be better and that they can hardly help getting worse.'[152] 'Shut your dear eyes and imagine that I am giving you the softest, coolest, tenderest, lovingest embrace in the world.'[153]

What in practice did this language mean? How completely intimate were they? Mrs Grundy evidently suspected the worst. A modern reader might well suppose that they enjoyed intercourse. We shall never know, but doubts remain. It may be that physical intimacy never went beyond the hugging, kissing, and petting to which both of them refer in their letters, but the language of their communications was passionate. In a postscript to a letter, written in January 1880 shortly after her return from Oxford, Meta, writing two years after Mark's death, asserted that 'A sentence here catching my eye ... I must explain that the Rector generally took a nap on the sofa in his study after lunch when poorly, and it is to this "tucking up" to which I referred. I never saw his bedroom until he had left home. It is necessary to say this as I hear rumours which would lead me to assume that this sentence has been copied and wilfully misunderstood.'[154] Meta was probably a virgin, frigid even. 'I don't

---

[i] Meta herself had written to Mark, 'By the bye, they say at Oxford that I used to tuck you up every night! and I never once went into your bedroom except the day I went all over the house to see it.'[155]

suppose', she once wrote, 'that there are many girls, if any, so absolutely fancy free as I have been.'[156] There was in her make-up, as in
that of Mark's, a puritan strain, both rooted in the evangelical teaching of their youth. 'I am always thankful', she wrote, 'when people
affirm that friendship, frank, legal and absolutely free from any conscious thought of sex is not only possible, but frequent between men
and women of healthy well-conditioned minds.'[157] Had Mark been a
free man, she would have loved to have been his wife, but the sanc-
tions were too great.

Mark's case is perhaps less capable of easy analysis. Until he
married Francis Strong, there was no evidence of a significant male
or female attachment. Yet he was interested in young women, writing them romantically worded letters, suggesting a measure of frustrated sexuality. His wife's refusal to share any longer his sexual life
had wounded him deeply; though it is not impossible that all this
may have represented on his part a rough awkwardness, possibly
even impotence.

By 1880 he was an ageing, if not an old, man. He was very alert to
the possibility of scandal and eager to avoid it. If circumstances had
been favourable, his inhibitions might have been less strong. But
there were too many people in the Lodgings, the housekeeper Mrs
Baines, the housemaid Ellen, who were loyal to their mistress, the
absent Mrs Pattison. Both Mark and Meta were probably too tied by
the conventions of their time to feel free to give full range to their
affection.

Did they entertain the idea of doing so? To have done so would
have aroused the strongest possible disapproval of all their relatives
and some degree of social ostracism. Mark was not simply the head
of an Oxford College, with an assured social position and a good
income, but a Clergyman in Holy Orders. Whatever the tenuous
nature of his beliefs, he could not or would not resign offices which
conferred dignity and provided for his comfort. Although modestly
well-endowed, like other ageing men he feared penury; natural
parsimony was deepened by the financial support which he had to
give his wife while she wintered in Provence. At one time he
pondered whether his sporadic separation from his wife might
become a permanent arrangement. 'I cannot', he confessed to Meta,
'go on with her [i.e. Mrs Pattison] much longer on the footing we are

now on, and must make some arrangement by mutual understanding. Supposing that she and I agreed to live apart, and there was a *de facto* separation, known to the world to be such, how would that affect people's view of your coming to stay with me? This is what is on my mind now, and I want you to help me go through it, before I make any proposition to her.'[158] Regretfully Meta had to say that the idea was impracticable, if only because even a visit from her would arouse the acute disapproval of her father.

'As long as I live in his house I can't go absolutely against his wishes. That she [Mrs Pattison] came home in the summer, and was absolutely obliged to live abroad in the winter has always been a point on which I have had to insist with him. He has very strong views on those sorts of subjects, and seems to think that two people had better make their lives perfectly wretched together when they could be tolerably comfortable apart ... You quite understand, darling, that I am wholly indifferent to anyone's opinion for my own sake. If I were independent of my father I should think that your pleasure and mine were the only things to influence us short of giving rise to absolute scandal.' Living together would have constituted 'absolute scandal'. Meta added naïvely that 'any downstairs backbiting would not affect our consciousness of our best friends confidence in the perfectly innocent nature of our friendship'.[159] Mark soon backpedalled on this at best tentative proposal. He could not face an 'open rupture'. 'I never intended to go as far as a legal separation, only to get her to agree not to come to Oxford.'

Francis Pattison was wintering in Provence. She was only too aware that relations with her husband were strained. 'I wrote', she told her friend Ellen Smith on 21 November, 'to Lincoln after careful calculation of every word as if I were indignant, saying that I did so feeling it was no use to appeal to "sense of what was due to me", that "honesty" had no chance. I could "not flatter" and that he "would always persist in putting confidence in those he would do wisely not to trust".' In this way Mrs Pattison revealed that she knew of Meta's presence in the Lodgings. She continued, 'It instantly brought forth the enclosed to which I answered that "I should be grieved to say anything that would look like a taunt, or make any representation which he could take as "recrimination"; but I must say that I invariably do and have considered all that is due to *him before*.' She reverted to her husband's objections to her wintering abroad, 'all medical opinion concurring in the view that I must practically become a helpless cripple if I did not—I spent hours weighing the question whether my duty enjoined me to sacrifice my whole future at the age of 33 ... He has never said 'It is "inconsiderate" of you to go abroad but only "I wish you would stay away altogether". It will now remain to be seen whether I have succeeded in clearing up the atmosphere and I write by the same post to you to get you, if possible, to see him alone and find out what effect my letters have had.'[160] She had, however, little hope of persuading him to think otherwise 'as long as he is under the charm of the "ever loving imposter", and I am very much vexed that Gertrude [Tuckwell] should be there now for a week, for I fear she either gets harm from, or will be harmed by her companion, who I am told has been spreading scandal about that most innocent girl, the niece Mary [Stirke] who was with him last winter ...'.

Mrs Mark seems at first to have believed that Meta Bradley was only another of the young girls who attracted the Rector, though she clearly thought her to be a schemer. After her letter to Ellen Smith, she had received '*a very underbred* but, I suppose well meant letter', some eight pages long, from another of the Rector's guests, Fanny Kensington. 'She begins', Mrs Mark wrote to her Oxford confidante Ellen Smith on 20 December,

by telling *me* (!) that *she knows* the Rector does not write fully and in detail and therefore thinks I may like a report of things at Oxford during this term etc. from her. She then fills three pages with Miss Bradley, not committing herself to the admission that Miss Bradley has been in the house nearly three months but saying that she is there now and that she, Miss Kensington, "hopes that she *has succeeded* in persuading Mr Bradley to allow his daughter to remain" till the end of January as otherwise the Rector says he must leave Oxford. The whole thing was clearly MEANT to draw me into some expressions about Miss Bradley which could be shown to the father. ... I answered that I was much pleased at her kind thought and that her letter came along with a long letter from the Rector but he was always so desponding that I was glad to compare the view of an outsider ... That I should be sorry if he remained on in Oxford throughout January as I hoped he would have joined me after Christmas in a visit to Rome ... I think, as the Rector has never alluded to her visit, and as I have some reason to believe that Mrs [Granville] Bradley does not like it—for she pointedly refrained from inviting Miss Meta Bradley to the dance she gave, I had better not say a word.

'I don't know the Miss Bradley of whom you speak', she informed another of her correspondents (and the Rector's friends), Mrs Thursfield.[161] 'What do you think of her? I am told she has given her family a great deal of trouble by repeated and violent sets at men of all sorts and sizes.'[162]

So guardedly did Mrs Pattison comment on Meta Bradley's prolonged stay in the Lodgings. She was none the less exasperated by what at the moment she felt to be her husband's folly, hardly a serious infatuation. Had she realized the impact which Meta had made upon his heart, she would have been more apprehensive. 'Does it cheer my sweetest', he wrote to Meta from Paris on 13 January 1881, 'to be told over and over again the same old story, how this aged veteran revived and felt young again when he found, oh how wonderful! a young heart turning to him with love. No, my own darling, nothing I can ever do can pay you for what I have derived from you.'[163]

The autumnal visit of 1880 was the only period in their four years' relationship during which Meta and Mark lived under the same roof. For both of them it undoubtedly had been an enriching experience, creating a reservoir of affection on which they were to draw in the agonizing passage of time. Meta, enthusiastic and tactless, lonely and frustrated, found in her elderly mentor not simply a store of heroic learning, which she adulated with all the fervour of a convert, but a craving for affection to which she responded with even greater eagerness.

In his solitary, insulated state Mark, egocentric and taciturn, had discovered in Meta a warmth which melted some of the wintry chill by which he was encased. A vein of love momentarily rejuvenated a crabbed spirit. Their relationship must surely have been stimulated by some degree of physical intimacy, an essential ingredient in mutual understanding and love, whether homosexual or heterosexual. This may have been no more than petting, fondling, and embracing (though the language of the letters might suggest a stronger bond), but whatever its nature, it crowned their friendship.

'Could anything', she wrote on 30 January 1881 'express my feelings
better than this extract from Guizot himself, in fact I believe I've
already said much the same to you. "I cannot tell you how happy I
was during the weeks which are just ended; I knew and enjoyed my
happiness at the time, I feel it deeply now that it is over, and I shall
enjoy it just as much when I return to you.

    ' "I carry you with me, you are present with me everywhere; you
and the happiness I owe to you. When I am away from you everything reminds me of you; when near you I forget everything else, my
very soul is yours". There dearest! Only I don't like to know that
anyone else has felt so exactly what I do. I thought I had it all to
myself. How glad I am that I can tell you so frankly just what you are
to me. I suppose most people would be ashamed of feeling or at any
rate speaking so strongly, but somehow I am proud of it, and love to
tell you how much I adore you. It is good for you, dearest, it must
prevent that wretched haunting suspicion that no one after all really
cares about you. You know you never must even say that any
more!'[164]

    Yet the shafts of sunlight, wintry in themselves, were already over-
shadowed by hovering clouds. Mark was forty years older than
Meta. His health and spirits were often depressed by illness, whether
real or imagined. He was very well aware that there was a foreseen
limit to their friendship which nature itself imposed, a limit narrow-
ing month by month, week by week, hour by hour. Where for Meta
the years still seemed to stretch out in endless procession, for the
ageing, introverted scholar time passed with unrelenting haste. Every
contact had to be cherished for itself alone. If he was engaged in a
battle against time, time was not on his side. Nor were circumstances. Meta and Mark faced, some might think justifiably, an
embattled array of critics, Mark's wife, Meta's father, the suspicions
of relatives and acquaintances, the conventions of public opinion.
The climate in which love could grow was cool indeed.

1 8 8 1

WHAT was to happen in the future was happily concealed from
Mark and Meta as they embarked on the New Year, their hopes
fuelled by the expectation of another visit to Oxford in the following
autumn. Wintry storms, high winds, deep snow, and bitter frost
gripped England and the Continent. Mark left Oxford for Paris on 5
January, his ship tossing in rough seas as it crossed the channel.
'Though I was sick, like every one else, I did not suffer such agonies
as I used to when younger. If I had not taken the extra precaution of
eating a whole buttered muffin for breakfast, I should have been far
worse. An abominable old boat took 2½ hours in crossing, while the
heavy seas every now and then swept the deck from end to end.
When we got over, more delay for delay's sake, and then we crept at
about 30 miles an hour, through 2 inches of snow, reaching Paris at
10 instead of 8.'

Once he had reached his lodgings at 26 Avenue Friedland near the
Champs Élysée, a well-stoked coal fire, hot soup, and the savour of a
cigar provided welcome warmth. Next morning as the sun sparkled
on the frost, he was stirred by the beauty of a city of which he had
fond memories. There were some twenty or so guests in his pension
whom he examined with academic detachment: some Americans
'belonging to the uncultivated class', though a Miss Burney,
daughter of the American minister to The Hague, was 'very pretty
and rather elegant', 'intelligent, éveillée à demi, likes to talk with me,
doesn't know much of what is going on, but understands what she
does know'; a Canadian family, a Scotch–Australian, a Frenchman
'who eats as much as all the rest of the guests together' and who was
looked after by an aged English spinster, an Irish family, an Anglican
'priest' and his bride ('two cretinous beings'), a Swede, a Corsican girl
from an aristocratic family, Colonna d'Istria, and a Persian. This
cosmopolitan clientèle was joined later by a Mrs Stewart, the wife of
the British ambassador to The Hague, a convert, or as Pattison

preferred to put it 'a pervert', to Roman Catholicism who brought her own confessor, an abbé, with her.

Although his own room was placed inconveniently next to the bathroom, the house was warm and comfortable. He lay long in bed, drinking his early morning coffee and reading the newspapers and periodicals. In the afternoon, goloshes on his feet, his great green cloak flapping in the wind, he emerged like some aged bird of prey, to make his precarious way along the slippery streets. 'How you would sprawl about on the roadway', he reminded Meta, to which Meta replied 'You only laughed when I sprawled, but I should weep bitterly, if you got hurt'. 'You'll know', she ended her letter, 'that my thoughts will always be with my dearest dear. How I'd hug him were he here.'

He called on old friends. Madame Renan brought her husband, the author of the then notorious life of Christ, from his study and 'he bore the infliction better than would have been expected'; Charles Thurot, crippled by a stroke but obliged by penury to earn a living by lecturing on comparative grammar; Paul Meyer, married to an English wife, 'artist, very pretty, aesthetically not mondaine', who was soon to die. He dined with the Langels, an Orléanist family, the secretary to the Duc d'Aumale and vigorously opposed to Gambetta; 'all chat and gamesomeness'. He went to the theatre to see the *Bourgeois Gentilhomme*, but the acting seemed to him 'loud, vulgar, stagey'. He attended a lecture by Bouche Leclerc on the colonies of Athens but was unimpressed: 'about 30 people, only 3 or 4 of whom students, rest middle aged gents of the class who have nothing better to do, 2 women, not young, lecture fairly average, but nothing more discouraging to the lecturer can be imagined. Just such new Professors whom the Oxford Commission is setting up.' The wintry weather delayed his departure, and he fretted at the waiting. 'I try to persuade myself that I am just as well where I am ... but a restless spirit stirs within and takes away all the interest of the surroundings which were attractive enough to a youth of 67 at first.' He eventually crossed on Saturday 22 January by the *Princess Dagmar*, a splendid boat which did the 28 miles in 85 minutes.[1]

After his departure his 'pearl of price' remained a little longer at Oxford, staying with her cousin at University College. She went round to Lincoln to deal with Mark's correspondence. Upset by his departure, she felt reluctant to join in the festivities which followed the Christmas season. 'When I got back to University I found a lot of Bartholomew Prices,[a] Max Müllers and Salters, dancing in the drawing room, and had to assist at that amusement till 7 ... This morning the others didn't come to breakfast till long after 9 but I got to Lincoln before 10. I collected, tied up and arranged ... in the cabinets all the newspapers and periodicals [she was sorting out, shelving and cataloguing all his books]. Then it was time to go to tennis. We didn't have a good game. The sun was *de trop*, one court was slippery.'[2]

The pain of separation seared, annealing the heart. 'How I miss my usual evening with you, my own love. You've made me hate two words more than any others in our language, viz. good-night and good-bye.'[3] 'I suppose', she wrote the next day, 'this should be a polite letter of thanks for my very pleasant visit but as you partly understand what the last 2 months have been to me, and as I wholly understand what they have been to you, thanks would be quite out of place. I need not even say that I shall always look back (alas) upon them as having been full of conscious bliss such as I imagine few people are capable of experiencing ... Life certainly is worth living for me while you make the greater part of my life! The knowledge that you value my love is quite enough, to say nothing of my having in you a friend who never misunderstands and who almost always understands! I lay awake for so long thinking of my dearest one.' 'My dearest', Mark replied, 'what return can I ever make for so much love.' 'Much love and many kisses to my dear who is never absent from me, even when I am not thinking of her.'

Meta returned to her London home on 11 January, 'a cold journey here, the railway people were nasty about a footwarmer, and I couldn't get one though I ordered three'. On her arrival home, there was an unaccustomed luxury, a welcome fire in her bedroom, 'a most phenomenal event' and her father 'seemed quite amiable! I played backgammon with him for an hour last night, and mean never to give him any pretext for being vexed with me', one of those New Year resolutions which she would find it impossible to keep.

Even in this self-same letter she confessed 'I already feel as if I

[a] Bartholomew Price (1818–98) fellow Pembroke College, Oxford 1844; Sedleian Professor of Natural Philosophy 1853–98; Master of Pembroke 1891–8.

must rush away tomorrow. I do thoroughly detest this life with these people.' Her stepmother, Mrs Bradley, 'gets daily sillier, and never stops dribbling inane remarks, not dribbling but over flowing them'. She took her young niece, Jessie's daughter, Lettice, to the dentist, but, with the best intentions, she found it a trying experience. To divert Lettice's attention, she told her stories, which proved a 'dreadful task in noisy streets'. All this, Mark commented sententiously, was an act of 'self-sacrifice without appreciation by anyone'. Meta then returned home to find that there was an Irish curate visiting the house. Even so, she managed to snatch a few minutes before dinner to read *Endymion*. 'It does feel so queer to be here again. My heart is certainly with you, and I find it difficult to make a decent show of interest in anyone or anything. My life seems so entirely centred in yours.'[4]

The tedium of Meta's existence was probably little different from that of many of her contemporaries, more especially if they happened to be unmarried daughters, but an iron of discontent had entered into her soul. The only outlet she would find was writing long letters to Mark. 'I always feel restless and uncomfy if I don't write a few lines to my dearest once every day.' Her screeds were sometimes as much as eighteen pages in length, once running to twenty-seven pages. 'When I am with you I'm sure I don't say $\frac{1}{3}$ as much as I write.'[5] 'As you say', Mark replied, 'the things you write are not the same things as those you *say* to me. This is very curious. I conjecture it is because when with me you follow the lines of my thinking, with the view of amiably contradicting them, but when alone, your original thinking takes its own course, and this is why you are vastly better upon paper, than in *viva voce*.'[6]

Mark, sparing on paper as in conversation, could not compete with the flood. He could never respond with equal quantities, 'nor can I get upon paper the welling up love and devotion every page of your's conveys to me. All I think of now is how to mitigate the frostiness of your home, and give you the surroundings you require from your heart to live and move.' Meta reassured him, 'I shall never think that silence betokens forgetfulness, and shall go on writing just as often as I feel inclined, knowing that my dearest friend cares for my chats. You surely could'nt imagine that I was complaining of the shortness and rareness of your letters! I paid some calls near Victoria, and, as I felt justified in going by train instead of walking, took all this year's letters from you to reread! I don't believe anyone ever had ½ such lovely letters. I can never feel so proud of anything as I do of having won your affection, my own darling. I woke early this morning, and thought of you, and nothing else for a whole hour!'[7]

Mark could not bring himself to tear up letters which afforded him so much pleasure. They were for reading and re-reading. 'Your love is the cordial of which I take a sly dram, every now and then, in the train or over the Club fire.'[8] 'The light', he wrote on 2 February 1881, 'did not serve my old eyes for reading my darling's letter in the train. But it was in my breast pocket and the thought of it kept my heart warm.' 'This writing almost daily to each other', as Meta remarked, 'will prevent one's feeling that one had lost some weeks from each other's life. I do wish I could have known you when you were a youth. I wonder whether you understand it yourself . . . I wish you would really try to give an account of your real inner self, think how intensely interesting it would be.' Meta's curiosity was to prove the incentive which eventually led Mark to write his *Memoirs*.

Yet if Meta thought herself 'lonely and desolate', in practice she certainly did not live the life of a recluse. She was frequently in the company of friends. For the Bradleys' acquaintances and relatives were serious-minded, Oxford-orientated men and women with keen intellectual and artistic tastes, and social consciences, Toynbees, Kensingtons, Kegan Pauls, Milner, Ilberts, Bryces. 'I went to the Toynbees at 9', she wrote on 13 January, 'and really liked my evening there. Music and the little Webberleys bored me, but I saw almost too many old acquaintances, and Willie Rendel . . . introduced me to the Pauls.'[9] Kegan Paul, a friend of Pattison, had had, religiously speaking, a peripatetic career. Ordained in the Church of England, he became first a broad churchman, then a high churchman, turned to positivism and landed up in 1890 as a Roman Catholic. In the 1880s, having already left the Anglican ministry, he was best known as a successful publisher.

'They are so different to what I had fancied', Meta commented on the Kegan Pauls, 'I imagined Nancy [his daughter] an etherealized Daisy! They look years older than they are, and I wonder at Mary's liking them. Nancy likes you best.' Mark had a soft spot for Nancy

Paul, but found her enigmatic. 'I am not exactly afraid', he told Meta,
'but not at my ease with her. She does not chill me, but she makes me
think what I am going to say, and considers if it will do, in a way
which makes intercourse not successful. On the other hand, she
brings out of me a side, which you do not and the only one you do
not tap, viz. the tendency to turn up the philosophical view of everything.'[10] 'Nancy', Meta commented, 'wants to stay with you as she
can't see you in any other way she truly says. She would be allowed
to go alone if you asked her. She says she feels afraid of you and
would rather I were there too ...'.[11] 'There is so much reserved
silence about her, that I can imagine *long* pauses when you're
together, not the pauses old friendship entitles you to, but pauses
during which you both wonder what on earth to say next.' She was
quixotic in character, 'a girl of deep nature, capable of intense [feel-
ing], too intense for happiness, affection, and hatred'.[12]

Victorian dinner parties, ponderous and protracted, abounded.
There were ten at table when Meta dined with her sister, Jessie Ilbert.
'Albert Dicey, Mr Watson from Wimbledon, a Mr Booth and Mr
Milner. Jowett had commanded J[essie] to make Mr Milner's
acquaintance ... I sat between Watson and Milner. The former Jessie
loves and I find very dull. All I got out of him was that he had spent
some days in the same house as Turgenev and George Eliot.'[13] Alfred
Milner, then in his late twenties, had had a spectacular career as a
classicist at Balliol where he had been one of Jowett's star pupils.
Subsequently he had been elected to a fellowship at New College,
but he decided against the academic life, was called to the bar and
worked as a journalist on the *Pall Mall Gazette*, under the editorship
of John Morley. They talked about 'wingless birds' and did not know
how best to define them; it was the sort of conundrum which
Pattison loved to solve. 'The Apteros (wingless bird of New
Zealand)', he commented knowingly, 'though now extinct, has been
seen alive by many persons now living.'[14]

Milner and Pattison had many friends in common, notably
Leonard Montefiore and Arnold Toynbee.[b] Meta was much excited

---

[b] Arnold Toynbee (1852–83), tutor of Balliol and disciple of T. H. Green, lectured on
industrial problems to working men in London. Died in 1883. Toynbee Hall in White-
chapel founded in his memory.[15]

by the forthcoming marriage of Grace Toynbee to Percy Frankland.[c]
She told Meta 'all about it'. . . 'Grace doesn't expect impossibilities
from life, which is often so fatal to happiness as content.' In such a
dubious project as marriage Pattison only took a reluctant interest,
perturbed by the thought of the wedding present he would have to
give. Another guest at one of these parties, a Mr Ricardo, spoke of
the architect, T. G. Jackson, able but 'atrociously conceited' who had
been commissioned by Lincoln College to design some new buildings and renovate old ones.[d] 'I wish', Meta wrote of Jackson, 'he were
as pleasant as he is clever.'

'I went to lunch at the Toynbees, one of the girls having a bad eye
and wanting cheering up', Meta wrote on 4 February. 'The married
one, with whom I stayed at Liverpool is there . . . I paid two calls and
went back to tea with the Toynbees. After which I read to them an
article on George Eliot, the moral influence of herself and her works.
It was badly written and only contained one or two remarks worth
reading.'[e] There was even an occasional outing to the theatre. The
Ilberts took Meta to see *Patience*, 'extremely amusing to me, who
have only seen that sort of thing once before. If it wasn't for the bad
air you really would like it. It is a skit on aestheticism. The girls . . .
had the loveliest garments on!'[18] With the Kensingtons she played
whist 'which has hitherto been the way I most liked spending the
evening, but yesterday I didn't care for it. Your sweet face got
between me and the cards. Mr K[ensington] and I lost 29 points', a
comment which evoked a sniff of disapproval from Mark; 'cards
always seem to me a miserable waste of the fire of life, absolute
repose preferable.'[19] The Bryces were other acquaintances. 'I spent an
hour with Minnie and Kate Bryce today . . . They looked quite
pretty'. When she had tea with them a month later, Minnie and Kate
'were tremendously got up. They can't spend less than £100 a year on
their clothes. I wonder James can afford to give Minnie so much . . .
Somehow her perfect self-satisfaction provoked me, tho I really have
a feeling for her'.[f]

[c] Percy Frankland (1858–1946), Professor of Chemistry, Birmingham University.

[d] T. G. Jackson (1835–1924), architect. Designed many Oxford buildings including the
New Examination Schools and new buildings at Lincoln College.[16]

[e] The 'married one' was Rachel Falk with whom Meta had stayed.[17]

[f] James Bryce (1838–1922), jurist and historian, fellow Oriel College Oxford 1862–89.[20]

Although Meta was isolated from Oxford, the Oxford connection was never far away. Uncle Granville Bradley called on his brother: 'he says Lord Salisbury is very much annoyed at having the patronage of Worcester taken from them.'[21] Jessie's husband, Courtenay Ilbert, was a close personal friend of Jowett who often visited their London house. The January snowfall frustrated Jowett's return to Oxford and Jessie was 'quite annoyed having him indoors chatting over the fire all day'. Oxford gossip kept creeping in. Who was to be the new Provost of Worcester College? To the disappointment of many, including Mark, Dr Daniel had failed to be elected. The new Provost, Dr Inge, was an unknown factor; 'Papa', said Meta, 'has never even heard his name'. 'I suppose he is about 50 and a mere Conservative parson. There'll be another head on the wrong side.'[22] 'Inge', Mark commented, 'has not shewn himself to a curious world as yet. Mrs Cotton [the widow of the previous Provost] having her month to move out ... Cotton's books are at Gee's in the High, mainly low church divinity. I couldn't find (hardly) anything to waste my substance on.'[g] Uncle Granville reported that Inge was a 'strong Tory, a connection of Lady Salisbury'. Pattison had his own pieces of gossip for Meta. Brodrick's election as Warden of Merton filled him only with gloom, 'as he is wholly on the side of the school-masters, and hates learning worse than toad or asp. Everything seems to be going against me, and it is high time for me to retire from the scene.'[h]

Mark responded sympathetically to Meta's continuing catena of complaint about the tedium of her existence. 'Yes, your life is a *gêne* [torture], but it is so, not because your surroundings are so much worse than other peoples, but because you are too great for them.'[25] That surely was laying on flattery with a trowel. She must find outside interests to take herself out of the rut. 'As I care for nothing for its own sake apart from you', Meta wailed, '(not music, drawing, whist, skating, even reading, not seeing people unless they say what will interest you) I hope really to do more for other people, and to be less selfish outwardly. . . .'[26]

---

[g] Richard Cotton (1794–1880), Provost of Worcester College 1839–80, was a strong Evangelical and critic of the Tractarians.[23]

[h] G. C. Brodrick (1831–1903), a Liberal but opposed to Gladstone's Irish policy, was Warden of Merton from 1881 to 1903.[24]

In spite of her complaints, she was beginning to take a real interest in social work, finding satisfaction in district visiting. She visited a 'luckless invalid in the Workhouse Infirmary. Such surroundings, smoke, noise, quarelling women, born cheerfully by a fairly educated woman for 15 years.' Some three weeks later she found her on her death-bed, 'isn't a bit evangelical or canting. . . . She reads French novels (nice ones, of course) and Morley's series, whenever the Toynbees or I hand her one. Fancy your Milton being read and fairly well understood in a Workhouse Ward! You don't like this sort of thing, I know, so I'll spare you any more.' She was right. Whatever his views on society, Mark's heart was hardly wrung by the injustices it perpetrated; he had no wish for the rag-bag to be thrust into the cloistered calm of an Oxford college.

Half-humorously, half-seriously, Mark suggested that marriage was the proper solution to her problems. 'Choose, don't be chosen, don't wait till you "like" or till you "care", as you call it, but choose a rich muff, who will do nothing and want nothing of you and then you can live your life and be yourself.'[27] 'When you talk of leading my own life!', Meta replied somewhat exasperated, 'Why, dearest, I haven't any now but in you!'[28]

Actually they managed to see each other fairly regularly since Pattison had many engagements, lectures, committees, which brought him up to London. She hoped somewhat naïvely that he would call at Orsett Terrace. 'I had such a cosy tea for you, and had put on all the clothes I know you'd like, and taken off those you hate, and made a lovely fire for us to snuggle over! . . . My own dear love, I do care so very, very deeply for you, words never could tell how much!'[29] But Pattison was wary of causing talk. 'Oh my dear I am so grieved I did not come to you last night when I read of the preparations you had made and think of all the loves and caresses which were awaiting me.' But he had been 'morally exhausted by people, and unfit for anything, but a sulk over the fire in my bedroom . . . but, my own, I was utterly worthless and unavailable, too done even to write to you.' Daringly she suggested the he might take a room in which they could meet, but he rejected it on the grounds that it would be prohibitively expensive, '4 or 5 guineas a week'.[30] With her and his friends, Fanny Kensington, Grace Toynbee, and Rose Nicholls, she went to hear him lecture at the London Institution on

31 January on 'The Thing that might be', 'a much better audience than at the Royal [Institution]'.[31] She sometimes came to see him off at Paddington, for her house at Orsett Terrace was only a short distance from the station. To his diary he confided on 2 February, one of the very few references to Meta that somehow escaped Mrs Pattison's sharp scissors, 'Down to Oxford by the 4.45, dear Meta coming to the station to see me off and wrap me up.' 'How I wish I were with you', she wrote on 26 January 1881, 'I should have met you at Paddington had I had your dear letter in time. I dreamt last night that I did so and was carried on to my great delight straight to Oxford while I was tucking your rug round you. What bliss it would have been!' 'At Lincoln at any rate 1000 things will be always recalling your little girl to you. What a heavenly feeling perfect confidence is! to *know* that misunderstanding is impossible!'

By and large then they did not do too badly. 'I shall come upon Monday morning', he wrote on 10 February, 'and if you are at liberty, will either go to the old masters or make a pedestrian excursion into the city.' He visited her at the Lewis Campbell's house at Wimbledon to play tennis or croquet. He invited her to a literary *soirée* at the Grosvenor, but she excused herself. 'If you had that paralysing headache you speak of you were just as well away from the Grosvenor, for the atmosphere was suffocating. Such a crush! The great Oscar [Wilde] the hero of the day. Wherever he moved, there was the thick of the party, and when he deigned to stand for 5 minutes talking to Rachel Huxley (she is handsome!) there was a regular ring of lookers on formed round them.'[32]

They both looked forward to Meta's visit to Oxford in the coming autumn and, if possible, an earlier stay together. 'I usually dislike all evenings not spent with you, darling', Meta reassured him. 'My plans', Mark told Meta, 'now all go in the direction of getting you to make a tour on the continent, and to get a house where you may stay with me in the summer.'[33] Mark was considering renting a house in Yorkshire for the summer, and persuading his wife to stay away. He knew that his wife hated both Yorkshire and his Pattison relatives. Consequently he hoped that she would refuse to contemplate a trip to Yorkshire. He raised with Meta another possibility. If her sister Jessie and her husband could be encouraged to take a house in Richmond and ask Meta to stay with them, everything would be above board. 'The summer sounds too delightful', Meta replied, 'and I shall try not to think much about it till you have had your answer from Draguignan [where Mrs Pattison was wintering] and actually got a house.'[34] She did not, however, believe it was feasible to suppose that the Ilberts would want to rent a house in England. Alternatively she suggested to Mark that they might join a friend of hers who was going to Switzerland for July and August. 'She is wholly uninteresting, very limited mentally ... but would be a very unobjectionable chaperone and glad to take me in the same pension.' This would provide neutral territory. 'I should *awfully* like to spend a week with you this term, but don't believe they'd let me ... I dreamt about you last night again! Not much to be wondered at, considering that I thought of no one else from 11 to 1.'[35]

Other possibilities loomed before their eyes. Perhaps a continental trip at Easter might prove feasible. 'I believe it could be done', Mark wrote, 'and with Mrs Grundy's full consent, if we assumed the right attitude towards each other, you the indispensable daughter and staff of my old age. That view once accepted, we may do what we like.'[36] But Meta considered that Mark had not taken into account the objections which her parents would be likely to raise. Perhaps Mark should make a direct approach to Charles Bradley. 'Darlingest, how heavenly it would be to have you again. If you knew how the bare possibility agitates me',[37] but Mark cringed at the idea of writing to her father. He greeted the Swiss scheme warmly, 'as I a little doubt your being quite happy for 8 weeks in Yorkshire with no entertainment, no society, no lawn tennis, nothing but books'[38] This, said Meta, would be 'bliss, so perfect that I must not dwell upon the possibility until it becomes a probability'.

This she was right to do, for all Mark's calculations were upset by his wife's reply. He was dumbfounded by learning that she would reluctantly accompany him to Yorkshire. Mrs Pattison had been staying at the Albergo di Molero in Rome, much lionized, visiting French archaeologists and through the good offices of Lady Paget, the wife of the British ambassador, was privileged to inspect the Poussins in the Doria palazzo.[39] She was, of course, aware of her husband's hostility, intending 'in a sort of cowardly way to cast me adrift'. When, therefore, his letter came, suggesting a stay in Yorkshire in the summer, she countered his proposal with an acceptance.

This was in part designed to maintain the artifice that they were still a happily married couple, and in part because in a mean and ineffectual attempt to keep her away he had offered her the ludicrous sum of £50 to maintain herself and her housekeeper, Madame Moreau, for five months. 'I did not take up or comment on the *nature* of this proposition', she informed Ellen Smith, 'or the *amount* on which he proposed Moreau and I were to live on (I to be clothed and her wages to be paid) for five months! I wish I had a better temper, or could manage to feel indifferent.'[40] 'I suppose', she wrote again on 23 March, 'we may consider the Yorkshire question settled and that the summer will pass as usual this year but how one is made to waste time and life by these perversities ... Much of what I suffer is rendered heavier by the sense of intense resentment which is I think justified by the nastiness and meanness of what I am forced into close contact with.'[41]

Mark emitted a shrill squeal of anger at his wife's decision. 'I merely proposed, on the ground of pulling down in the Grove [the replacement of an eighteenth-century cottage building at Lincoln College by new undergraduate accommodation, designed by T. G. Jackson, in proximity to the Rector's lodgings], to take fishing quarters for myself in Yorkshire, and, as it would be impossible that she should spend the summer in that rough style, offered her £50 to find herself during the period. Now she writes back to say of course I shall be ready to go with you where you may settle to spend the summer months. This is the very thing I want to avoid. If her presence is a misery to me here in Oxford where I have all sorts of resource and refuge, it would be intolerable if we were shut up together in a country house. So I have written back urging the unfitness of picnic quarters such as I should find in Yorkshire, for her and hinting at Richmond as the chosen locality, a place of all others she must detest, as it abounds in my relations and acquaintances. If that doesn't frighten her off, nothing will.'[42]

The Rector had been hoist with his own petard. His sister, Sarah Bowes, offered him at very low rent a house at Richmond. The prospect was attractive, but only if Meta would visit him there.[43] Much worried, Meta pleaded for time. Mrs Pattison would surely, Meta thought, be hurt by hearing that the Rector intended to have Mary Stirke and herself 'to stay at a place which you call fishing

quarters and too rough for her.'[44] Now and later, Meta cherished the
hope that Mrs Pattison might be persuaded to accept her as an unobjectionable companion to Mark. 'I would give almost anything to
have Mrs Pattison like me. Of course she wouldn't but if she only
would it would make everything quite straight.' It was certainly a
pipe-dream to suppose that Mrs Pattison would like Meta. To
Mark's disgust, she now intimated that she would, if reluctantly,
come to Richmond. 'I can hardly think she means it, as I know there
is nothing she would detest so much. I am almost disposed to think
she is persisting in order to make me drop the scheme altogether.
And this I shall be driven to if she holds on, for I should be miserable
shut up there with an antipathetic person for 4 months.'[45]

It seemed unlikely that Meta and Mark could now meet before the
autumn, but 'November is a dreadfully long time ahead, perhaps it
will be October'.[46] Meta's father had told her that he did not wish her
to stay with Mark during the summer, thus putting full stop to any
possibility of the expedition to Yorkshire. They were left with
occasional, fleeting meetings and correspondence. The sense of loss
which she experienced through Mark's absence formed a constant
refrain. 'I always go to sleep thinking of you, and when I awake I am
still with thee, my own darling! I suppose you think of me every day.
My state of mind would be better described as being always
conscious of, and generally thinking of you. I wonder whether that is
what some people feel about God.'[47] 'I read your letter 3 times last
night, and put it under my pillow, darling. I didn't sleep at all, but it
was lovely that your dear words were close to my head. You're so
wonderfully sympathetic and responsive, much more like a woman
in your quick tenderness.'[48] It was a view of Mark that many of his
friends, let alone his wife, would have found difficult to recognize. 'I
entirely agree', she wrote three days later in reply to a letter from
him, 'that no one appreciates me as you do, or can love me as you do
... How I wish that we two were basking in some sandy bay with
smiling waves rippling at our feet.'[49] Outside, as she wrote, a harsh
wind blew the snow along the terrace, and the cosy evenings
together were never to materialize.

With her father it was now a form of guerilla warfare, for her
resolve to make an effort not to provoke him soon subsided. After
strolling with him, she went to his study to talk in a friendly fashion,

but he simply grunted and handed her a newspaper to read. Then he enquired, knowing perfectly well the answer, as to what church she had attended, for it was a Sunday, adding, before she even answered, 'one advantage of this life we lead is that neither of us can miss the other when either of us has to leave it'. 'Of course, I said sweetly "speak for yourself", not wishing him to know that I prefer his absence to his presence.'[50] 'There is', Mark, who had plenty of experience of strained family relations, felt obliged to comment, 'something peculiar in your relations to your family, not a mere negative froideur, but a positive repulsion exists between you.'[51] With an ingrained respect for paternal authority, which he had certainly not practised, he besought her to be more conciliatory. He was aware that she could be prickly. 'I think', he said frankly, 'you would irritate me were I your father.' She found the long dinner, which usually took an hour at Orsett Terrace, peculiarly purgatorial. 'I seldom open my lips so I can think about you! If I do try to say anything my father says "don't you cut in" or "I didn't ask you."'[52] 'My father', she wrote at the end of January, 'is gouty, poor thing. I'm very sorry for him, but I prefer him when he is not well.'

Then consternation struck the Bradley household when in early February 1881, he had a slight stroke. Unfortunately Mrs Bradley was away, and Meta's fussing irritated rather than soothed him. 'He couldn't let me stay in his room at all. I could only sit in the next room and go in every half hour to poke the fire!'[53] Fortunately his favoured daughter, Jessie, lived sufficiently near to minister to the sick man. He recovered slowly, but his doctor, Andrew Clark, warned that any sudden shock might cause a recurrence. 'He must never preach again or use his brain, or be contradicted', a prescription which was to make life even more intolerable for Meta than it had been before. In practice he was at least well enough within a few days to entertain some of his 'yachting girls'; 'you would have been amused at seeing him talking hand in hand with one of them, and kissing them all round when they came and went.'[54] He had recovered sufficiently to tell Meta brusquely when she offered to play backgammon with him, 'Not with *you*, thank you, send up my wife.'[55]

All this was the more disturbing since a few days after her father's stroke there came an anonymous letter, in the course of which the

writer, evidently a woman, criticized Meta's relationship with Mark.[i]
At first Mark reacted sorrowfully, 'Dear! how unhappy I have been
made all this day by the malignity of a spiteful world when both our
happiness depends on our being together.' Yet he did not seem to
show much fight. 'I do see that this state of public opinion on the
point cannot be treated with contempt; it must be allowed to
influence our behaviour towards each other.'[56]

Meta thought that Mark's judgement was mistaken. 'I am only
afraid that you should mistake the opinion of the few for that of the
many. If it were not so horrid it would seem laughable that anyone
should see anything improper in a friendship between you, a philosopher scholar etc. of 67 and me, a very ignorant girl! But we may
quite console ourselves that *none* of our *friends*, certainly not one of
mine, but thinks our intimacy very good for *me*, at any rate, and I
beg to inform you, Sir, that I won't give it up to please any human
being, so don't flatter yourself that you won't have to scold me many
more times at Lincoln.'[57]

This was putting a brave front, perhaps too brave a front on the
matter, for its ramifications were manifold. Yet even Mark by the
evening of the same day on which he had written his earlier comment was beginning to take a less pessimistic view: 'an anonymous
letter does not speak for anybody except the writer'. It should surely
be ignored. But could it be? It was the worm in the bud. It niggled. 'I
trust', Meta wrote, 'you'll lock up these letters with those I wrote to
you before you went abroad! How the contents of them would
surprise and puzzle the world! though no words on paper could give
any one idea of how I love you, still less could they realize that I
really am some heart comfort to you.'[58] Aware as he was of Meta's
affection, Mark had no desire for it to be blazoned forth to the world.
Who else beside the anonymous letter-writer knew of the contents
of such letters? 'It haunts me', Mark confessed, 'and if the malicious
sender knew how she had destroyed my peace she would reap the
full gratification of her malice. It is well for me that I have such a
beneficent atmosphere of literary thought and occupation round me,
or I should be thinking of nothing but the letter all day.'[59]

Two questions were uppermost in their minds. How and where

[i] 'Said my relative to the unknown "Were her letters very gushing?" "Gushing is
nothing to it."'

had Meta's letters been seen, read, and evidently copied, and who
was the anonymous writer? Was the Lodgings the seat of the infection? Mark kept Meta's letters in a locked tin box, but from time to
time he left his own unfinished correspondence on his study table.
But what was at issue was not a letter from him to her but from her
to him; incidentally the letter-writer mentioned also letters to him
'from other girls'. Mark pondered the loyalty of the staff. He found it
difficult to believe that his housekeeper, Mrs Baines, who certainly
had access to his rooms, could be guilty of such treachery. 'I have
often told you that Baines does read my papers, but I have always
had such confidence in her fidelity and regard for the interests of the
family that I never believed in her repeating what she knew.' His man-
servant, Hans, not especially efficient and sometimes given to drink,
was about to leave, but he had neither the opportunity nor the
interest. The housemaid, Ellen, was an unlikely candidate. 'I cannot
suppose Ellen either would read, or if she did, would or could,
repeat, or even understand our words.'

Meta had sometimes requested Mark to burn her letters, a request
which he usually ignored, but he had on occasions torn up her letters
and thrown them in the wastepaper basket. Could some one have
pieced them together? Conscientiously after Sunday chapel he
plodded down to the cellar to examine the box of waste paper, but
the scraps were intact. Since the writer had described Meta's
language as 'gushing', he supposed that they must refer to letters
written during the autumn rather than in the previous summer when
her wording had been comparatively restrained.[60] So he concluded
that 'the letters in circulation do not emanate from here'.[61]

If not Oxford, where else? In London Pattison wrote his letters
usually at the Athenaeum but he would not have left letters from
Meta in his club. Could it have been some place where he was visiting, for one phrase in the letter referred to the 'house where the
Rector was staying'. Could it have been Waltham where he stayed
with the Montefiores or the pension in Paris where his friend, Miss
Rowland, '*had* opportunity of reading, and had time to do so. But
even if she read, she knew nothing of you, and was on too good a
footing with me to do anything to injure or annoy me behind my
back'.[62] It was just possible that she might have sent such letters to
her aunt, Mrs Thursfield; he would prod gently. Meta had warned

him that 'you must send the letters I write while you're in Paris by post, in case you lose them during the journey home. They really would not do to leave about'.[63] Yet as the anonymous writer 'knew your father well', that could not refer conceivably to Miss Rowland or Mrs Thursfield.

Meta came to the conclusion that Mrs Pattison herself might be the root of the matter. She enquired of Mark whether he knew of a mutual friend, a Mrs Hullah, who might have been in contact with her, but Mark pooh-poohed the idea, for Mrs Hullah had cooled towards his wife since the development of the 'liaison with Dilke', the first direct reference in the letters that he had made to the counter-affair.[64] Meta still wondered whether Mrs Pattison might have seen the letters in the summer of 1880 when she had been staying at Lincoln. 'I can't help hoping that the letters read aloud were those I wrote to you in the summer, which you doubtless left in the wooden box by the smoking room window with your other 1880 letters, and that Mrs Mark Pattison might have read them in your absence to a circle of friends.'[65] Mark believed that this was out of character, and held correctly that the adjectives used to describe the letters suggested that they were those written in the autumn rather than in the summer.

But Meta was, of course, right in thinking that Mrs Pattison had read her letter to Mark, if wrong in supposing that she had engineered the anonymous missive. 'Privately to you', Mrs Pattison was to write to Ellen Smith on 23 March 1881, 'I say what I *would* say to Mrs B[radley] (since I can *openly* avow having seen the letters which came under my notice in the course of last summer when according to custom I opened *all* arriving in the Rector's absence) that they betrayed a perhaps *unconscious* condition the cravings of which are *cheated* by relations such as those in *which* she placed herself with the Rector.' But though she knew of the correspondence, she speculated that Meta herself could have been the authoress of the anonymous letter, writing 'to *accaparer* exclusively and to be *known to do so*'.[66][i]

The identity of the writer remained an opaque matter. Pattison decided to throw out what may be described as series of baits to his

---

[i] She commented that Sir Charles Dilke had learned of what had occurred from Mrs Cyril Flower at Lord Rosebery's.

female friends in Oxford, but his efforts were cumbrous and the
ladies too quick-witted to take the offering. They did not conceal
their dislike and suspicion of Meta whom they plainly regarded as a
scheming young adventuress, engaged in snaring their beloved
Rector with her flirtatious wiles. Meta was hurt by their unfriendly
attitude. Apart from the Daniels and the Arthur Johnsons, with
whom she had played tennis, she had hardly met them. 'The others
must make up their minds about people on *very* slight acquaintance
if they could express or have any views about me.'[67] The Oxford
ladies could take Mary Stirke or Gertrude Tuckwell, but Meta had
designs. Rhoda Broughton and her sister, Mrs Newcome, Mark
reported, 'vented their intense hate for you about which there could
be no mistake, only in seeming tones and sarcasms aimed chiefly at
me. They were too savage to descend to detail, or to pick holes in
you'.[68] Yet earlier he had also written 'Rhoda doesn't dislike you (i.e.
not more than she does everyone) but she dislikes my being "so
fond" of you which she has found out'.[69]

Two days later, Miss Broughton brought a note from her sister,
Mrs Newcome, inviting the Rector to dine, an invitation which he
refused, pleading pressure of work and ill health. 'She behaved over it
as naturally and as pleasantly as possible, jested about seeing me with
you at Burlington House, said she meant to punish me for not
coming to dine by talking of me etc. I was all the time turning in my
mind whether I should hint at the letter on us, and before I could
make up my mind she was gone, and no break in our cordiality yet
made!' He wondered whether he should have made some allusion to
the letter but came to the conclusion that it was better not to do so,
'as she is more likely to betray herself thus if put on her guard from
the first. She certainly acted innocence most admirably! and is as
good an actress as she is writer, for acting it undoubtedly was ...
She'll now go back to her sister, and chuckle over my unsuspecting
simplicity'.[70]

Firmly convinced of Rhoda Broughton's guilt, he made a new
move, after talking it over with Meta, when the Irish novelist, May
Laffan, came over from Dublin to stay a few days at the Lodgings.
Pattison admired Miss Laffan as an intelligent woman and an
excellent letter-writer. 'I can sincerely write "affectionately" to the
Laffan because she's a woman who has thought me worth her

notice, and one can always love a woman, especially if she's young and good-looking, though love in one case means much more than it does in an other.' Meta was critical of Mark's liking for Miss Laffan. 'By love I think you mean a mild feeling of interest and gratitude in a case such as the Laffan's. However, you men are inscrutable, and I shall never fathom your natures.' She insisted that Miss Laffan's attraction was based simply on the intellect and was lacking in depth. Indeed the Rector's actual greeting to Miss Laffan was qualified. 'Miss Laffan is a most interesting experiment,' he wrote on 14 March 1881, 'but she takes up too much of my time . . . I have not had an hour to myself the whole of the day . . . She gives a kind of Irish sympathy, very ready and real, but superficial, understands the human part of me, but not the cultivated and artificial part, and at times I almost fancy she is only making fun of me. She got me, the very first night, to tell her a great deal, more than I have told anyone, except you, and I don't feel sure that she won't talk it out to the next comer.'[71]

His choice of her as an emissary to Miss Broughton was therefore strange. He sent her to Rhoda on 11 March, the very day after her arrival in Oxford, 'with the commission to see by mention of the name what the animus of the house towards Meta was', though this was something which he should surely have known from his earlier conversation with Miss Broughton and her sister. 'What did the blundering thing do but tell Miss Broughton that I suspected her of having written the anonymous letter, and naively asked her "if she had".' 'So bad is made worse — never employ an Irishwoman in a diplomatic mission', the truth of which he should have foreseen before he sent her on her mission.[72]

Miss Laffan's indiscretion rankled. She was his guest. He had to walk with her. Professor Smith and his sister, Ellen, were invited to dine on the Saturday, Hatch and Bywater on the Sunday. 'Inflamed mucous membrane from eating meat and drinking wine' left him 'jaded and worn out'. 'Oh! amici quam parum amici.' What with chatting and walking with his guest, entertaining undergraduates to breakfast and attending the Council for the Higher Education of Women, he found his days 'wholly unprofitable'. 'I am dreadfully plagued with 2 visitors [Mrs Thursfield had joined Miss Laffan as a guest] in the house for whom I have to provide dinner every day at 7.'

'Much as I have liked Miss Laffan and glad as I have been to have Mrs Thursfield here' it was with relief that he saw them go 'and I got a quiet evening!' 'At such expense of the intellectual life, do I do the small amount of entertaining which I do do.'

May Laffan's interview with Rhoda Broughton was bound to have repercussions. At first he seems not to have confided the failure of Miss Laffan's mission to Meta, but the news filtered through Mrs Toynbee that he and Miss Broughton 'had quarrelled about some letter' and 'weren't on speaking terms!' Meta hoped that they would soon be friends again. She could understand how Rhoda Broughton had felt. 'Most people would be hurt at being even suspected of a mean action like that by a *friend*.'[73]

More dangerously Rhoda Broughton, furious at the accusation, told Mrs Pattison what had happened. 'It is perfectly monstrous to suppose either of those two women Mrs Newcome and Miss Broughton capable of such a villainous act' was Mrs Pattison's comment.[74] 'From London', she wrote on 27 March, 'I hear of the "ever-loving" one cheerful in picture galleries with "the person who has shewn her that she still has a heart" so the anon: letter has not produced much effect.' His wife's reference to quotations from the letter which Meta had written to Mark indicated that the bitterness had cut deep.[75]

She was furthermore still much exercised by the proposed expedition to Yorkshire, seeing through in some measure the stratagems which her husband was employing. 'I have at last heard from the Rector', she commented in the letter of 27 March, 'I thought when you [i.e. Ellen Smith] told me of his pleasantness and amiability that it was a bad sign because he is never so sweet as when he is hatching a trick. The letter is very unpleasant. He announces to having taken the house from middle June to middle August, still in spite of reiterated positive assertions to the contrary, in the expectation of my going to friends for that time . . . I suppose I must stand firm and *go*, but it is in the highest degree offensive to me. It is not only the loss of just the two months I counted on for books and Bodleian, but the being forced to live with people whose habits and ideas are equally distasteful to me and with no relief of resource.'

How Ellen Smith replied we do not know, but it provoked a furious outburst from Francis Pattison about her husband's conduct. 'I think you must bear in mind that the Rector has never informed

me of Miss Bradley's visit or alluded to her in any way . . . Then I am
suddenly told "to provide for myself during the 5 summer months
and I offer you £50 for doing so". I *am* very indignant. I do not see
that patience and affectionate tone have *now* the least effect under
these circumstances. Can he ask a favour of me? Supposing he did—
at your suggestion—and I received Miss Bradley thereby facilitating
her return next winter, I should like to know what would be the
course adopted by Mrs Bradley. If she continued to disapprove, and
to forbid her daughter from going to Lincoln I think I should have
[put] myself distinctly in the wrong. I don't think I could ask her to
the house without first seeing her and telling her I have seen her
letters of last year and that flattery of a man near seventy by suggestions that he is not in old age and by assuring him that he is the first
who has shewn her that she has a heart is something worse than out-
rageous bad taste.'[76]

Meta's hope of mollifying Mrs Pattison, and the Rector's belief
that Miss Smith's good offices could be used to make a stay during
the autumn possible were thus swept away. Mrs Pattison ended her
letter by giving vent to a snort of outrage. 'The fuss about the Carlyle
Reminiscences reminds me that when some idiot asked him 'Why he
said the Rector has a strong accipitral head', he replied 'joost a
human birrd of prey', and I feel sometimes as if my life would never
hold out against the incessant peck, peck, peck, of the cruel beak.
The weakness of nerve which the life at L[incoln] created disappears
only to be fretted into being again by these incessant worries. For
nineteen years I have been struggling to keep down the longing for
deliverance. I cannot, it is always there. I can stifle it by working but
it springs up stronger than ever.'[77]

Meanwhile, in early March—Mrs Pattison's last letter had been
dated 30 March—Meta and Mark had been much perturbed by what
may have been the delivery of another anonymous letter. Unfortunately Meta's letter of 4 March is missing, but next day the Rector
'Wrote long letter to Meta on this unfortunate business of some
woman having got hold of her letter to me'.[78] 'Your's just received',
he wrote in this letter, 'has so upset me that I feel it difficult to sit
down to my usual quiet evening of reading.'[79] Since the original
anonymous letter had come some three weeks earlier, this suggests
that there was reason for a fresh perturbation. It may, of course, have

been simply that Meta had become so sensitive about security that she had once more charged Mark with carelessness, so suggesting that he had some responsibility for the crisis. 'Such a night' was Saturday 5/6 March, 'as I hated: feverish, constantly waking, and the presence of you throughout. I should go mad if I had often such nights.'

He decided to go up to London the following Tuesday to talk over the matter with Meta. 'Meanwhile, be of good courage, dearest, we shall get through this storm and the main thing is that we are so much to each other! No slander can reach that inner bond by which we are bound heart to heart.'[80] 'I think', he wrote on the eve of his visit, 'we had better now have it out, and proclaim that we are fond of each other, and don't mean to be separated, I being your grandpapa, and you my dear and attached grandchild.'[81]

'To town by 9'o clock train', he wrote in his diary for 8 March 1881, 'to see Meta about this unlucky business—excellent behaviour of Mrs C. Bradley, who advises that we should not write to each other just at present nor see each other often—she entirely kind and sensible.'[82] From Orsett Terrace, he went on to a meeting of the Council of Aberystwyth College, left cards on some of his friends and joined the Kensingtons for a stroll in the park. On his return to Oxford he at once wrote a consolatory letter. 'How sweet was the sight of your darling face . . . though traces of grief visible on it gave me a pang, grief caused by my carelessness, yet you never resented it, by word or by look, never once imparted it to me, though I was feeling all the while like a guilt-stricken thing. Then the drive with you in the cab. Oh heavenly! . . . I think it all over, and think "Is it possible that I am so fortunate as to have got a being in the world who thinks and cares, and sympathises with me so keenly as this one does!" How different is my life become since I discovered you.'[83] He was sufficiently free from the agitation, which had so unsettled him during the past few days, to read Freeman's *Essays on Thucydides* on the journey and was amused rather than irritated on his return to find the undergraduates celebrating their victories in the Lent Races or Torpids, as they were called at Oxford, 'by tom-tom music' and 'by going about the quad beating the bottoms of their baths [i.e. hip baths] with the fire shovel! Ain't they big babies?'[84] Fed by whiting and coffee, he read Tozer's book on Armenia before he went to bed at half-past ten.

Meta was feeling the strain more than Mark, so much that he began to be worried by her morbidity. She was in danger of permitting her 'imagination to dwell and centre on one thought'. 'Every day a tyrant thought is tolerated in the brain, its dominion becomes more established.'[85] She was, he thought, no longer the 'robust, vigorous, strapping lass' that he had known at Grasmere.[86] She must, he felt, develop some interest that would make her less introspective. To encourage her, and to demonstrate his affection, he told her that he had left her a small legacy in his will. 'I want to give you more than it would be advisable to leave you, as it might expose the legacy to comment.'[87]

Meta at first demurred, preferring that the legacy might be given 'to encourage research *in your name* ... I should like my grandnieces' generation to be familiar with your name in connection with something at Oxford. Don't you wonder whether hundreds of years on someone will take the trouble to do for you what you did for Casaubon.'[88] But Mark was adamant. 'As to endowing research, I would not do it even if I could, as I am at present minded.' 'It is the only sum which I have any satisfaction in leaving behind me. You would not deprive me of the one pleasure I can have in connexion with my testamentary dispositions. It is a sum which I had left in my will to the College. Since the Commission I have executed a codicil transferring it to you.'[89]

The next move in the crisis of the purloined letter was not made by Pattison but by Ellen Smith, probably prompted by his wife. She called at the Lodgings on the evening of 22 March, remarking casually as she was leaving that 'she had had a person making representations to her about Miss Bradley staying with me'. She refused to name the person and said that she made light of it. 'She spoke very kindly, and without any spice of feeling against you.' His curiosity aroused and his feelings flattered, he relaxed his guard and wrote a long letter stressing Meta's usefulness to him, more especially in rearranging his books, 'the only one of my visitors who knew how to be "victorious over disorder"', in the hope that he might leave an impression that he was simply an 'egotistical brute whose one thought was his own comfort, to which I was ready to sacrifice you'. He urged that his comfort next winter would depend greatly on Meta's staying with him at Oxford. He enquired into the insinuations that had been made against him, and expressed the hope that Miss Smith's 'sympathies' were 'on our side'.[90]

Given her close friendship with Mrs Pattison, this was an unlikely eventuality. In reply Miss Smith sent a 'masterly letter', 'excellent, quite human, yet so sensible'. Clever woman that she was, she had managed to persuade the Rector that it would be inadvisable to have Meta to stay with him in Oxford. 'I fear', he told Meta, 'we shall have to surrender all prospect of doing so in Oxford, for any but very short visits from time to time.'[91] Miss Smith did in fact put Mark's case to his wife, provoking the reply of 30 March in which Mrs Pattison wrote strongly about her husband's conduct. 'No one knows', Francis Pattison told her, 'not even you, all that I've had to bear—it seems very weak to complain but it is safe with you, and you know that I soon make fight again as hard as ever. Do you remember the American parrot who was shut up with a monkey. They found her without a single feather even in the tail. She remarked as the door opened, "*Oh* I've had a *Hell* of a time" and then proceeded beak and claws undaunted to go it again. When I feel bad, I try to reflect on that parrot. I don't know whether she got the better of the monkey, but I think she deserved to. May *I* deserve it?'[92]

None the less Mark still placed some trust in Miss Smith's intervention and encouraged Meta to do likewise. He had more or less agreed to Mrs Bradley's request to limit his meetings with Meta and to write no more than twice a week. He asked Meta to forgive him for making it appear that she meant nothing to him save a useful assistant. 'I . . . afterwards reproached myself for having even said so much in disparagement of the thing I love so dearly and have such reason to value so highly.'[93] Meta was more apprehensive about Miss Smith than the Rector. 'If I could only see Miss Smith instead of her having to take other people's opinion of me it would be a good thing . . . I must say that I'm sure she would not dislike me! She is so downright and independent herself . . . It is so new to me to be looked upon at all as a doubtfully proper young woman, not a desirable companion for girls!' Why not get Mrs Arnold Toynbee to come to tea when Miss Smith was there. 'Mrs Arnold Toynbee knows so much about me and would put things truthfully and sensibly.'[94][k] Meta sighed but if Miss Smith's intervention made it possible for her to stay at Oxford in the winter, it would be worth it. 'I didn't get to

---

[k] Arnold Toynbee married Miss Charlotte Attwood in 1879.

sleep till 6.30!, owing I suspect, to some bad claret. You and Miss Smith kept up a duet in my head for hours which even Shelley repeated persistently couldn't silence.'[95]

Meta remained in a desponding state. She felt that the attitude she had taken had somehow depressed Mark, and that she had allowed her suspicions to range too widely and even too wildly. 'You say you "did all you could think of for me, and were of course little use and comfort". Dearest that is little to say. It was much more than "doing" anything. Mary [Stirke] "did" though nothing to what you did, but she "did", but you gave the heart of affection that warmed up again my chilled nature which had not known *love* for 5 years, and was craving it and so terribly!' 'Dearest', he concluded, 'I forgive you all little suspicions, your burden of misery is too great.'[96]

Meta moved down to Wimbledon to stay with her sister, but was irritated by Jessie's attempts to cheer her up. 'One can't exactly be merry when one's heart is nearly broken, and one's dearest hope dashed to the ground.'[97] I never still feel at home with Jessie and I'm sure I gave a ghastly grin today when she was sympathetic! If I have a wound she always gives it a blow.' 'Jessie drives me half-wild with perpetually (most kindly) harrying me to eat more and nagging at one for not talking.' Jessie was nothing but persistent. She and Meta drove in an open victoria paying calls for three hours. The day was cold and windy. No one was at home except at their last port of call where they were given tea. But, for the most part, Meta sat and shivered. 'Jessie's presence', as she confessed later, 'always has an evil influence on me and shuts me up or makes me absolutely foolish.'

Not so Mark. He had taken advantage of the ending of the Hilary or Lent term to breathe the fresh air of Wensleydale, staying at the Cover Bridge Inn near Bedale where he had a length of the river Ure for fishing, ten hours bed and six hours out of doors and still abundant time for reading. 'They get me a daily paper the *Yorkshire Post* ... everything is primitive, simple rather than poor, the materials of food excellent, only the elements of cookery unknown, bread, butter, cream, cheese, eggs, all of the true country sweetness and freshness.'[98] 'So the solitude is complete, not so appalling as the wilderness solitude of a Highland moor, but sufficiently cut off from the world to make one fall terribly on oneself, and consider "Whither"?' Wensleydale as usual proved a tonic. He felt immensely better, almost exhilarated. 'This regime of open air, such air! and sleep, is a marvellous medicine. Today I walked up the fell, where patches of snow still are, and over the moor to Colsterdale, 4 hours there and back, and never saw a human from the moment I began to mount the brae, but in the heather the grouse were pairing, and calling to each other on all sides, making the moor alive with their amorous glee. Oh! how I wanted you to share the pleasures and exhilaration of the walk with me ... a real moor solitude, not a tourist haunted moor like those at the lakes strewn with empty soda water bottles and torn *Daily Telegraphs*, but the peculiar thrill which passes through my nervous system when I look down on the panorama of these scenes of my boyhood. That I have to myself, and I don't suppose there is another human being to whom it comes. I began to fish these water in 1829, 53 years ago. Here I can feel the quick heart of the great world pant, how different to the petty air of an evening party.'[99]

He walked the four miles to call on the Stirkes at Grazing Nook. It was the first time he had met the second Mrs Stirke, 'a very presentable, properly behaved person'. Mary, whom he had traduced so sternly earlier in the year, walked part of the way home with him, 'just the same, not altered, cheerful, unemotional, matter of fact, simple, unaffected, uninteresting.' But, as Meta commented, his thoughts were with Mary's mother, his dead sister Rachel. 'Almost every valley and stream has its special association for you, connected so intimately with those long ago lost and with your old self, so different from your present self.'[100] As rooms were booked for Easter he was turned out of 'my lair by some Huddersfield chaps—seven of them', and moved for a few days from Cover Bridge to Tanfield until, at least temporarily refreshed, he returned to Oxford. 'I had 10 days of entire silence in Yorkshire', he told his friend, Mrs W. D. Hertz, 'during which I entered into possession of my own soul, and felt myself. It is a strain, quite as much as society is, and I could not support it for long at a time, but, like cold bathing, I should be better for having it at intervals all through the year. The contrast of Piccadilly, when I came up yesterday, with the solitary bank of the Ure which I had left in the morning, was a sensation which was worth the journey of 7 hours. No retirement so complete is nearer than Yorkshire, I believe.'[101]

Nancy Paul, with whom Pattison strolled through Kensington Gardens, had suggested that Meta might resolve her problems by taking a post as a governess in Mlle Somestre's teaching establishment at Fontainebleau in France. Pattison passed on the suggestion approvingly to Meta who at once turned it down.[102] Although 'I hate my life at home ... I do feel at the end of the day that I have done my best to do my duty to my people. It's a dreary look-out for the best part of my life to be spent as it now is, but I see no help for it.'[103] Mark was critical. 'You go on saying you are dissatisfied with your life at home. If that really is so, why not try what a new sphere will open to you.'[104] Meta replied promptly the very same day that Mark did not 'realize how extremely hurt my father and stepmother would be at my preferring to live with strangers to living with them. If you had a daughter would it not go to your heart, even if you weren't devoted to her, that she should manifestly be thankful for any chance of leaving you? My staying with you was different (and even that rather hurt Papa's feelings) ... Now my only motive, which he could apprehend, in going to France would be to get away from home ... if his feelings were not considered nor hers, and I could leave home, I should much prefer regular hard work among the lower classes.' As her relatives were to discover later, Meta was not very easy to help. There was a strain of intractability in her that made her stubborn. 'As a happy life seems out of the question I want to lead a useful one if I am ever free to do this.'

Meanwhile Mark's discomfort was made the greater by Miss Smith's seeming inability to bridge the gulf between himself and his wife. She had done her best to put his case, but Mrs Pattison had responded strongly. Ellen Smith passed on some of Mrs Pattison's comments. Meta was 'inane'. She had assumed too important a position in the Lodgings during her stay. With characteristic insensitivity Mark passed on these uncomplimentary remarks to Meta. 'I am extremely amazed at Mrs Pattison or anyone else thinking that I or you wished my visit concealed from her.'[105] Her reaction, was as so often, strangely naïve. Yet she did not take offence. 'What has she [i.e. Miss Smith] said against me really unkind? In fact if nothing else has been said I think my relations foolish to have made such a fuss ... I do hope, dear Rector, that I haven't lessened anyone's respect for you.'[106]

Mark was much touched by her response. 'I must say I never met with your equal in respect of freedom from vanity or egotistical irritability . . .', faults that must be said were intrinsically his own. Nor had his position in Oxford been harmed by the gossip, 'I have no reason to think that people are less friendly disposed or less inclined to welcome me in their homes than before the fracas.'[107] He held that the Bradleys of University College and Mrs Bonamy Price were responsible for the malicious circulation; though he was later to learn that Mrs Price was in no way responsible.[1]

An uneasy situation was made worse by the unexpected return of Mrs Pattison herself. She travelled to London the very day, somewhat ironically, that Mark was himself dining with Sir Charles Dilke, a 'witty and lively enough party', which had been followed by a soirée at Burlington House.[m] 'After my carefully trying all my places', Mark commented angrily on 5 May 1881, 'a fortnight beforehand and arranging everything for her going down on 12 May, she has insisted on returning with me today. It was in vain represented the upset it would be to the whole household, no room ready for her, no servant, no food, no windows cleaned. . . . She yielded at first, and then began to cry about the wish to be "at home", a place she has hated and abused for the last 5 years, and made as though it hurt her not to be wanted and welcomed back. Of course I gave way, though I knew it was all acting, admirable acting though.'[108] 'You and I might have had 2 games [of tennis] this morning . . . I was so upset yesterday evening that I could think of nothing else all the evening.'

Life in the Lodgings could hardly be described as cheerful. 'Not a word has passed between Mrs Pattison and myself about anything that interests me', he told Meta on 7 May 1881, 'She talks when I am with her, of her own writings, and visits to Museums etc, but avoids touching on other things or persons, about which confidence would be necessary. Of course, I on my part, am as reticent, as anything I

---

[1] He recorded in his diary for 27 October 1881 that he had been told by a Mrs Nutt 'in a good natured way' that neither Mrs Bonamy Price nor Dan Fearon had anything to do with the gossip set afloat in Oxford about Meta', one of the few entries in the diary relating to Meta not deleted by his wife after his death. Bonamy Price was the Professor of Political Economy.

[m] Other guests included Lyulph Stanley, Thursfield, Stebbing, John Morley, and Kegan Paul whom Pattison accompanied after dinner to a soirée at the Royal Academy.

might confide would be used against me hereafter. You can't imagine anything so dreary and heart barren as my fireside. Fortunately, she doesn't come down to breakfast, so I never see her till 1, and at 9 p.m. she goes to bed, but I am looking forward to the 2 hours, 7 to 9, with dread and disgust.' His resentment may have been further fanned by May Laffan who was staying at the Lodgings and observed to him that his wife 'never shewed the least desire to know where I had been, and what had befallen me while I was away'.[109] Mrs Pattison perceived the drift of Miss Laffan's sympathies, and indicated that her room might soon be required for another guest. 'I fear', Mark noted, 'she has incautiously let it be seen that she takes an interest in me, and she is made imperceptibly to feel that she is no longer as welcome as she was.'[110] Meta, a little jealous of Mark's admiration for May Laffan, commented a trifle sharply to Mark, 'Perhaps she'll reproduce you in her next novel!' 'Much waste of time this week', he entered into his diary for 14 May, 'in consequence of London, Miss Laffan's visit, F[rancis] . . .'.

None the less Mrs Pattison was making a conscious effort to be conciliatory in an effort to pacify her errant husband. Although she was still unwell, she had left a pencilled note of welcome for Mark when he came home from a visit to London. Even Mark was obliged grudgingly to admit that she had 'quite turned over a new leaf', adding, however, that she 'can't think of anything, and is always tendering the very thing I least want, of affection not a grain.'[111] It was in accord with this policy that she had agreed to Mark's suggestion that she would at least talk to Meta's sister, Jessie. She had told Mark that she had read two of Meta's letters, which she thought were written in a 'very bad style', another piece of information that the Rector somewhat tactlessly passed on to Meta. 'I daresay', he said truthfully, 'you won't think that I stood strongly up for you, but I did, speaking of yourself, and your good sense and tact and practical qualities.' Mrs Pattison was not thus easily placated. 'Though her tone was moderated, she is not mitigated towards you, nor will ever be. Make up your mind to that.' She consented, however, to see Jessie when she was in town.

For Mark the future seemed irretrievably bleak. 'She cares', he said self-pityingly, 'nothing for what may become of me next winter.' If Meta was not there to look after him, how he would suffer. Neither Mary nor Jeannie Stirke nor Gertrude Tuckwell could be regarded as adequate substitutes. He would shut up the greater part of the house, live solely in the study and spend the Christmas vacation in Paris. 'Is it not a curious consequence of having tasted the sweetness of life last winter that nothing else has any savour for me?'[112] 'The enemy', he added, 'never will be conciliated; nor will your words and acts ever be judged fairly, not to say leniently, by them.' 'As for ever living together again, that you see is never to be, and that thought makes me sick! I care for nothing now, and find myself unable to take any interest in anything. Everybody else is odious to me by comparison.'[113]

Once more the future was overshadowed by gloomy speculation. 'As to you and I being with each other in the way we want *that*, it seems, it is settled must not be any more. As to just seeing you for 10 minutes in the presence of witnesses, that is not at all what I want nor, I suppose, you either. Letters are now all that are left us. 12 months ago, I thought writing to you, telling you everything, in confidence of its receiving all your sympathy, was very delightful. But after the happiness of our daily life last winter, where every hour was soothed and sweetened by your presence hovering round me with a protecting and provident care I had never known, after this gracious time with you close to me, to go back to letter writing seems like being exiled from Paradise, and all for what?'[114]

Meanwhile Meta had been staying in Wimbledon, in part to act as amanuensis to the classical scholar, Lewis Campbell, Jowett's favourite pupil. Campbell's talk of Jowett led inevitably to a comparison of his career, in some respects so parallel, with that of Pattison; failure to obtain the headship of the College first time, association with university reform, hostility of the conservatives and clericals, some erosion of religious faith.[115] 'It's curious that you both were within an ace of becoming Catholics, both wrote in E[ssays] and R[eviews], both had a near shave of being head of your Colleges before you were actually elected, and yet that your experiences haven't made you great friends.'[116] Mark did not deny this. 'The separation between Jowett and myself consists in a difference upon the fundamental question of University politics, viz. Science and Learning versus Schoolkeeping. Two men who are opposed on this point cannot as things are now, be in sympathy on any other.'[n]

Mark believed that Jowett had deliberately avoided him. For when he called on Meta's sister, Mrs Ilbert, who was staying at Balliol, the Master, 'who was sitting there, rushed out'.[118] For once Meta was irked by Mark's suspicious nature. A few weeks earlier she had told him: 'you know you're very like a girl in her teens in your very great sensitiveness! You're always unearthing in people's most innocent remarks, looks and actions, some hidden and (I maintain) nonexisting unpleasant feelings towards your dear old self! Then you shrivel up when the unconscious offender next appears and he or she wonders what can have happened, or imagines that you're being bored, and in her turn freezes and decamps, leaving you convinced that no one cares about you. I daresay that's happened to you scores of times.' Now, in Meta's opinion, it had happened again. 'How I long to shake you! What could be more schoolgirlish!!! You know in your heart that it was simply his awkward way of being considerate. He knew that you'd come to call on J[essie] and he purposely left you alone ... I will not let you nurse such tiresome, morbid, untrue, unsensible delusions! There, Sir!'[119] But Mark would have none of it. 'I'm certain Jowett's evacuation of the premises, was a fleeing from me, as St. John fled from the room when Cerinthus entered it.'

Mark's call on Jessie Ilbert was intended to try to get Jessie to view his own relationship with her sister more sympathetically, and to persuade her to use her good offices with his wife so as to enable Meta to stay in Oxford the following winter. But Jessie was a woman of strong views who disapproved of her sister's close friendship. 'Jessie', wrote her sister, 'does mean and try to be kind to people, but I never met any woman who so frequently contrives to probe your unhealed wounds, for their good as she would say! to tread needlessly on their corns I should say.'[120] Mark asked Jessie whether he might walk with Meta in Kensington Gardens, only to

---

[n] Oxford, Pattison recalled later, had become 'a school for young men who have outgrown school.' 'Our young men are not trained; they are only filled with propositions, of which they have never learned the inductive basis. The youth is put in possession of ready-made opinions on every conceivable subject; a crudeness of matter which he is taught to regard as *real knowledge*.'[117]

receive a blunt No. 'What am I do to? I don't suppose I shall see you again! This is free England and yet the one woman I wish to be with, and who wishes (in all purity and innocence) to be with me, I cannot be with!'[121]

All Mrs Ilbert could suggest was that Mark should himself try to get his wife to 'befriend' Meta and so get her permission to stay in Oxford.[122] But when Mark showed his wife Jessie's letter, 'her pent-up indignation burst out, and she said some hard things'. She regained her calm, 'more dangerous than the stormy weather', and eventually agreed that she would do what she could to suppress the 'idle gossip', allowing that the principal responsibility for its dissemination lay with Mrs Granville Bradley.[123]

Mark gladly made his escape from the unusual June heat of urban Oxford to the cooler climate of Richmond. After spending a night at Darlington, he arrived there at an early hour to be greeted by his sister, Mary Roberts. He settled in the small house which his other sister, Sarah Bowes, had procured for him in the Spring; 'the house itself is in a street, and there is no view from the windows, but then the street is grown with a thick crop of grass'; and there was a small garden. He called on Sarah, by now a confirmed invalid, who 'poor thing can take nothing but milk, and is kept alive by a goat, a miraculous goat, which yields 3 pints of milk per diem.'[124]

As always, Richmond and the surrounding area acted as a refresher. 'What is an essential of a summer tent-life', he told his friend, Mrs Hertz, 'for me, viz. the element of wildness. Where *you* would walk out, it must be between hedges, at most by a field path across enclosed, mostly subdivided ground. I must have moor, wilderness, flood and fell ... I can see from my bedroom window a clump of battered pines which is within the parish in which I was brought up! Associations of childhood ... become very strong as one gets older, and it has come to this now that, with the best will to stay away from Yorkshire, I *cannot* do it, and find myself, inevitably and fatally, here or hereabouts, at least once in every year, this year longer than usual, inasmuch as we are pulling down and re-building, a piece of the College, and I am consequently driven from my lair for a time. I never read—nobody in Richmond ever does—I never talk, or hear any talk except of local affairs, but the valley with its ever varying colours, sounds, harmonies, is always insensibly playing upon the emotional part of me in a way which promises much heartache during the coming winter if I live to see it.'[125]

At Richmond he seemed, though with reservations, to enjoy some of the distractions of society which at Oxford he found so infinitely tedious. 'I had only been 3 days in Richmond, when I had already been to 2 garden parties, and might have been at a review, and a military lunch (with brass band!) only that I preferred the riverside, and solitary meditation, to the hideous blaring of wind instruments.'[126] Tennis provided recreation: 'we had 3 hours of tolerably good games, my partner and I winning a set from a Balliol undergraduate who is down here and his partner.' He was struck 'by the great preponderance of young women over young men ... Girls abound, Mary [Stirke], out and out, the best-looking, but there is a deplorable absence of anything which can be called cultivation, style, fashion, dress, elegance even, one could do without, but it is impossible to get over the emptiness and frivolity, with which they all sit down, so perfectly content. I have not yet succeeded in cornering one of them so as to discover if there is any depth of nature to be found in such a general appearance of shallow water.'[127]

He could not conceal that Richmond was very provincial. 'There are 2,000 people in the place, and not a single one with any outlook upon the world of thought as we [he was writing to Mrs Hertz] know it. There is not a copy of *The Athenaeum* or *Academy* in the place except my own — all interest is local, and when they are not at work in their respective professions they are devoured by *ennui* ... the total want of education and culture of the humblest kind is a bar to any intimacy which satisfies the requirements of a human soul.'[128] There was another disagreeable aspect of his stay. His brother-in-law, Canon Roberts, the Rector of Richmond, had been taken seriously ill. He felt obliged to offer his assistance in church, 'and this on my peaceful Sunday, and forgo my Sunday ramble over the moor' to 'listen to the bawling of a choir, and the howling of an organ instead.'[129]

None the less he was more than content. 'The first maxim of my life now is to be as many hours in the open air as I can. Yesterday e.g. I was 8 hours, and I am never less than 5. Fishing is the pretence. It is little more than a pretence but it serves. I start at 8.30 and am driven up to a point 4 miles up stream, and deposited. The pony-trap comes back to Richmond, and picks me up again at 4 p.m. by which time I am pretty tired. I go down to the Reading room where we have all the morning papers ... I dine at 1—fishing days not at all, but take a cold chop in my pocket, and eat it at a sitting on a thyme bank, and watching the rising of the trout below me.' 'I am often 6 or 7 hours by the waterside, and do not in all that time, set eyes on a single human being! This is a situation for an intellectual epicure.'[130] Solitude afforded time for contemplation and reflection. If he had asseverated that he read nothing, this was less than the truth. He was particularly attracted by reading a work by a Mrs Ellis, with an eighteenth-century background, *Sylvestra*; in fact Jeannie Stirke had been reading this book to him at Lincoln at the end of May. 'It surpasses all my expectations!' 'The authoress revels in her wealth of knowledge—nothing seems misplaced—the stream of consciousness flows on its way as from the lips of a pleasant talker.' He thought he would like to meet her but wondered whether he would be disappointed, more especially when he learned that instead of being a young girl she was a woman of a certain age, the sister of Canon Raine. 'I know the risk I run of disappointment. Walter Scott (with his feudalism) would have been offensive—and Wordsworth (with his egotism) unendurable—yet their books have been, and are, sources of greater enjoyment to me than any others.'[o]

In such a way the Yorkshire countryside acted as a salve for his tortured spirit. 'My life here must be agreeable to me without my knowing it. It certainly is healthful and peaceful ... I live but I *do* nothing. That thought would grow upon me in time, and drive me back to the mill, even if wintry winds, and wet, and miry roads did not soon arrive to drive me indoors. This life is an essentially out-door existence ... I find that a stiff day walking, or fishing, of 6 to 8 hours cannot be taken oftener than 3, or at most 4 times a week. If I fatigue myself one day, it does me good, but if I do so 3 days together, I get a headache ... Then I have letters to write, read in *The Times* (in the Newsroom) and the *Pall Mall* (take it) daily, and make visits, give tea and strawberries, and now on Sunday have to read prayers twice.'[132] All in all, existence might well have seemed relaxed and pleasant. 'The 2 things which have made my stay

[o] Annie Raine Ellis, *Sylvestra, studies of manners in England from 1770 to 1800* (1881), 2 vols.[131]

agreeable to me, are the old associations of the district and the town and the opportunities of absolute solitude during long days spent by the waterside in the lovely upper valley of the Swale. The trout fishing is not worth speaking of . . . but . . . the streams and deeps are the same as were so well known to me as a boy, and by favour of the proprietor Darcy Hutton, his great uncle first gave me my permit in 1825, I have it almost to myself.'[133]

There was, however, one obvious disincentive to a more prolonged stay, the presence of his wife who, as he confessed, did not 'add to the satisfaction of the encampment. She is now wholly unsympathetic, reserving all her interest for the other man and his affairs. She shuts herself up in her bedroom (which I never enter) all the morning, and is in a perpetual state of scornful antagonism to all her environment, all the while holding herself to be a notable example of wifely dutifulness, in having followed an aged husband into savage and icy climes.'[134] Whenever he returned home from the rushing waters and winds of the moor, he was aware of the glacial disapproval of his 'cara sposa'.

'You have', she had written to him at the end of March, 'exercised your right in selecting the place of a home for June, July and August. I accept your decision, and if it is disagreeable I shall try to make the best of it as you must also.'[135] Yet she found it impossible, however much she might to try to conceal it, to screen her dislike of a place which formed so striking and bleak a contrast with the warm, rose-scented air of Draguignan. There was no point in unduly prolonging the exercise. The *bon viveur* and *litterateur*, Lord Houghton,[p] had invited the Pattisons to stay with him at Fryston Hall during the forthcoming meeting of the British Association at York. Pattison was much tempted. His wife reminded him that if she went she would certainly require two new dresses. Frightened by the threat of such additional expense, Mark decided to return straight home.[136]

So they came back to Oxford in late August. Mark had already been discussing the possibility of a continental holiday, a Swiss 'Wandermonat', with his friend, the classical scholar, Ingram Bywater. 'Are you in earnest?', he asked him, 'I am very cowardly about it, though aware that the reluctance is only a form of constitutional

---

[p] Richard Monckton Milnes, Lord Houghton (1809–85), see James Pope—Hennessy, *Monckton Milnes*, two vols. (London, 1949–51).

idleness, or limpet adhesiveness to native rock. I don't know whether I really want to be let off going or no.' They agreed that they would not necessarily travel together, but meet up at selected places.[137] Accompanied by his niece, Jeannie Stirke, they set off for the Continent on 5 September, intending to join Bywater at the Insel Hotel, Constance. Their outward journey was delayed by floods, for August had been an unusually wet month, and by a breakdown of an engine of the train in front of them. When the train halted for two hours near Chalons-sur-Marne, Mark, who had alighted to take a brief walk, was surprised to be addressed by two fellow Oxonians, D. B. Monro of Oriel,[q] and a young scholar from his own college, J. E. King,[r] both of whom had joined the train at Laon.[138]

Mark and his niece arrived at Basle, but the date of their stay was too close to the anniversary of his honeymoon which had brought him there to evoke happy memories. Schaffhausen, with the neighbouring Rhein Falls, swollen by the recent rains, left an awe-inspiring impression before he moved on to join Bywater at Constance.[139] After the bad start, the trip seems to have been modestly successful, though no more than that. 'Once set a rolling', Jeannie said in a postcard to Bywater who had left them, 'we cannot stop. Here we are at Chur. The uncle well and *playful*. Next move gloriously uncertain. Landquart strikingly uninteresting being absolutely devoid of cigar-shops. Natives support life on bad tobacco. Chiefly remarkable for uncivil big dogs, nervous females and involved roads. We are living on intimate terms with the clouds which are in the habit of strolling down casually to look above us.'[140] From Landquart they crawled up the Prattigau to Davos where though the 'air was simply *delicious*', everyone seemed 'in the last stage of consumption'. They took coffee with the Symonds[s] and even did some walking. As so often, however, 'the uncle', annoyed that he had failed to meet Bywater at St. Gallen, wasn't 'quite as well as he ought to be ... in spite of the blazing burning sun which came out for him to bask in up the valley.'[141] Fretful he commented on his return to Oxford for

[q] D. B. Monro, fellow Oriel College 1859–82; Provost, 1882–1905.

[r] J. E. King, matriculated Lincoln College 1877, fellow 1882–92, later High Master Manchester GS. (1891–1903), H. M. Bedford (1903–10), H. M. Clifton (1910–23).

[s] J. A. Symonds, English man of letters and historian of the Renaissance, had been living in Davos since 1877; see Phyllis Grosskurth, *J. A. Symonds* (1964).

the start of the Michaelmas term that he was 'in worse health than when I left, and spent the 2 first days on the sofa in nursing myself'.[142]

Meanwhile Mrs Pattison was congratulating herself that her visit to England had paid some dividends. 'I cannot', she told her friend, Eugene Müntz, 'regret a period which in certain ways has been very useful to me. Family affairs and troubles have very much set back my work, the cold and the damp have not been good for my health, but, on the other hand, I think that in future I shall encounter fewer obstacles and find greater tranquillity'—a hope that was speedily to be falsified.[143]

Fortified by this modest optimism, Mrs Pattison, accompanied by Cyril Flower, had returned to Paris to work on her book on Claude Lorrain in the Cabinet d'Estampes. When she was in Paris she had a visitor from Oxford, Ellen's brother, the mathematician Henry Smith. She was surprised, for she knew that Henry, unlike his sister, was sympathetic to Mark rather than to herself. 'I am of course much gratified but also a little puzzled by the attention which he is now good enough to bestow on me, and even the thoughtful solicitude which he expressed as to the hardships of my life here [at Draguignan]'. 'If there is not a real change in his attitude of mind, why does he think it necessary to change his manners?'[144]

She was, however, still smarting from her husband's failure to recognize her existence. 'My second long letter to the Rector which I risked to Poste Restante Constanz still remained or remains unanswered. Mr Bywater had left them, and I feel rather curious as to what had determined the break-up of the party and have written to him for news, as since Sir Charles [Dilke] tells me he was in Paris I suppose he is now probably in Oxford.' Whatever the 'hardships' of her life at Draguignan, the southern warmth formed a splendid antidote to the chill of Yorkshire. 'At present I feel nothing but the intense enjoyment which the south is to me so that I can sit down by the burning wayside and bathe in the golden heat, and renew the ravishing sense of being one with the earth and sky which never comes to me till I am past Marseilles.'[145] Surrounded by her books and flowers, in touch with her artistic and intellectual friends, she revelled in her freedom from the tiresome angularities of life with Mark; Sir Charles Dilke was not far away in his villa near Toulon.

That long summer, often dreary and damp in England, Meta had been moving from house to house, making herself useful. She stayed with her sister at Wimbledon, acting as amanuensis once more to Lewis Campbell and helping Jessie to look after her children, walking and riding. 'I had a pretty ride on Saturday on a decent hack with an uninteresting companion. Nancy [Paul] came before 4, and we thus had such a pleasant drive, a capital pony, quite willing to go and easy to manage. We drove a long way about Regents Park and got home at 6, before the rain began. All the evening Nancy read to me, bits of Victor Hugo, Daudet, Keats, Browning, and a good deal of the Task.' 'We have been reading and talking nearly all day, as it was too wet for much walking. We had tea and a toddle with the Campbells ... This evening Nancy read me Browning's "Blot in the Scutcheon". I don't think I have ever felt any poetry quite as much before. It has quite got hold of me ... and will keep me awake to-night.'[146]

Life was mildly social. 'Yesterday we, the Campbells, Mr J. C. Morison and a Mr and Mrs Cock dined at the Bridges. The dinner was dull to me because I sat between Lewis [Campbell] and Courtenay [Ilbert], who had lost his voice, and I was dying to hear what Mr Morison was saying.'[t] James Cotter Morison, a former member of Lincoln College, was an author and journalist who contributed articles to the *Saturday Review* and, like Pattison, had written a volume in the *Men of Letters* series edited by John Morley. 'There dined here also', she wrote of another Wimbledon dinner party six days later, 'a young Balliol man, such a creature! as common as any of your Lincoln men! I did so long to snub him! ... To day we had a short walk and then played Lawn Tennis at the Lawrences with the Arthur Pearsons, good exercise. How I hate this sort of life though!'[148]

June opened unusually with a hot and sultry spell, and for a short time she returned to Orsett Terrace where her stepmother was at home; her father was fortunately on his yacht. But the pattern of her existence remained much the same. 'Dined at Mrs Sanders [this was presumably the mother of her friend, Christina], ... Such a queer woman there, very loud and vulgar though apparently very amusing

---

[t] J. C. Morison wrote a penetrating, if laudatory, obituary notice on Pattison in *Macmillan's Magazine* (Oct. 1884), 401–8.[147]

as she kept Mr Sanders roaring all dinner, and they made such a hideous noise that no one else could hear what their neighbour said! She was a Miss Sassoon, now Prodgers. You should have seen her dress!... I sat between 2 very dull creatures, one of whom could only speak of yachts and the other of politics, and the wretch was a Protectionist...'[149]

She called on Mark's sister-in-law, Margaret, at Burwood Place. 'How fond she is of you and she understands you better than most people do', a verdict which Mark doubted.[150] 'I think', he agreed, 'she is attached to me in a dumb sort of way.'[151] But in all this there was disquiet which Mark and Meta's common agreement to restrict the number of letters they wrote to one another constantly evoked. Jessie brought pressure to bear on Meta, urging her sister that it would be ungrateful not to keep her side of the bargain in view of 'all the worry and trouble I had given her and every one'. Jessie suggested that Meta should write only once a month. 'I might go the Devil my own way, and probably should do so if I insisted on writing often and by dreary letters for which you [i.e. Mark] couldn't possibly care.'[152]

Mark fumed and fretted at the absence of Meta's letters. 'I have been for three weeks in a misery of suspense, daily intensifying and not without an underground current of irritation against you, at not getting a line from you.'[153] If there was no letter to which he could reply, his own correspondence with her would suffer. 'It must flow from me as a living stream.' 'I see already the chilling effect the suspension has upon the tone of your letters ... When I return I must have a recurrence to the old footing or our correspondence will die out altogether.'[154] Meta was pained at Mark's complaints. 'It's rather too hard to reproach me for my coldness in my letters, when that is caused by you leaving some about!! Besides, surely you don't want assurances of my affection. You must be absolutely certain of its depth and duration.'[155]

Meta's letters drifted into diaries. In early July she went to stay with her friend, Christina Sanders who had married a Mr Hilton, the rector at West Lavington, near Midhurst. 'It is a real satisfaction when one's friends marry suitable men and have a fair chance of leading happy, useful lives. Tina was vastly pleased that her husband liked her friend, that I could play Lawn Tennis, his songs and music, chat to him.'[156]

Thence she moved to a girls' school, Polygon House at Southampton, run by a Mrs Daniels who had stayed often with the Bradleys when Meta was a girl. The Principal was a woman of indomitable perseverance, conceited, vain, and humourless, who addressed her guest as if she was one of her own pupils. 'I certainly have never met anyone so rude, and I quite admire my own angelic conduct towards her.' The weather was hot and oppressive. Meta found the atmosphere uncongenial. The pupils 'seemed cowed and submissive'. 'Imagine the void in me.' 'Mrs Daniels wishes she always had me here, and I'm sure the girls agree with her', but she was relieved to get away on 4 August, 'never more glad to escape'.[157]

Thence she moved for ten days to stay with her aunt, Mrs Grove, the wife of the musicologist, whom she helped occasionally in writing down articles for his musical dictionary, at their house at Sydenham. 'I spend an hour pottering over the flowers, write a duty letter or two, read to my aunt for an hour or more while she darns, go out with her after lunch, play Lawn Tennis from 5.30 to 7., reading aloud after dinner, and play dances for the children from 9 to 10.' But she felt distrait. She did not much like her young teenage cousins. 'Somehow I can't be merry and bright as I was at Lincoln.'[u]

And the return to Orsett Terrace left her even more depressed. In response to one of her letters, Mark sharply commented 'What are your trials to mine, and death galloping towards me all the while?'[158] But Meta was not persuaded that his lot was worse than her own. 'If you knew what I have been feeling for many months I don't believe you would think the advantage so much on my side. Never have I been free from conscious wretchedness almost sickening in intensity. Death would be more a friend than foe to me.'[159] This was a view which the Rector, so often melancholic as he was, would have strongly repudiated. 'Why I find life worth living', he had written frankly the previous June, 'is because I have never let my mind go to be the passive scene of impression from without, but have always nursed a secret self-assertion, not as against people, but as against

[u] Mrs Grove (Harriet Bradley) married Grove in 1851. Her husband had been at school with her brother, Granville, at Clapham. She collaborated with her husband in making a complete index of all the proper names in the Old and New Testament. Apart from his exhaustive *Dictionary of Music and Musicians*, Sir George Grove (1820–90) was an indefatigable student of the Bible. He was a close friend and literary executor of Dean Stanley. See Percy M. Young, *George Grove* (London, 1980).

things. It is an end to me always worth attaining to subject the forms of things to the images of the mind, as Bacon has it. But I admit that the thought of the fleetingness of things is very painful. And it is this thought which makes what you call my "fear of death". I won't say quite that fear does not enter into the feeling, but at bottom it is the chilly shadow which the rapid approach of the end throws over the present, so marring what is otherwise most acceptable in and for itself. Life does not seem to me in itself "poor" but only too soon over. All the more so, if you assume, as you say, that it is all the life one is to have. The racing railing pace at which my days are now slipping away from me quite appals me, when I can stop to think of it, which I sometimes do.'

Meta surely can hardly have been a cheerful companion for her father and stepmother when towards the end of August she went with them to Southgate. Her father, however, seemed 'wonderfully well and seems happy here'. A few days later the scenario changed dramatically. She accompanied her stepmother on a walk one Sunday morning, for Mrs Bradley was too deaf to attend church and Meta greeted any opportunity to abstain from this disagreeable duty. When she returned home, her father, as usual offended by her failure to share in divine worship, launched into a tirade, telling her, among other things, that she could not expect him to leave her money when he died 'to live in idleness . . . and that he couldn't let me live any longer at home without something to do'. 'I believe he is quite capable of turning me out of the house altogether and cutting me off with 1s/- instead of £5000 (which is what he had often told me I was to have)! How dreadful it is to feel hate instead of love for one's relatives.'[160]

The threat was a serious one, since Meta had hoped that he would leave her enough money to forward her interest in philanthropic work. But she would find it difficult to live on £100 a year. Next Sunday she went to church 'but survived the infliction by dint of sitting in the free seats and reading *The Water Babies* during the sermon (the most biblically covered book in the house). An old man by me asked me, as I did up my umbrella, whether I wasn't "going to the Table", and whether I "knew the Lord". Ten years ago I should have answered with a fervent "yes" '.[161]

The news of her father's meanness reached Mark at the Athenaeum just as he was setting off for Switzerland. Naturally he had been greatly perturbed. 'It makes me wretched to think of you wanting every comfort to which you have been used from childhood, and living in narrow, pinched conditions . . . As for earning your living, my poor girl, you can't do it. You have not got any special qualification. Think of your being matron to a Gaol! Surely Mrs Bradley will not allow you to want bread while she lives. You know that I will aid you to the utmost of my power, but that goes only a little way. Everybody's hand seems to be against you, and now that of your father.'[162] Since he was writing on the fatal anniversary day of his own wedding, his thoughts lingered on the past, recalling his strained relations with his own father. 'My father', he mused, 'did me out of all he could! but then I had been put in the way of earning my own living and at his expense.'

Meta and Mrs Bradley returned to Orsett Terrace on 16 September. In spite of everything Meta soon fell back into her old routine. She visited the Frank Pattisons, 'Mr Frank very chatty', saw the Humphry Wards who had taken Jessie's house while she and Courtenay were staying at Cogne, the Alpine resort in northern Italy, and went out to Sydenham to see Mabel Bradley who was staying with her aunt, Mrs Grove. Mabel's father had been offered the Deanery of Westminster in succession to his friend, A. P. Stanley. At first he had been inclined to refuse it, partly because of his wife's ill health and his own lack of private funds, but had been persuaded by George Grove to accept. 'He is a lucky fellow', was Pattison's comment, 'to come in for the best piece of preferment in the Church of England, without family interest, without distinction of any kind.'[163] Feeling a little guilty at her breach with her father Meta made a surreptitious call on Mr Kempe—John E Kempe (1829–1907) was Rector of St. James, Piccadilly from 1853 to 1895—or rather his curate as he was not there—at Piccadilly to explain that it would be unwise to ask her father in his present state of health to preach for him five times in October.

Doubtless prompted by Mark she began to read some of Miss Laffan's novels, finding *Weeds* well written and witty but her earlier novel *Hogan* of indifferent quality. 'She certainly has the power of graphically drawing a situation' was Meta's comment, to which she could not prevent herself from adding that she was 'fought shy of by the best people and the book reads as if she were showing up people against whom she had a spite. None of the characters are interesting, and all are innately vulgar.' Perhaps, then, she recalled Mark's liking for May. 'She must be a very amusing person- I wonder at your preferring a dull friend of ours who shall be nameless.'[164]

It took very little to reopen the old wounds. 'All this time I never lost the consciousness of intense misery.'[165] A conversation which she had with Daisy Woods and Mabel Bradley caused her acute embarrassment, for they reported that Miss Smith had told their father and mother that Meta 'made love to you before her face and wouldn't let anyone else speak to you'. 'I couldn't have imagined that an educated woman could have *thought* such nastiness. She must have got that way of looking at people from being so much among the poor. The day we dined at Jowett's I certainly didn't look at or speak to you, and the few other minutes during which she saw me I certainly did not monopolise the conversation which I left to her.'[166] If, for all her radical views, Meta revealed her class consciousness, she was perhaps right to feel that the Rector's trust in Miss Smith was ill-advised. 'F[anny] K[ensington]', she added 'is right in calling her pre-judiced and Daisy and Mabel in calling her low-minded ... what a nasty feeling hate is.'

In default of anything else Meta started on her round of autumn and winter visits, first to stay with the headmaster, Mr Hart, and his wife at Sedbergh.[v] The change of scene and occupation pleased Mark. It would help her to cast off her sense of depression and uselessness. Truth to tell, though he could only express his feeling indirectly, he was beginning to be a little fed up with her constant moaning, which seemed to him to be fringing on morbidity. 'Cast off', he told her, 'your sighing *fainéantism* ... Be sure that the more you throw your-self out of yourself, the more interests in life will open themselves out to you. To shut yourself up and complain of fate is not only unheroic, but an error in self-conduct, as the very life we wish for closes itself against our imprecations.'[167]

Her letters certainly became rather more chatty and a little less introspective. After she had met Mark at her home in Orsett Terrace,

---

[v] Henry George Hart (1843–1921), fellow of St. John's, Cambridge, Headmaster of Sedbergh School, 1880–1900, married H. L. Lawrence, daughter of Sir Henry Lawrence, KCB.

with Mrs Bradley acting as chaperone, she declared that 'instead of
feeling more wretched after it than ever, I feel what you said has
stirred me up and will help me to struggle back into life again for as
long as I have you to write to often. I don't mean of course, that I
shall long any the less for what I can't have, or think the less of you,
or enjoy things which I can't share with you. I don't think you must
blame me for having felt so utterly wretched for so long. You know
better than anyone what I have missed all those dreary months and
what I shall miss all the winter. But this summer without letters has
shown me how much remains while we can correspond. So, dear
Rector, I won't any longer be the dull, uninterested creature I have
been for so long.'

What especially pleased her about Sedbergh was its comparative
nearness to Mark's own beloved dales. 'I already am quite in love
with what little I've seen of its scenery. It was misty during my
journey ... but I caught glimpses of tantalising loveliness, especially
at Clapham and Ingleton ... The trees haven't nearly shed their
leaves, which are particularly red, I fancy, so they make capital fore-
grounds, and throw back the hills, which were many-coloured
today.' The headmaster's wife, Mrs Hart, proved to be a congenial
companion. 'She has a decided talent for putting people at their ease,
and drawing out the best of them. There's nothing small about her,
and she's as bright and merry as possible, with a great deal of depth
and earnestness. To tell you quite the truth she reminds me more of a
fine edition of myself than of anyone I know! ... We chaff and laugh
(I, sadly at heart) much as we used to do at Lincoln.'[168]

With Mrs Hart's sister, 'quite young but as stout as Miss Smith',
and brother-in-law, Henry Lawrence, Meta made several expeditions
into the country-side round Sedbergh, once descending from
Winder in the autumnal twilight, 'only dim shapes of hills and sheep,
and lights below to be seen'.[169] She talked to the masters, two of
whom, a Mr Lovells and a Mr Wise were candidates for All Souls
fellowships, and she discovered that Hart's uncle, Sir Bartle Frere,
and his daughter were staying as guests of honour.[w] 'She is very plain,
my height, has long arms which she moves about angularly when

[w] Sir Bartle Frere (1815–84), Chief Commissioner of Sind, Governor of Bombay,
Governor of the Cape and first High Commissioner of South Africa; recalled as result of
the Zulu War 1880.

talking, even at meals or when driving . . . very self-possessed and talks a great deal, but too slowly, and will err, err, as he does . . . What amuses me is the naive way in which she takes one's interest for granted, and gives one lengthy explanations of his policy.' Sir Bartle himself seems to have been in the running for a prize bore. 'Sir Bartle is most unhappy about England, says the Conservatives have no good leader, and that the younger Liberals have such bad private characters that one can't trust their public actions. He hesitates most aggravatingly in the simplest conversation, but when he gets warmed up and has the field to himself he doesn't stick at so many ditches . . . He is . . . very ready to be turned on, like a tap I tell him! He gave me twenty minutes all to myself today on the opium question. They are so very friendly that I feel a brute for picking them to pieces (but it's only to you). I don't agree with the world that he's a humbug. We had a dinner party yesterday and today, and a lot of people to hear him give an address. It was awfully stupid to me, only about Livingstone. Do you know much about ostriches? If not, I'll teach you someday! second hand.'[170] But, in the Hart household, it was possible to find time for reading and quiet meditation.[171]

At the end of the first week in November she went to Edinburgh to stay with the Sellars.[x] Mark sent her small presents of money which, as her hosts were not rich, enabled her to hire the occasional cab. At a dull drinks party she was offended by having to sit by 'a got-up woman, Mrs Balfour, *née* Woodhouse, with a rather pretty daughter there, and another lovely one married to Lord de Clifford', and her thoughts wandered back to the same time the previous year when she had been sitting in a corner of the study reading to Mark. She thought correctly that the smallest detail would interest her reader, recounting how she had lunched at a *café* in Princes Street, 'quite as good as the Grosvenor for 1/- each, cutlets, potatoes, bread and butter, coffee with milk and cream and served by charming handmaidens with black frocks, and red aprons and red caps'.[172]

From foggy Edinburgh she moved to the Lewis Campbells' house, The Scores, at St. Andrews, 'where I think I shall be as contented as I can be anywhere away from the Paradise closed by Mrs Grundy's

[x] W. Y. Sellar, matriculated Balliol College 1842; fellow Oriel College 1848–53; Professor of Greek at St. Andrews, then at Edinburgh University; Lewis Campbell succeeded him at St. Andrews.

flaming sword!'[173] Lewis Campbell became Professor of Greek at St. Andrews in 1865. He was a prolific writer and editor of classical texts. Pattison thought him somewhat uninspired, ponderous and learned rather than elegant and penetrating. By comparison with Oxford tutors, he was, in Pattison's opinion, 'above the average in knowledge and extent of reading' but 'when we ascend into the higher regions of scholarship, the science branches into several specialities. In none of these specialities can Lewis Campbell be considered strong, as Ellis or Hugh Monro[y] . . . Lewis Campbell seems to be precluded from the highest quality of an interpretative critic by a want of logical discrimination of the forces of words. He sees many possibilities of meaning, owing to the delicacy of his perceptive faculty, by the width of his sympathies, and amid these possibilities, he loses himself, when to an intellect of more distinctness the writer's meaning sufficiently declares itself. Hence Lewis Campbell's own English is always more or less foggy. I should not think that with this mental weakness he can be a good teacher.' Jowett had tried unsuccessfully to get him elected to a tutorial fellowship at Balliol but, Pattison added, 'though it sounds like blasphemy to say it of the Regius Professor of Greek, he has not shown himself to be a good judge of other men's scholarship'.[174]

Meta found him kind and sensitive but not very approachable. 'What a gentle, lovable creature it is, Lewis, I mean! He is dreadfully thin-skinned . . . I wish I could find him more interesting to talk with. He won't begin and doesn't always go on.'[175] He lacked the capacity for common conversation and often failed to put people at their ease. What he, like so many Victorians, really enjoyed was the now lost art of reading aloud. Rather to Meta's surprise, though at her solicitation—'I thought one of those old novels which neither Fanny nor I have read would suit us all three'—he selected Fielding's *Joseph Andrews* as an after dinner book. She thought it coarse but interesting. To ease the susceptibilities of his female hearers, he skimped the more explicit passages. 'The first part makes me cry

[y] Robinson Ellis (1834–1913) was fellow of Trinity College, Oxford, in 1858, Professor of Latin at University College London in 1870, and Corpus Professor of Latin at Oxford from 1893; Hugh Monro (1819–95), fellow of Trinity College, Cambridge, Kennedy Professor of Latin (1869–72), authority on Lucretius, one of the best Latinists of his time.

with laughing ... It is far too clever not to be read because its language happens to be coarse.'[176] Mark strongly approved of the choice, for it showed Campbell's broadmindedness. But Lewis's wife Fanny missed the witty insights and listened with glazed eyes, so that Campbell's own enthusiasm began to lapse and the novel was not pursued to its end. 'We wonder', Meta mused, 'whether morality (used in a narrow sense) is really very different now to what it was in Fielding's time. It is hard to know. Certainly immorality blushes more. I never heard anything like the brazen way in which he makes his characters talk.'

Above all Lewis Campbell enjoyed reading Shakespeare aloud. 'Fanny says I'm too stimulating for Lewis!', Meta told the Rector, 'That's because I suggested reading a play last night, and Lewis would take Lear, Kent and the fool! so no wonder he was tired after the first act, especially as he would read Lear as if he were mad and the fool in a simple voice.'[177]

From her letters a portrait emerges of university society in this small Scottish town. 'Besides sea and sand and rocks, castle, cathedral and abbey (now turned into a burial ground) there are charming bits of colour in a dirty, fishing part of St. Andrews. Wooden stairs and balconies outside like a Swiss chalet.'[178] There were long walks along the links and the windy seashore. 'We went along the links and faced furthest off snow hills, a decent height half hidden by blue purple points of hills nearer us, whose base was hidden by mysterious mist. Then nearer came cold, greeny grey, thin grass, and sickly sand showing thro' the grass, then warm, glowing sand, and water, part light blue, and part a rich dark green with dark brown rocks jutting into it.'[179]

There were 'at homes', teas and dinners, attended by university dons and mistresses from the girls' school, as well as the inevitable tennis parties. 'I've just come back from our 'at home' to all the world of St. Andrews', Meta wrote to Mark on the 19 November 1881, 'where some queer faces, dresses, shirts, hair, and beards appeared. There is a fair proportion of prettyish girls here, and they're chiefly unadorned.'[180] Tea parties 'at which the husbands seldom appear' were in Meta's view, 'the chief dissipation here'. Dinner parties gave her an opportunity to provide the Rector with pen portraits, not always very felicitously achieved, of the other guests. The Knights were among the guests at a dinner party given by the Campbells, the wife 'an insignificant, quiet, oldish little woman, with plenty of good, hard sense', whom she came greatly to like. 'I don't know when I have met a decidedly middle-aged woman whom I like better. I think she's too good for him.'[181] She found Mr Knight 'decidedly clever' but too prone to talk of his acquaintance with celebrities. 'Mr Knight can't take in the simplest chaff, and listened gravely to our brilliant banter. It's quite comical to observe the literalness of many of these Scotchmen—the women are a shade better.'[z]

She knew that the Rector would be interested in the personnel of the University of which, by and large, he had already a low opinion. Among the young fellows recently elected at Lincoln was Andrew Clark who had been Lewis Campbell's assistant at St. Andrews.[a] He had told Pattison that only Lewis Campbell, Tulloch and Baynes were exceptions to the 'low level of most of the professors there'. Yet even Spencer Baynes 'has but one set of lectures, the set namely which he wrote when first elected to the professorship. This brown yellow fly-spotted often illegible MS he reads perfunctorily every year. It was never good for much and is now entirely obsolete in its subject. There are thirty or forty copies of it in the hands of students handed down from one generation to another. So that when as sometimes happens the Professor cannot read his own writing a student from the back benches will help him out from the copy in which he is following.'[183] The Professor of Latin, Roberts, who had never apparently heard of Grimm's Law, 'is not thought anything of by anybody, and I suppose he's another barbarian as one never meets him'.[184]

John Tulloch, the Principal of the University, at first made an unfavourable impression on Meta. 'He strikes me as capable of bad taste, not to say brutality, of course he's not a gentleman. I'm sure he is most dreadful to live with, and I don't wonder at his daughters marrying fast. His laugh is peculiarly disagreeable.'[b] When she sat next to him

[z] William Knight, Professor of Moral Philosophy 1876–1903.[182]

[a] Andrew Clark, fellow Lincoln College, 1881–95; honorary fellow 1905; Rector of Great Leighs, Essex, d. 1922. College and university historian. His war diaries, edited by James Munson, have been published under the title *Echoes of the Great War* (Oxford, 1985).

[b] John Tulloch (1823–86), Principal and Professor of Theology of St. Andrews 1854; chaplain to Queen Victoria; Moderator of General Assembly 1878; broad churchman, founder of Scottish liberal church party.[185]

at a dinner given by the second mistress of the girls' school, she found him little better company. 'He likes being chaffed and teased, but he never says an interesting word ... He evidently dislikes disapprobation and wants constant slaps on the back to make him speak up like a man.'[186] She admired, however, the broadmindedness of his opinions and the liberal scholarship which he displayed in his lectures. Johnnie Shairp, who occupied the chair of poetry at Oxford from 1877 to 1885, was another luminary; he had been Principal of the United College at St. Andrews since 1868. In Meta's opinion he was a 'poor performer'. 'I never heard such a vile delivery. I listened with the greatest attention, but couldn't follow all. I don't think Shakespeare's songs ... nor his sonnets voluptuous, do you? ... Mr Shairp ... told me you had been to hear him at Oxford, and he spoke so warmly of you that I forgave him his slipshod utterance. As for your Milton and Pope he couldn't find words to express his appreciation of them.'[c] A glutton for intellectual punishment she attended courses of lectures. Professor Nicholson 'passed on titbits of obscure zoological information. I don't believe I knew that birds' bones were filled with air in connection with their lungs.[188] [d]

The advent of Sir Theodore Martin, the university's rector, and his wife formed the occasion for much social activity.[e] 'Lady Martin', she wrote of a dinner party at the Tullochs, 'glided about the room in a queer and unsuitable garb, with her hair fearfully and wondrously dressed and a curl tickling her neck dreadfully I should imagine.' Her

[c] J. C. Shairp (1818–85), won Newdigate Prize at Oxford, Professor of Latin, St. Andrews 1861–72; Principal of United College, St. Andrews, 1868; Professor of Poetry, Oxford 1877–85.[187]

[d] H. A. Nicholson (1844–99), biologist, Professor of Natural History, St. Andrews 1875–82; Regius Professor of Natural History, Aberdeen, 1882–99. 'Did you know that with savages the part of the tooth where the nerve lives gradually gets filled up by bone, so that the nerve is killed?' 'Snakes' jaws', she told Mark, 'are divided down the middle so that they open to right and left as well as up and down, which explains to me how they can swallow such huge things.' Nicholson 'makes the hardest subjects as clear as day to the dullest mind.' But like his colleague Professor Meiklejohn, he was 'too poor to give dinners, and so foolish that they let their poverty prevent their dining out, so one never meets them.'

[e] Sir Theodore Martin (1816–1909), parliamentary agent and writer. Prepared for Queen Victoria a life of the Prince Consort. Lord Rector of St. Andrews University 1881. Married a Miss Faucit at Brighton 1851. At Stratford, the diarist A. C. Benson observed, 'It is *just* opposite, on the blank wall that that pestilent old man, Theodore Martin, wanted to put up his wife's bust.'[189]

husband, a *littérateur* who attained some fame by writing a five-volume eulogistic life of the Prince Consort for Queen Victoria, gave an address which Meta described as 'commonplace, prosy, inappropriately political and much too full of quotation'. His wife, however, half-reading, half reciting from the *Merchant of Venice* and *As You Like It*, drew applause, 'every letter clear as a bell yet nothing forced. She has a pull over most actors in being a lady'.[190]

It was at Principal Tulloch's dinner party that Meta met again Florence Sellar, the daughter of the Edinburgh professor, with whom she had stayed early in November, 'a very talkative all there young woman, with strong religious opinions but not bigoted'. 'She's not clever but has been properly taught and is intelligent.' Florence invited her to stay for a week-end with her family in Edinburgh. Meta found the money that Mark had sent her had come 'at the nick of time' 'as Papa wouldn't see paying for it'.[191] Yet the visit proved to be something of a disappointment. Florence's constant prattle got on Meta's nerves. 'She can't', she complained, 'hold her tongue, cares more for what is beautiful, pathetic, comforting than for truth, can believe, for instance, in religion, just what she thinks noblest and loveliest, regardless of obvious contradictions, is certainly by nature a conservative, thinks me flippant, which is possibly true! raves about a sister's engagement as if no one was ever engaged before. Insists upon arguing without first defining her position.'[192] Florence grated. Meta went to St. Giles on Sunday, 'I to propitiate Florence, she because she liked it'.

If Edinburgh had its compensations, among them a meeting with the Forbes Robertsons, it was with some relief she returned to St. Andrews. What intrigued her in early December was a visit there from the Donald Crawfords. Donald had been elected to a fellowship at Lincoln College in 1861 but as a practising lawyer—he was secretary to the Lord Advocate from 1880 to 1885—he was mainly non-resident, and on his marriage he resigned. His wife, Virginia, was a daughter of Mrs Eustace Smith who had been intermittently Sir Charles Dilke's mistress. Her childhood had been unhappy; she was thought intelligent—her sisters teased her by saying that her initials V.S. stood for Very Scientific—and she took the escape route of marriage, as Francis Pattison had done, to a man some years older than herself, conventional, ponderous, prosaic, set in his ways. Predictably it would be disastrous, but when they visited St. Andrews in the winter of 1881 they had only been recently married. 'She is', Meta gossiped, 'quite a girl, very young looking, and it's hard to believe she's married. She's bright, merry, happy and sharp enough.'[193] If on the plump side, Virginia Crawford had a beautiful, clear skin, 'milk-maid looks', which made her attractive to men. It is in some sense a mystery why she had agreed to marry Donald Crawford. 'We trotted', Meta told Mark, 'the Crawfords about to-day and I had some talk with Donald about you. He spoke quite comfortably and is very friendly, so he has ceased to think me "a designing young woman"! He made a remark I've often thought, i.e. that he didn't know anyone more capable of being wretched than you! He is decidedly attached to you. She has, I fancy, no depth of character, had never had any sorrow or trouble, nor felt any feeling strongly, looking upon marrying very much as a matter of course, a business to be got over at 18. Still I like her and think she and Donald have a very fair chance of commonplace happiness. He's a thoroughly good fellow, though of course rather heavy, and doesn't seem selfish, goes about more than he likes for her sake.'[194] A glance into the crystal ball would have shown that even at this early stage in their married life the clouds were beginning to gather.

All in all St. Andrews, if provincial, was an agreeable society, more liberal in attitudes than the majority of Scottish towns, 'very very advanced according to the received notions of a Scotch town'.[195] At one tea party Meta met a Scottish spinster who talked with such frankness that even Meta was worried lest their conversation should be overheard. She 'ran down the Bible as a book for the young, wanted to kill instead of keeping alive the diseased, touched on the wrongness of having large families and wanting fines instead of doles for such folk, discoursed on compulsory national insurance and so forth'. Nor was Meta expected to go to church, for though Lewis Campbell was in Holy Orders neither he nor his wife appear to have been regular church-goers. On Sunday evenings they often entertained young men to music or to play letter games, and once a guest had even played lawn tennis on the sabbath 'and nothing happened'! 'He ought to have been stoned by the poor and ostracised by the rich.' As December drew towards Christmas, Meta dutifully packed her bags and returned to Orsett Terrace, ever mindful that a year ago she had spent the festival in Oxford.

The Rector had, of course, been mainly in Oxford since the start of the Michaelmas term, supported in his loneliness by a succession of young female guests, his niece Jeannie whom he somewhat presumptuously decided should henceforth be called Joan, his wife's niece, Gertrude Tuckwell, Grace Toynbee, Helen Colvill. 'Jeannie', Mrs Baines, the housekeeper, informed Mrs Pattison, 'suited the Rector well.'[196] Gertrude Tuckwell compared Jeannie's influence on the Rector to that of Meta Bradley, in favour of the former: 'he has not been *horrid* once.' Gertrude's 'description of Jeannie Stirke', Mrs Pattison thought, 'is very just. She notes the "penetration" and coolness, but adds her "manners are sometimes astounding". The worst of that minor point is that they can never be improved, which if you look at her as likely to be a permanent inmate is a very unfortunate matter. I am writing to the Rector once a week, but he never answers.' But Jeannie was unlikely to be permanent. She was thinking of teaching, even allowing that this was in some respects a socially degrading career, and was engaged in studying French and German. Momentarily the Rector was strongly in favour of his niece, but his affection tended to be both demanding and capricious. It remained to be seen how long Jeannie would retain it.

For the time being the Rector was lulled into a not disagreeable routine by his young friends who accompanied him on his walks, acted as his amanuenses, played lawn tennis with him, helped to entertain his guests and read to him in the evenings. 'Very interesting evening in reading', he had noted on 31 October 1881, 'with the 2 girls [Jeannie Stirke and Grace Toynbee] both of them entering in the most animated way into everything.' To celebrate Milton's birthday on 9 December the Rector decided that they would each write an epigram of four lines to commemorate the occasion which would be read out at supper; afterwards Mark read extracts from Milton's poetry and Jeannie continued with her reading of David Masson's life of de Quincey. Helen Colvill whom Pattison had at first shied away from when Meta suggested that he should invite her was inhibited by shyness from much conversation but her visit passed pleasantly enough.

It did, however, lead to a temporary break with the redoubtable Miss Laffan who proposed a visit to Lincoln at the same time, and was told that there was no room in the Lodgings. 'Miss Laffan', he told Meta, 'is in a towering rage with me because I don't have her this week. But she would have entirely spoiled Helen's visit. When she is here she must be the centre of attention, and everything must be addressed and adapted for her. And though I don't want to act the part of teacher and mentor towards Helen, yet I like them always to feel that they have been done good by being here. And this would not have been the case had she to listen to the chaff and rhodomontade, which goes on when Miss Laffan is here. Yet it will be vexatious if it turns out, that as I quarrelled with Rhoda Broughton, for the sake of the Laffan, that I should now have to quarrel with the Laffan for the sake of Helen (not of Troy).'[197] His letters revealed how in his mind he fused the didactic and the avuncular in his attitude towards young girls. It was the theme which pervaded his correspondence with them, and which had led Mrs Pattison evidently to believe that Meta Bradley was only one further acquisition of this sort.

Pattison celebrated, though the word is hardly appropriate, his 68th birthday on 10 October. There was a card from brother Frank, greetings from sister Fanny, a line from Jeannie and a 'sweet' letter from Meta. 'Dear old thing, I know so well just what you'll feel all day, and wish we could spend it together.'[198] He found her devotion reassuring. As he was soon to write congratulating her on her 28th birthday, 'No words can express what you have been to me, what you are, the one dear plank to which I cling in the wreck that broke up my home and happiness. I know we thoroughly trust each other; so entirely trust, that all words put forward for the purpose of saying so, seem an impertinence. But on this one occasion in 12 months, I think it may be permissible just to renew the oath of fidelity for love's sake. My time is now short, running out every day, but as long as I live you must always be my dearest and most precious treasure.'[199]

Over the years the Rector's life at Oxford had become a routine existence. The College Chapter Day, which he dreaded as a waste of time, passed off on 6 November uneventfully. 'They did one or two things I would not have done, but not any of their worst things. I did not struggle against, never do now, having learnt that it is no use, and that I only expend nervous force in vain. Perhaps too I am weaker, and shrink from combat, where at one time I should have rushed in! at 7 I go back to the C.R. [Common Room] to see them guzzle for

2 hours.' He was back in the Lodgings by 9.30 p.m. 'with a listener in J[eannie] S[tirke] ready to enter into all I had to tell'. Jeannie who had been with him since October, gave satisfaction but had not entirely won the Rector's heart. 'She has done very well for me so far, is very ready and intelligent', he wrote at the end of November, 'but she is not loveable. You can't imagine me petting Jeannie as I did Mary.'[200]

She had been joined by Grace Toynbee whom Mark had at first described as 'incurably superficial' but by whom he had been gradually won over, so that he could describe her as a 'candid, genuine soul, and quite lovable'.[201] 'You will be pleased to know', he wrote two days after this verdict, 'that Grace and I have made prodigious strides towards friendship—on my side it is truly *love* . . . She has a quick apprehension, and a genuine delight in the things of the mind which was quite catching. We have never had anyone here who had entered into the evening readings with so much zest as Grace.'[202] Her approaching marriage (to Percy Frankland) filled him with some dismay. 'It is a sad reflection that such a bright little love of a thing should be given over to childbearing and nursery pursuits.' 'Other girls I have had more original, and more thoughtful, but none who so fully enjoyed to sit and read round the fire with which we always close the evening.'

Grace was, however, soon to leave Oxford, and the Rector had no wish to be left only to Jeannie's mercies. He sought to rally his friends. Helen Colvill could not come because of her invalid mother. Nancy Paul was taken ill. Fanny Kensington peremptorily refused the invitation and was promptly put into the black book.[203] 'I shall never ask her again, her excuses only trumped up ones', a condemnation which, since the invitation had been given at short notice, Meta thought unduly censorious. Eventually he fell back on his wife's niece, Gertrude Tuckwell. Happily she proved 'excellent! vastly improved and her fine nature coming up to the top, forcing one to love the creature'.[204] Gertrude confessed that she could no longer stand living at home, and was determined to leave, though the only prospect was that of nursing at Great Ormond Street.

Gertrude Tuckwell was much devoted to her aunt. Earlier in the year Mrs Pattison had cautioned her as to how to behave when staying at Oxford. 'Be careful in every way' was her advice.[205] 'A little confidence will carry you through any demand of that kind which is

likely to be made at Lincoln, whereas if you show timidity or *look* as
if you weren't attending you are utterly lost.' Gertrude was in some
respects a scatter-brained girl, failing, for instance, to sign her name
or to date or stamp her letters, who sometimes drew her aunt's criticism. 'These things vexed me very much because it seems to show
that you do not take pains to attend to what you are doing, and that
you have got into thoroughly bad habits of mind. If you do not
conquer and control these straying thoughts you will never bring
your brains to any state of real use and strength.'[206]

With two such mentors as her uncle and aunt Gertrude had no
easy task, but she seemed to have won their sympathy. While she
was at Lincoln she wrote to her aunt to ask if she thought that
marriage should be the object of a woman's life. In the circumstances of Mrs Pattison's existence the question might appear naïve
if not embarrassing, but she was an honest and intelligent woman
who had no desire to escape the challenge which Gertrude's
question raised. She began by quoting a verse from Tennyson:

> Then said the fatfaced curate Edward Bull
> I say God made the woman for the man
> To keep him tight and warm and snug o'nights

'That view', she told Gertrude, 'takes too little into account that the
woman is an individual, having claims and rights of her own and
duties to *herself* . . . One of the great problems of life is to learn how
to conciliate one's own claims and rights with the respect due to the
claims and rights of others. It is *not*, as Tennyson's Mr Bull sup-
poses, all claim one side, all duty the other. The woman's first object
should be I think to make herself in mind and soul and body the *best*
that she sees the possibility of becoming, and if she can marry in
such a way as to satisfy the requirements of her own nature, if she
and the man whom she marries are drawn together not only by that
strong physical attraction which is commonly called love and which
is indispensable but can also strive together after the same moral and
intellectual ideal, *then* marriage is the greatest bliss that life can
offer. Where there is the possibility of realizing such a state I think
each has a claim on the other to which all other claims ought to be
postponed. In the ordinary marriage which is a matter of social
convenience I see no such exalted obligations . . . The nobler the

woman is, the more she has done for herself, the more splendid and valuable a human creature she is . . . let us even suppose marriage *the* object of fancy, even those who say so would agree that it is not undesirable that the woman as well as the man should be a free agent in contracting it.' So coolly and even dispassionately did Francis Pattison look back on the hopes and disappointments of twenty years before she turned to Gertrude's more immediate problem. 'These are the grounds on which I should urge all penniless girls to strive to make themselves independent, but I'm not sure that they lead me to say to you "Go and nurse sick children *at* once" . . . certainly don't go in for teaching.'[207]

Although Mark lived in the very centre of the College, the life of his society washed around the Lodgings without more than a few rivulets making their way into its internal recess. A contract for the new building in the Grove to the design of T. G. Jackson was signed the day Grace left. He dined as usual at the College Gaudy on All Saints night, sitting once more next to the theologian, Dr Ince, 'very sensible but not interesting', and 'impatiently' he watched the clock 'till I could get back to my 2 sweet girls who had an armchair and bright fire for me.' He took Communion in Chapel the following Sunday and commented on the surprisingly good attendance of the undergraduates 'when nothing whatever is said to the students on the subject, nor any notice taken of their presence or absence'. The next day was one of the two statutory College meetings, an occasion which he dreaded. Fowler was the only fellow present at the morning service in chapel and was elected Sub-rector; the bursarship, vacant through the resignation of Washbourne West, was not filled.[f]

The death of his old friend, J. M. Wilson, the President of Corpus, 'the oldest and . . . truest man friend that I have in the world', was a grievous personal loss and a grim reminder, if he needed one, of the remorseless passage of time, for Wilson, as he noted in his diary, was actually a year and a half 'younger than me'. 'This comes very close home, and makes me tremble at every sensation of the bodily frame, that calls for my attention and added to some other things, as well as the average worry of term time depresses my spirits, makes me

[f] Washbourne West, fellow Lincoln College 1845–97; strong Tory; Thomas Fowler, fellow Lincoln College 1855–82, President of Corpus, 1882–1904.

determined to be away from Oxford this Xmas.'ᵍ But Wilson's death
was not without some gain since the fellows of Corpus elected
Lincoln's Sub-rector, Tommy Fowler, as President in his place. This,
in Pattison's view, was a most extraordinary decision on the part of
the fellows of Corpus. 'What can Henry Smith [another friend who
was a fellow of Corpus] be thinking of?' For years Mark had
resented Fowler's influence in the College as well as his courteous
but insinuatingly critical treatment of himself. 'How glad you'll be if
Fowler goes to Corpus!' Meta exclaimed, 'you'll have his fellowship
and Donald's to fill up. Do get good men. I should awfully like
Lincoln to be more worthy, or less unworthy, of its Rector. You
should elect Wise and my Sedbergh friend Wells, or Althaus, in
default of better men! Anyhow they'd work with you.' 'I daresay',
he admitted to Meta, 'you're the only person who understands what
a relief it is to me that Fowler has removed to another College, but it
is too late in the day to be of any use in the College point of view. I
am too old, my energy gone or what little remains of it diverted into
another channel ... Besides Merry [another fellow of the College,
classical scholar and future Rector] remains and the future elections
to fellowships in 1882 will have to take place under the Commissioner's statutes which are much more unfavourable to a College
struggling for reputation than the old statutes.'²⁰⁹
He was, perhaps, even more put out when, in her reply, Meta
suggested that Fowler's removal gave him the opportunity to exert
himself as Rector. With some exasperation he wrote, on Christmas
Day, 'This only shows that you have not ... as yet apprehended the
situation. When some twelve or fourteen years ago I began to withdraw from active administration within the College, it was partly
from the vexation of being so constantly thwarted by the Tutors in
little things, but it was also in a greater degree because I had found
that I was misspending my time in giving it to a trumpery business
which anyone else could do better than I could while all the while
there was opening for me a more considerable and more interesting
sphere in the world of letters. I have now an audience far wider than
any mere Oxford audience, and all I want is the vigor and elasticity
which is alas! fast leaving me to address the public I have got. Last

ᵍ J. M. Wilson (1813–81), President Corpus Christi College 1872–81. Whyte's Professor of Moral Philosophy 1846–74.²⁰⁸

week was our Audit and I spent 2 days of it in close attention to the business of the College, compelled to do so because West [the bursar, who had resigned] was not there, and I felt all the time how little I was fit for such work and how little worth it was to occupy my time, and how distasteful to me. I am sure that it would be most unwise in me to descend again into the arena of College disputes, and to fight with beasts at Ephesus . . .'²¹⁰ʰ

He was little better pleased when Meta innocently suggested that he should send his sister, Mary Roberts, a "fat Xmas box". The Rector, parsimonious to a degree, exploded. 'I wish before you make these suggestions you would ascertain exactly what my income is. One thing I can tell you that my receipts as Head are little more than half what they were ten years ago, and what my necessary household expenses are you cannot pretend to know, and yet you think yourself competent to recommend me to give money to other people of whose means you know less than you do of mine.'²¹²

Rapped vigorously over the knuckles, Meta felt obliged to reassure the exasperated Rector that her remarks were only intended humorously. Mark's mood was, however, sour. In mid-December he had slipped on a library ladder in his dressing-room, and catching hold of the travelling tin box had sustained several bruises and injured his finger. It was not a matter of great moment, but he thought that he might have to change his plans for Christmas and postpone his intended visit to Paris. Jeannie Stirke, who was to return to spend Christmas with her family in Yorkshire—'as I think it good for a growing filly to have its shoes taken off and be turned out to grass for a few weeks',—was persuaded to stay on to look after her uncle.²¹³ He abandoned his intention of spending Christmas 'among the Jews' with his friends, the Montefiores, at Waltham. Meta was afraid that he might visit his ill-temper on his long-suffering niece. 'I'm sure you won't be so unutterably cross to her as you were to me!', she wrote on Christmas Day.²¹⁴

Worst of all, there was the aching memory that Meta had actually been at Oxford the previous Christmas. 'I know only that you

---

ʰ The new statutes did not come into operation as a result of opposition from the College's Visitor, Bishop Wordsworth of Lincoln, who held that they attacked his proprietorial rights. Consequently he raised the question in the House of Lords which, to Pattison's chagrin, nullified the statutes.²¹¹

surrounded me with the tenderest care and affectionate watchfulness of every moment and that I owed to you the first Xmas for five years which could be called a happy one.'215 But what had been achieved in the previous twelve months? He was ageing. They seemed further apart than ever, their relationship encapsulated in a weekly letter.

Similar thoughts were in Meta's mind as she prepared to celebrate the festival with her father and stepmother in the Victorian if Christian gloom of Orsett Terrace. 'I'm not in a fit mood to write you', she told Mark on Christmas Day, 'as I've been in the lowest depths all day. I'd give a year of my life to live this day year again and be thankful for the exchange ... It is so awfully hard to feel absolutely alone in the world, to have no God to breathe a prayer to, still more not to be able to feel that one is working on his side and in absolute submission to his will. If I could only know that there was some Power whom I could love, say as much as I do you ... I am horribly wretched and actually cried this afternoon.'216

So, for two lonely, rather unattractive people, drawn to each other by their loneliness, the year moved towards its close. After eight months in which he had not seen Meta, Mark came up to London. Where should they meet? Mark suggested the Smoke Prevention Exhibition in South Kensington, but providentially they decided against it: 'Uncle G[ranville] was there! What a race there'd have been, writings possibly to our friend abroad [i.e. Mrs Pattison], certainly to us, and extreme embarrassment when we met.'217 More prosaically they met in the open at Orsett Terrace with Mrs Bradley acting as an unwanted chaperone. To Meta's annoyance, Mark tried to delay the time of his departure which looked 'very bad to Mrs Bradley, and makes it uneasy to me'. But the irritation receded in the delight which she felt at seeing him again. 'Feel peaceful, like a baby who has been rocked to rest on its mother's breast.' It was an odd, even inappropriate, metaphor.

What the New Year had in store neither of them could say, but the sky was overcast. The past year had been so tantalizing and wearying, a few shafts of sunlight soon giving way to cloud, some of it portending thunder. 'This year', she wrote on 1 January 1882, 'can't be much worse than the last has been, for me at any rate.

Thank God it's over. Whatever this one has of wretchedness for either of us, our confidence in each other can't be called in question. I am so thankful that . . . you have quite ceased to wonder "how long it will last"!'[218]

IV

1882

THE terraced house in Orsett Terrace and the panelled rooms of the Rector's Lodgings in Oxford were enshrouded in sluggish routine in the early months of 1882. Even affection seemed to blend into blandness. Yet if Meta's letters lacked prima facie the ardour of yester year, this was in part a cautionary manœuvre designed to avert the prying eyes of any unauthorized reader. The danger was still a real one. In February Mark had been perturbed to learn that one of his own letters to Meta had fallen into the hands of his wife. His informant was Miss Smith. She 'read me a letter she had received from *her* [i.e. his wife] in which was much, most disagreeable to me, but what I want to tell you is that a letter by me "to one of his young female friends, after being passed from hand to hand, had at last come into the possession of some one" who brought it to her, in which was a satirical allusion to C[harles] D[ilke]. Now this can only have been one of my letters to you, as only to you could I have used those initials .... Have you, like me, left your letters about?'[1] Doubtless Mrs Pattison was more irritated by the reference to Dilke than by the affectionate tone of her husband's letter. Meta could not remember any letter from Mark in which he so alluded to Dilke, and wondered whether the letter had been addressed to Miss Laffan, who was 'much more likely to evoke sarcasm on your part'.[2] For if Pattison was secretly pleased to find that he may not have been the only one to leave his letters about, Meta was put out by the suggestion that she may have been the culprit.

It so happened that both of them met again Mrs Donald Crawford, in the New Year. They were struck by her childish attitude, and agreed that she and her husband had little in common. 'I like her', Meta declared, 'she's very young and has never felt anything very much. It amuses me to hear such a child babble in her fresh way. I can't imagine what they can have in common.'[3] 'I knew', Mark replied, 'Mrs Donald Crawford, if one can know of such a

child before she was married . . . she and her husband have nothing
in common, and from her eagerness to contradict him, one might
infer that there existed at present a secret antipathy, but this she will
no doubt get over when she finds that her interests are identified
with her husband's, and how necessary it is for a pair to make
common cause against the world.'[4]

If their correspondence seemed more matter of fact, it screened
an aching heart and a lost horizon. 'I never pass a day' he declared
'in which I do not feel your presence, like a tutelary saint, hovering
over me.'[5] 'Oh, dear Rector', Meta wrote on 13 February, 'how very
hateful this world is. I can't say, as many people do, that everything
you want is vanity when you've got it. My complaint is that I can't
have what I want! I'd thankfully take my chance of my desire
turning into dust! But a truce to melancholy. I know you hate it — in
others!!'[6] She was right. If melancholy was natural to Mark, he liked
to be cheered. Meta continued to write long, informative, shapeless
scrawls, which gave the Rector such pleasure that he complimented
her on her descriptive powers. She should try to write a novel. He
read and re-read her letters before handing them back to her for
safe-keeping. 'They are too good to be lost. They would be
interesting even to persons who didn't know the parties.'[7]

A bout of chills and colds kept the Rector in Oxford in early
January: 'cold and fever. . . This in addition to gout, rheumatism, no
teeth and inactive liver! Is life worth preserving?'[8] But they continued to meet whenever an opportunity for doing so occurred
when he came up to London to attend meetings of the Hellenic
Council, the Vigilante Association, the committee of the London
Library, or the Council of Bedford College. Then they strolled the
streets, lunched cheaply or sat in the National Gallery, and even
occasionally met under the kindly surveillance of Mrs Bradley at
Orsett Terrace where Mark scoffed cream and muffins, strangely
unsuitable fare surely for one who suffered such digestive troubles.
To see Meta gave him pleasure, but there could be no exchange of
confidences in Orsett Terrace. 'I should only see you in that unsatis-
factory way', he wrote of a future possible meeting there, 'in which
we meet now and which is hardly the shadow of the life we used to
lead together. For my part I find writing gives me more satisfaction

than such half-hours as I have snatched with you this winter, and 3 miles to get them.'⁹

Happy as she was in the warm serenity of Madame Moreau's house at Draguignan, engaged in writing and researching, Francis Pattison was at least made uneasy by the barrier of silence which her husband had erected. She did not believe that his relationship with Meta would give rise to open scandal, but she was worried. She even began to consider whether she ought not to try to spend the next winter in Oxford. It was an unwelcome prospect. Oxford 'society' in which you say I "have no part"', she told Ellen Smith, 'is not more distasteful to me than any other sections of middle-class life (which is always ugly and unfinished), except for the dash of pretension which always accompanies officialdom, however small, and which makes its items less pleasant than simple country folk', but the thought of spending the winter there was abhorrent. 'I can hardly exaggerate the intense repulsion for the atmosphere', she told Miss Smith in another letter, 'and *that* must seem morbid or even absurd to you who thrive upon it so happily, but I am trying quietly to bring my mind round to what in the tamest moments seems like digging my own grave. To most people no doubt, the life here would seem more trying, but I find a joy in the full glory of the sun, the blaze and barrenness of the South which is an immense satisfaction to me and is like a cordial bath to one's weariness either of men or books ... the chill of English scenery ... depresses me ... this at once sobers and stimulates.'¹⁰

Ellen Smith pressed Mrs Pattison to winter abroad. Her presence in Oxford would add neither to her own happiness nor to that of her husband. Her arguments were not lost on Mrs Pattison. 'I cannot help questioning myself rather more closely than I should if my inclinations did not point to my taking my rest here and making it as long as possible. *I am thankful to claim all the respite that is really necessary*; but *I will not claim more*.'¹¹ She was touched by the fear that somehow or other Mark might allow his animus to involve Dilke, though on the surface he remained on friendly terms with the Liberal politician. 'It is very odd talking to you as he has done', she commented to Ellen Smith, 'that he should at the same time receive a visit from the person in question [i.e. Sir Charles Dilke] with MORE than courtesy ... I am glad you said what you did although he will make believe to himself that we are in a plot. There is something monstrous in this attitude, but I am learning to look at it without that passionate resentment which it naturally provoked and which poisoned so many years of my young life and drove me to desperation and the verge of utmost folly. I feel as if I could never be sufficiently grateful to you for having divined the terrible struggles which were behind the recklessness and levity and for having believed that I should work through.'[12a]

'Even his beloved Mrs Lathbury', Francis Pattison exclaimed, 'now speaks of him as a "malignant old man".' 'I work', she wrote in an exasperated fashion, 'at a kind of work which calls for distraction and relaxation and I turn from this to the querulous self-pity and fretful exactions with which it is very difficult to live in charity . . . It is very difficult to know how to deal when you can neither count on any natural feelings or chivalry, nor appeal to any *usage du monde*.'[13]

Whatever Mrs Pattison might feel or write, she was far away in the warmth of southern France while Meta clattered in hansom cabs through the thick yellow fog to the teas and dinners which she described in such detail for Mark's edification. There was, for instance, dinner with the Nicholls, the husband a brother of her friend Rose Nicholls, on 27 January; '10 Jews and 8 Gentiles. I sat next but one to your Mrs Lucas, who was very quiet and looked intensely bored and weary all the evening . . . My man was rather pleasant company for 100 minutes, our chat was booky and sanitary mixed! . . . My man lets his bright young bride coach at the Working Women's College once a week, very good of them both . . . I suspect that Mrs Nicholls has a good deal of stuff in her. She is rather taking, tho not lovely nor pretty, smiles sweetly and happily and is gentle and modest . . . She certainly draws well and is very persevering, has done a set of titles which go all round a large drawing room . . . There was also a huge man, a friend of Rose's [i.e. Rose Nicholls] who when introduced to me said "Rose is a great friend of yours, isn't she"! I really could not say "yes", so got out of it by replying, "I've known her all my life." Rose is an excellent girl, forsooth, but one's great friend must be a lady, I opine.' Such a remark showed that Meta, however

---

[a] After dining with the Grant Duffs at Twickenham in 1881, he had been driven back to London by Sir Charles Dilke 'in an open carriage trembling for my life at every blast, though wrapt in a huge black bearskin.'

broadminded she essayed to be, was not as egalitarian as she liked sometimes to make out. 'Then the giant said how delightful it must be to stay with you, though he supposed you were the reverse of a lady's man! He also supposed that your extreme views stood in the way of your being made a Bishop, or with a sly smile, a Dean! I was inwardly convulsed, but gravely replied that from a boy you had wished for exactly the position you now enjoyed.'[14]

Such functions were not unrequited pleasure. 'How very dull most amusements are', she yawned on 3 February. 'I've just come back at midnight from a French recitation at the Toynbees. The Cohens, Pauls (old), Kensingtons (young), Mallets and about 50 others. The Frenchman was distinctly good, and I could perfectly follow him ... But I found other people very slow ... F[anny] K[ensington] had a quite pretty frock on! I drove home at a furious pace in a hansom with the glass down in a dense fog, so you can hardly wonder at my being extremely frightened. Worse still, before I could clamber down, a brute, who must have been partially following, rang the bell. I was so furious that my voice positively trembled with rage, which so impressed the wretch that he slunk away without demanding a tip! But of course the luckless servants were awake. I only trust my father wasn't.'[15]

'Yesterday', she wrote two days later, 'I lunched at some fashionable cousins and was so bored. Four young men came also, and their talk all the time was of horses, racing, bettings, jockeys and the like.' Meta's puritanical instincts gained the upper hand. 'I sat dumb and vowed I'd never go there again. If the army young man is generally of that type I pity people who live in garrison towns ... Dull as my father's friends are, they're far superior to the gay and giddy.'[16]

Dinner with the Beddingtons, six Christians and twelve Jews, proved to be much more entertaining. 'I was taken down by Sir David Salomon[s], grandson of the first Jew M.P. and the wretch is actually a Conservative! ... He is great in science, especially electricity, experiments largely himself, was nearly killed by a shock ... Has a splendid place in Kent, which is now being pulled to pieces in order to be lighted with electric light. He thinks that what we call life is probably electricity ... We had a hot dispute about scholars. He happened to say casually that the most selfish and useless folk were those who spent their lives in the pursuit of knowledge for its own sake, and didn't communicate what they knew! He said if he had the choice of annihilation or an undefined future existence he should certainly choose the former. I said ditto. After dinner I had a chat with an artistic Miss Patterson ... a great want of animation about her, but I became convinced during the singing of a very sentimental song ... that she had had some love affair. Then I had a very lively sanitary conversation with a Mr Mocatta.'[b] The mind boggles slightly at the liveliness of a discussion which turned on so drab a topic as sanitation.[17]

At another dinner party Meta sat next to a young Dr Harper, a son of the Principal of Jesus College, Oxford, who spoke feelingly of the purity of Dean Stanley's character. 'A singularly, pure, passionless man, that no one could say a coarse word in his presence or gossip nastily'. On the previous Sunday Harper had visited the Zoological Gardens in the company of Tennyson. He commented to Tennyson that Gladstone still retained 'such a strong provincial accent, very noticeable in a long speech'. 'Tennyson stopt dead, and said "Is my accent like that, do I speak like Gladstone?" Harper actually said "Yes!!" Tennyson proceeded to explain that people who had north country nurses (I think Lancashire) always retained their accents.'[18]

The evening which she spent at the Drews was 'oh! so dull'. 'I sat between Mr Drew ... and a very ugly, rather nice barrister, late of Brasenose. But all we had opportunity of discussing was Weatherly, a contemporary of his ... I had to cope with Mr Drew, who is very heavy. The Lakes and Poor Law Guardians seem his only topics! The other diners were 2 of the girls, a married son, a heavy cross looking lout with a cheery prettyish wife who warbled most of the evening and two other men. One of them slouched about the drawing room with hands in pockets, yawned right in one of the girl's faces un-disguisedly, said "Ay" rudely to Mrs Drew, leant his hands and arms over the back of the ladies' chairs ... The Cub turned out to have been at University.'[19]

The Bradley household had much been flustered by the appoint-ment of Jessie's husband, Courtenay Ilbert, as legal member of the Council of the Governor General of India. It was a handsome

---

[b] Sir David Salomons (1851–1925), 2nd Bt., Engineer, contested Mid-Kent as a liberal candidate in 1874, author of Scientific Works; pioneer of the 'horseless carriage'; designed motors; recreation, 'four-in-hand driving'.

preferment, carryng with it a substantial salary, some £8,000 a year; but to Meta it meant the departure of her sister and her nieces to a period of exile in a still semi-barbaric country. Meta often criticized her sister, but she had grown to depend upon her. She was devoted to her nieces, fussing over them in ways that they later found embarrassing. 'For six miserable weeks', one of her nieces, her god-daughter, Olive, later recalled, 'Aunt M . . . took charge of the house—Aunt M, who advocated practising before breakfast and put down afternoon tea, and who, when famine overtook the children after a protracted concert, took them to a place called Lockharts, where they ate, standing up, little cakes covered with ants. Aunt M, who usurped Judy's bed and made sleep impossible by her habit of crunching biscuits and crackling newspapers, which she read by preference the last thing at night.'[20] But the nieces were then still very young children for whom Aunt Meta envisaged horrid fates. 'It is too dreadful', she said of Lettice, 'to contemplate that child's going to India. Of course she'll die there.'[21]c 'These children are so sweet that being with them is pain and grief. I wake with horrid visions of another mutiny. In fact mingled thoughts of you and Lettice keep me awake many a weary hour.'[22] She seems to have communicated her anxieties to her sister who herself became 'possessed with the fear there should be a general Mahomadan rising, is awfully worried by visions of the children being massacred before her eyes'.[23] 'Disordered livers, fiendish offspring, the decease of at least half a dozen relatives in their absence'; such were the possibilities that temporarily diverted Meta's melancholy from one misery to another. 'It is very trying to have people perpetually talking about this Indian affair. I fancy that I now pretty well realise what a man feels like when innocent people discuss the approaching marriage of the girl who has refused him!'[24] To avoid Mrs Bradley's constant chatter about the subject, Meta went and sat in her sealskin coat in a cold room.[25] Courtenay was to leave for India in April. Jessica, who was pregnant, was to follow in the autumn. When another daughter, Margaret Peregrine, was born, the suggestion was mooted that Meta might accompany the Ilberts to India, thus setting up a new ferment in Meta's mind.[26]

c Lettice Ilbert was eventually to become the wife of H. A. L. Fisher, historian, later Warden of New College, Oxford.

Fortunately her growing interest in social and philanthropic work, on which she seems to have so often expatiated at dinner parties, formed an outlet for her energies, even if they only served to take her mind off Mark. A Mr Congreve, with whom she had a long talk in the 'back-drawing room after dinner' told her that he had 'a great belief in the saving power of work, but I tell him that work may keep one sane but won't give me an idea of happiness. I daily feel more longing to die. I am so tired of yearning for what I can never have. Everyone says I look ill and my ring, right a year ago, falls off now'. By immersing herself in social work, she did manage to fill the day. 'There is a sort of demon of unrest always urging me on.' She had been approached the previous winter by the secretary of the National Health Society, Fanny Lankester, the sister of the eminent scientist Ray Lankester,[d] to give talks on different aspects of sanitation, 'air, ventilation, water, babies etc.', to mothers' meetings. 'I know quite enough for a few talks ... Rather a joke for me to give advice to aged women on the food and clothing of infants, but as long I hadn't to feed and dress one as an example, my ignorance wouldn't appear.'[27]

Henceforward, though the subject was for Mark (who had however contributed the information that women's 'stays' had been first mentioned by the classical author, Synesius) evidently infinitely tedious, her letters were full of allusions to district visiting, the plight of the poor, the need for hygiene, the proper size of a woman's waist, the wisdom of wearing long skirts and similar problems of a sanitary nature. She was modestly pleased with the reception of her lectures, though the falling attendance might suggest that her audience was less entranced. 'I had only 30 women for my audience today. If they don't get their pill well jammed with stories they won't swallow it all. They much annoy the lady who collects them by saying that they know all I told them (quite impossible!) yet by not practising any of it.'[28] The hot weather in May led to a further drop in attendance: 'Instead of 1 or 200 poor people there were 8 poor and 22 rich, mostly friends of mine! You can imagine how tiresome it was to give them the lecture intended for the great unwashed.'[29]

---

[d] Ray Lankester (1847–1909), fellow Exeter College Oxford 1872; Professor of Zoology, University College London 1874–9; Professor of Comparative Anatomy, Oxford 1891–8; Director of Natural History department British Museum 1898–1907.

The 'great unwashed' were less than enthusiastic about the virtues of sanitation and hygiene than their patrons. Meta did her best to encourage them. She persuaded the shopgirls from Whiteley's store to attend a meeting at Kensington Town Hall where the speaker discoursed on the evils of stays, suggesting that 25 to 20 inches was the proper size for the waist of a well-developed woman, and of high heels.[30e] Yet it was an uphill struggle. When Meta lectured at Hoxton on skin and cleanliness, her audience consisted mainly of the affluent, 'besatined, besilked and bevelveted women', though one of these asked her later to come on another evening to talk to her factory girls.[32] 'I wonder whether we shall do much to prevent tiny waists and heaps of heavy petticoats.'

While Meta immersed herself in sanitation and good works, Mark was passing a relatively uneventful, painless winter. A persistent chill kept him for the most part indoors, so that he did not dine out until mid-March when he went to an 'uninteresting party' at the deanery.[33] Friends came to stay, but his welcome was sometimes grudging. Of James Morison he conceded that there was 'no one with whom I have such good conversation'; but of his oldest friend, David Horndon he was obliged to confess 'we have no idea in common'.

College life continued to bore or frustrate him. He found Fowler's successor as sub-rector, W. W. Merry, almost as irritating as Fowler himself, grooming himself to take Pattison's own place.[f] A dispute over the filling of vacant fellowships at the college led to an appeal for a decision to the College's visitor, the Bishop of Lincoln; I 'found myself', he confessed, 'in the old way beginning to care how things in the College go—which must be guarded against.'[34] Perhaps, indeed, there was no great need for this since his personal life at the Lodgings was of greater moment than what happened in College.

As usual during his wife's absence he was attended by his youthful ministering angels. But his Stirke nieces, Mary and Jeannie, were in Yorkshire, helping to nurse their young sister, Pippa, who was ill with scarlet fever. Pippa died. Meta pressed Mark on the desirability of inviting Mary or Jeannie to Oxford, if only for as a much-needed change after the harrowing weeks. But the Rector's grudge against

---

[e] Compare 'I'm sorry to see that the majority of women still wear low dresses. No wonder consumption is rife among us.'[31]

[f] W. W. Merry, fellow Lincoln College 1859–84; Rector 1884–1918.

Mary persisted. She was not educated enough to write his letters.
Jeannie's extravagant expressions of affection aroused his suspicions.
'Anywhere with you', she had told him, 'would be perfect bliss.' The
Rector was too shrewd an old bird to be taken in by such flattery.
Meta tried to persuade him that Jeannie really meant what she had
written: 'I have always found you better company than anyone I
know ... Then you've been very kind to her, and there's something
about you peculiarly likely to win the affection of a clever, observant,
strong girl, who feels herself useful to her mother's favourite brother,
whom she sees is fragile, who she feels has mind and heart.'[35] But the
Rector was not persuaded by Meta's special pleading. 'That she likes
life with me, I don't doubt. It suits her, but that is a very different
thing from liking me. No, that can't be quite sincere, and if it isn't
you see what the fact lets in upon me!'[36] Poor Jeannie, she was to
have a rough road to travel with her grudging uncle. Meta suggested
that he should invite Mary and Jeannie to the Lincoln Commemora-
tion Ball, the first in the long history of the College, and 'fork out a
trifle'. Neither suggestion found favour. 'The ball is given by the
undergraduates, and is calculated to cost them £80. The Dons have
nothing to do with it, though Katey Merry will be asked—she's
getting quite pretty.'[37] The present had so little to offer, but when he
ruminated about the past he became equally depressed. On a
Saturday evening in February, he read through all the letters which
he had received in 1861, congratulations on his election as Rector of
the College and on his subsequent marriage: 'most melancholy! Of
how much forgotten goodwill have I been the object in my life-
time!'[38]

As the Hilary team neared its close, he became eager to get away
from Oxford. But he could make no plans until the Visitor, the
Bishop of Lincoln, adjudicated on the appeal; eventually he ordered
that the vacant fellowship should be filled by 26 April. Then his
departure was delayed by the entrance scholarship examination. 'My
chance of getting to the sun is almost vanished.'[39] As so often
happened, his natural pessimism proved to be unfounded. Towards
the end of March he left for a month's trip to France.

The holiday was evidently a success in spite of the ill omens which
marked its start. For the steamer broke down three miles outside
Boulogne and drifted to Calais in high seas, 'making everyone on

board, even those who are never sick before ill'. At Bordeaux, where he spent a night, he left his dark suit in a drawer in his hotel bedroom. At Biarritz his intention to stay at the Grand Hotel was frustrated by an outbreak of scarlet fever, of which he learned from young Theodore Althaus who came to greet him at the station, and he was obliged to resort to the Angleterre which he had tried to avoid as he knew that the Duke of Connaught was occupying a suite there. The weather became wintry rather than spring-like, with little sun and high winds.

In spite of all this he was actually enjoying himself. 'For pure lotus-eating, which is about the best thing for me just now, I don't know where I could have pitched my tent more advantageously.'[40] Although the mass of the hotel residents were 'ordinary British philistines ... harmless and unaggressive bores', there were at least five people whose company he found sympathetic. Edward Lowe, one of his earliest and brightest pupils at Lincoln, later Headmaster of Hurstpierpoint College, 'though gone for clericalism has not thought it his duty to foresake me', and Mrs Lowe 'mothered' him.[g] But it was Lionel Tollemache[h] and his wife, accompanied by a Miss Hardcastle 'intelligent without being intellectual', who delighted him. He basked in Tollemache's wide reading, acute judgement and intellectual power. 'They have birth'—he was the second son of Lord Tollemache—'manners, savour wine, simplicity, she accomplishments and reflection, though not charm, he wonderful knowledge, and inexhaustible resources of intellect, a Balliol scholar and a 1st class man, but not like Ilbert forgotten it, but one of the most interesting men I have ever known.' Pattison shared the same table with them, after dinner went to sit with them in their private apartment 'till the strain of the conversation becomes too much for me'.[42] 'Their society was a rare treat for me, and worth coming here on purpose for.'[43] Once the Lowes and Tollemaches had departed, there were others whom he found adequate as congenial companions, Mrs

[g] Canon Edward Lowe (1823–1912), IIIrd Literae Humaniores Lincoln College Oxford, 1846; Headmaster Hurstpierpoint 1850–73; Provost of Denstone 1873–91; Provost of Lancing 1891–8.
[h] Hon Lionel Tollemache (1838–1919), 2nd son of 1st Baron Tollemache, educated Eton and Balliol. Writer; near-sighted; married Hon Beatrice Egerton. A critical portrait of Pattison in his *Recollections*.[41]

Haigh, sensible and well-informed, Miss Black, very pretty and free-thinking, the Dunlops, he 'an ex-diplomat, well-posted up in foreign politics, but common at bottom', Major and Mrs Addison, very rich, his talk of lawn tennis, she evidently used to high society, Dr Hume, who had been dismissed from Netley Hospital, civilly and with a pension, because he was an agnostic.[44] 'It is years since I have lived the life I do here—au grand jour—with no moment to myself except before I get up, and after I retire at 9 o'clock too tired to do as you do, who begin your letters at midnight ... ∴. I breakfast in bed, reading, and have not, in the cold mornings, been downstairs much before 11. Then there is "good morning" to say to those delicate ones who like myself haunt the salon until the sun has softened the air. At 12.30 comes *déjeuner* and then more lounge in the drawing room or read newspapers till the time comes to go out with some one, or make calls. After calls comes 4.0 tea, which is universal in all the English villas. Then comes dress for dinner, which is at 6.30 ... There are about 100 visitors in the hotel, the Connaughts occupy their own pavilion, and we see nothing of them. They have a visitors' book, and I suppose I am almost the only Englishman in the place who has not entered his or her name in it. The rest of the visitors may be divided into two classes, the interesting and the uninteresting. The number of the former is 5, the latter therefore must amount to 95, or more.'

At the end of the first week of April, in the company of the Cornishes and Mrs Lloyd, he moved to Bagnères de Bigorre, having given up the idea of going to Spain, '1650 feet above sea level, the air cold, not too cold, and sun is there to warm me up, very cheerful place, good hotels quite empty, consequently we have a monopoly of attentions—40 people however assembled in the Anglican Temple this morning.'[45]

He returned to England on 19 April to find that Meta's life had erupted into a new crisis as a result of a further quarrel with her father. For some months there had been a kind of armistice in the relations between Charles Bradley and his daughter. Yet he still harboured a grievance against what he regarded as her unfilial behaviour. At the end of March they had a serious talk, 'too private to risk other people knowing about it' which only showed that they were more at loggerheads than ever. 'Our idea of duty of children to parents and vice verse being hopelessly at variance.'[46] The following

Thursday Meta had a long conversation with her friend, Daisy
Woods. She would not reveal what was said but it was on a subject
'very unpleasant to us both', evidently her friendship with Mark.[47]
Shortly afterwards she had a headlong collision with her father—the
letter which Mark praised for Meta's dramatic descriptive power
does not survive—in which Charles Bradley once again made plain
his strong disapproval of her relations with Mark and more or less
forbade her to admit him to Orsett Terrace. Indeed he stressed his
wish that she should not see him at all, recognizing at the same time
that this was a request with which his daughter would not comply.
'What annoyed him so hopelessly was the knowledge that she [i.e.
Meta] would not do so to please f[ather] or anyone else. His profession has fostered all his faults and made him expect to be considered
Supreme Wisdom in his own house! The alienation is of long standing, and the feeling between them is that of armed neutrality. At
breakfast the other day he informed her that her life or death would
make not the least difference to him! and this not at all in anger!'[48]

Mark was both worried and irritated by the renewal of the
conflict. He felt he was the predestined loser. 'It is most cruel, this
determination of the world to keep us from each other. As I am at a
loss to know *why* it is done, everything around me feels full of
treachery.' But he could not avoid allocating some of the blame for
this new upheaval to Meta. From his own experience he knew her to
be tactless and impetuous. Whatever the nature of his own relations
with his father, Pattison was too imbued with Victorian principles to
approve of filial or marital disobedience. 'You might', he told Meta,
'have given the dialogue a more gentle turn had you been a little
more yielding in speech and manner. You refuse too point blank.
Could you not have reasoned with f[ather] and asked him to say
what there was in me that made me an objectionable acquaintance
for his daughter; instead of falling back on first principles, and the
rights of children against their parents. I should like to know *what* he
would have alleged against me. If, as I suppose, he had only been
stimulated by Mrs Granville G. Bradley's poisoned insinuations, it
would have weakened the impression in his mind of these if he had
been called upon to repeat them in his own words. He would have
felt that they were calumnies. I am more than ever disposed to
believe that it is not your opinions and decision of character which

have alienated Mr Charles Bradley, but your lack of tact and brusqueness of speech.'[49] 'I wish', he ended his letter, 'we had from the first acted as I proposed and written and spoken of, and to, each other, openly and frankly, shewing all the world that we were friends, and nothing more.'[50]

When he was in France he had bought a 'hand knit tricot, for throwing over the shoulders natural colour of the wool' as a present for Meta's stepmother. Now that he was *persona non grata* at Orsett Terrace, he wondered whether he should send it to Mrs Bradley by parcel post. He did so, and both to Meta and Mrs Bradley's mortification, her husband ordered her to return it to the donor. 'Of course', Meta wailed, 'you'll never darken his doors again. Every scrap of his food chokes me and I hate him with what will be a lasting hatred.' Once more she wondered whether she ought not to leave home and take a job. 'I know quite well that poverty is most dreadful for a woman who has never been accustomed to it, but even that is better than daily life with a person you hate and who has been unpardonably and causelessly rude to your dearest friend. He and I shall not openly quarrel. I shall look in on him occasionally, but I hate being indebted to him for my paltry allowance of £32.'[51]

Mark urged Meta not to break openly with her father, which would have tragic results for her and would naturally react upon his own reputation. 'On no account should you leave his roof, that is your place, and you will only quit it for worse. Hate him, if you needs must, but do not put yourself in the wrong with him before the world.' He could not blame Mrs Bradley for obeying her husband. 'Of course she had to do what her husband required.' 'Dear love', he besought Meta, 'make life bearable by doing right, and don't be thinking whether you like it or not. I have heavier troubles to bear than ever you have. I get through by regarding it as a game which has to be played, though I confess I don't think I should be so composed, had I not my loved books to bury myself in.'[52]

The 'heavier troubles' looked alarmingly near, for Mrs Pattison announced her intention of returning from the South of France. She arrived from Paris on 5 May, staying with her friend, Theresa Earle, at whose home Sir Charles Dilke was being entertained to lunch.[i]

[i] This episode had a significant part in the later evidence in the Dilke divorce case: see Mrs Crawford's evidence in Queen's Proctor *v*. Crawford and Crawford.[53]

There was, perhaps, a hint of irony in that on the same day Pattison, waited on by his wife's niece, Gertrude Tuckwell, was entertaining Donald Crawford and his young wife, Virginia. The Crawfords had left before Francis Pattison returned. 'She has been home a fort-night', Mark moaned, 'and her egotism is now so fortified that she can talk of nothing but what has some relation to herself. She never exhibits the smallest interest in anything which happens to me, or has asked me a single question as to my winter.'[54] '"She" is in great force, in powerful health and vigour, so that there is no escape from her consuming egotism. She can talk or think of nothing but so far as it concerns herself. About me or my concerns she never enquires, or knows. She has taken into her head to give this dinner when for 6 years, we have not had a party during the summer months while she is at home. Worse than all she threatens me with the prospect of stay-ing till December! So that I shall not be able to have any of my friends to stay with me, and shall be afraid even to ask Jeannie as the girl would be exposed to an influence which would not be wholesome for her.'[55]

Even so, they both maintained the façade of harmonious union. To escape the 'wretchedness of the ghastly gaieties of commemora-tion', for neither Mark nor Francis was attracted to the festive side of academic Oxford, they went up to London and dined with the West-lakes 'in order that we might be seen to be dining out together'. Mark did not dare to call at Orsett Terrace even in the absence of Charles Bradley. He lunched with the Montefiores but was much put out that Claude Montefiore who had recently sat by Meta at a dinner did not even mention her name. The Rector, paranoiac, could only comment: 'Is it that people won't mention your name to me? What mischief Mrs G. G. B[radley] has done!'[56]

He escaped occasionally to London, to dine with friends—'with Frederick Macmillan, had a capital seat between Mrs Clifford and Lowell, the Excellency very gracious ... to everybody but did not talk literary, the political instinct being evidently the uppermost with him. Mrs C[lifford] and myself sympathetic, she greatly worth cultivating'—and to attend a Hellenic Council Meeting, 'long and tiresome'. He met Ruskin in St. James's Square. 'We embraced but as he was walking with R. with whom I'm in antipathy I didn't stop.' At Oxford his quiet was disturbed by the new College building and other 'botherations', and he missed Bodington's support and help. 'If I didn't adopt the maxim "don't care" they would soon be the death of me.' 'Our pecuniary troubles through defaulting tenants are becoming very serious.' Too fearful of declining income, he wondered whether it was worth continuing as Rector since 'the income of the headship is not more than half what it was ten years ago and even that remnant seems likely to vanish', fears that were as usual much exaggerated.

Some relief was, however, in sight, for, unaccompanied by his wife, he arranged to go down to Richmond for two or three weeks. At least it would now be possible for Meta to write to him more frequently since his wife would be unable to keep any check on the letters he received. 'O! if you could be at Grasmere again in July.'[57] 'Shall I be permitted to call at Mrs Ilbert's at Wimbledon to see you? It was the 19 August, I think, 1880 that I went to Ambleside (Bowness) and the day after to Grasmere. Mrs Ilbert was very good to me then.' But Mrs Ilbert had joined the ranks of her sister's critics. She now viewed Meta's friendship with Mark with growing disfavour and determined to do as much as she could to weaken it before she left to join her husband in India.

At first the Yorkshire dales failed of their normal therapeutic effect. 'Richmond is losing its charm, and Swaledale is dead.' He suspected that he was unwelcome. He had only warned his lodgings of his expected arrival. When he met his sisters, 'they didn't seem glad to see me'.[58] Mary Roberts, always somewhat distant and aloof, was more tiresome than ever. 'Unlike 1880, she has failed so far to go through the courtesy of asking me to a meal at the rectory.' 'She has not asked after you, or named you, for which, as you may suppose, I don't like her the betterer.'[59]

Slowly, however, the air and scenery, the familiar environment of childhood, seeped into his consciousness. 'I am getting old and know it', but 'loafing in the sun, real sun, and pottering over books and calls, and gossip' calmed his nerves. 'It is good for me to be here', he wrote after he had been a week in Richmond, 'Not only are my nerves in better tone already, but the whole style of life is refreshing, rejuvenating . . . One curious result is that instead of growing weary of the life, I grow to like it more. It is just the contrary of my Oxford experience. There I like the first week the best, the excitement,

1. Mark Pattison, Rector of Lincoln College, *c*.1880

2. Mrs Mark Pattison (later Lady Dilke), by Charles Camino, 1882

3. Meta Bradley as a young woman, May 1888

4. Meta Bradley in later life, July 1910

5. The Reverend Charles Bradley, father of Meta Bradley

6. Sir Charles Dilke, by G. F. Watts, 1873

7. Lincoln College, Oxford, c.1880. The Rector's Lodgings were in the right-hand corner of the front quadrangle

GxC 1865

Mr Pattison
Rector of Lincoln Coll
Oxford

8. Rector Mark Pattison, 1865, a drawing by C. W. Cope, Professor of Painting
to the Royal Academy (1867–75). Cope was commissioned to prepare murals
for the House of Lords and Westminster Palace, and used this drawing as a
model for the central figure in the fresco entitled 'Explusion of the Fellows of
a College in Oxford for refusing to sign the Covenant'.

constant change of person, and incessant demands on one's energies is stimulating. After a fortnight or so, it begins to jade, then to pall, and finally to nauseate, and I must escape, or languish in imbecility. Coming to Richmond, the first aspect of the place was that of a dead city. The first drive up the dale was still more disappointing. I felt as if the charm had passed away from it ... Gradually this phase of feeling has disappeared. The market place, my windows look out upon it, has recovered its interest, my curiosity is awake again, and fastens on the shabby figures that pass up and down with a desire to unlock them, and know who they are, and what moves them in their various directions. Swaledale yesterday shewed itself as lovely as in old time. Remember this experience of mine, if ever, when you go out of town into the country, this looks stale and unprofitable, it is only that the sudden withdrawal of the wanted excitement, while the mind has not had time to turn to the new.'[60]

At the end of the month he returned to Oxford to attend a College meeting, but the familiar scene drew him back to the North Riding. He even agreed to read prayers for Canon Roberts and donned his black suit to accompany the Rector's curate in a dogcart to a bazaar at Marske designed to raise money for a new organ. One of his congregation at prayers was Mrs Barclay Thompson who was holidaying with her husband at Helmsley, walking '17 miles in light boots', he noted that her beauty attracted all eyes in church, 'the interest of the Rector's extemporal address not being absorbing'. And in the evenings he read Tom Mozley's *Reminiscences*, recalling the fierce battles of bygone Tractarian Oxford, to write a review for *The Academy*.[61] But even the 'most agreeable' vacation had to come to an end. 'This loafing life in which I can be all the day in the country, with all the resources of a town, is most attractive, and I only resolve to go away from it by persuading myself that I shall return in a month's time. Who knows if I shall ever return? One thing, I am pounds stronger and hardier than I was when I came, eat and drink like a young man, and sleep 8 hours off the reel.'[62] But on his last day he was attacked by rheumatism, brought on by sitting on a wet cushion in the dogcart which brought him back from his fishing.

Meta's summer was less agreeable, though largely uneventful. It was overshadowed by preparations for her sister's departure for

India and all the fears that that evoked in her mind. She indulged herself in a spate of good works, lecturing to mothers on bringing up
their babies, justly struck by the paradoxical comicality of the situation. It was equally ironical that she should have been called in to
console a young man, a gasfitter by trade, who had been jilted by a
nurserymaid. His mother feared that the boy in desperation might
take his life. 'Then I went to the youth, and we mourned together for
a long time with tears in our eyes over the inconstancy of women!
Then you may imagine how I discoursed on the necessity of not
letting that spoil one's life and of trying to take an interest in other
people's happiness if one's own was irrevocably smashed, how much
worse it would have been had they been married etc. I talked *to* him
as if it was at myself.' The boy thought that he would emigrate and
join a cousin in Utah.[63]

There was a 'quiet' period in her relations with her family, in part
because her father had gone on his yacht. 'On Monday', she wrote on
25 April 1882, 'he goes on his yacht, and I hope I shan't see him again
for many months.' To Mark's sardonic amusement, he had invited
Mary Stirke as a guest. 'Suppose', Mark commented to Meta on
learning of his invitation, 'you were to go with me on a driving
excursion about the dales in a pony trap? What a commotion there
would be. I wish you would ask Mrs C. Bradley to explain the
difference. Mary goes alone all the way from Yorkshire to Dart-
mouth to meet him.'[64] Meta was not convinced by the analogy. 'Mrs
Bradley will receive M[ary] gladly and other damsels will be on board
with her.'[65]

None the less the troubles set in train by the anonymous letter still
lingered below the surface. Incautiously Mark suggested to Miss
Smith, of all people, that Meta might be a suitable person to succeed
Fanny Kensington as secretary of Bedford College.[66] Miss Smith was
definitely not amused. Meta was 'so badly behaved'. Meta thought
the suggestion mistimed and mistaken. Mark was so, 'utterly
unaware'. 'It would only be giving an opportunity to the enemy, viz.
Miss Smith to abuse me. Anyhow it was not worthwhile to run the
chance without knowing what *I* should say to it, and I should not
think for one moment of assenting! Already I have as much work as I
can possibly manage, and if I consented to give up any of it ... it
would only be for *paid* work ... do you think I would ever work

under Miss Smith! Every time I looked at you she would say I was "making eyes". I certainly prefer to work, as I now do, with people who know and value me, not with one who calumniates me!'[67] Under the barrage of two affronted women, Mark hastily withdrew his proposal. 'No one heard her [Miss Smith] "abuse you" but myself, and you may be sure she did not hit out at you with impunity to herself.'[68]

Mark still thought that if he was able to conciliate Meta's sister, Jessie, a major obstacle to their continued meeting and to regular correspondence would be removed. There seemed little or no hope of winning over her father. 'He would be thankful to know that we should never see or write to each other again. Only the certainty that I would sooner leave his roof than obey him prevents his demanding this. Not that he bears you the least malice. The only step which you can enable us to see each other is to remind "her" that she expressed her intention of inviting me to Lincoln this year. Until she has done so you must see that my f[ather] will always think that she disapproves of our friendship, and can take that ground on which to base his own disapproval. As long as my f[ather] lives I feel sure that he'll never let me stay with you when she isn't there. It's a question which of you has the greatest staying power. His father lived to be over 80.[69]

Since there seemed no remote possibility that Mrs Pattison would invite Meta to stay at the Lodgings, Mark concentrated his efforts on winning Jessie's goodwill. He arranged a visit to her, ostensibly so that he could bid farewell before she left for India. It also enabled him to see Meta and go for a 'lovely long walk'. 'I think', Mark wrote plaintively, 'I shall take the opportunity of coming to a clear understanding with your sister as to how much you and I are to see of each other in future. Life is slipping away from me, and I am having none of the society of the one person whom I most care to be with.'[70] Even after the invitation for a visit had been issued, Mark remained deeply critical of Jessie's behaviour, 'abusing me to various people'. 'She has', Meta agreed, 'a very strong way of expressing herself', but she begged him to come to Wimbledon. 'I don't suppose', he wrote on the eve of his visit, 'it will be worthwhile my bringing a racket, as we couldn't play more than half an hour.'[71] 'How blissful', Meta replied, 'to have you on Friday!'[72] 'Don't ring at the door as J[essie] tries to sleep from 2.30 to 3.30 but toddle round to the drawing room where you'll see me! You shall have a frugal lunch, then a long walk, and tea with the family.' As Mark had a meeting in the city, he would lunch in a cafe before catching the train out to Wimbledon. It is doubtful whether the meeting in any way removed Jessie's doubts.

Jessie had not found her sister's stay at Wimbledon a pleasurable experience. Meta, she told her husband in India, 'is less doleful than when she first came, but still I must say it is a burden to have her in the house. It is a great pity she does not take pains to be really pleasant. She ... makes endless observations on every occasion on the dreariness and wretchedness of life and looks the picture of woe. She is also looking very delicate.' She found Meta exasperating, 'most tiresome', and 'so eaten up with selfishness that she is never out of her thoughts and is always posing as a marytr, and refusing to believe, that any of her unhappiness is her own making.' Jessie admitted that in part their father was to blame for this, 'his own bringing up of Meta, than which since Mother died, nothing could have been worse'. The possibility of having Meta and the Bradleys to stay for two months filled her with dread. 'It is such a torture to me to be present in such constant bickerings and quarrels ... I shall be nearly killed by it if things don't go on pretty peacefully.'[73]

Meta's letters, for all her occasional depressions, were, however, also full of sprightly gossip as in accordance with her usual practice she moved from one house to another. She had been a bridesmaid at Grace Toynbee's wedding to Percy Frankland from which the Rector had thankfully escaped by being in Yorkshire. He had, however, done his duty with the gift of a silver salver which, Meta reassured him, stood out among 'more showy but inferior plate'. There were long and stately dinner parties—eighteen guests sat down at the Cohens—followed by music. 'It was a grind', she wrote of such an occasion with the Lankesters, 'going there by train but I'm glad I made the struggle ... I sat by Ray—he certainly is most objectionable in his manners ... We touched on Miss Smith who Ray thinks a better man than her brother! ... Somehow our conversation turned to suicide which Ray defends ... I never sat through such a noisy meal. The youngest Lankester who is walking Barts is a pleasant lad. Chas and another son are very common. The dinner was long and bad ... At 11 I tore myself away but it was so wet that I didn't go by train, but instead let Mary drop me here in a hansom en route for a dance. The thing rattled so that we couldn't talk much.'[74]

She knew how much Mark was interested in other peoples' conversations. She reported how James Bryce, staying with the Lawrences, had spoken out strongly in favour of letting children read the Bible unabridged. It had happened that Meta's niece, Lettice, had been 'lying down reading the Bible. Whereupon we all enquired as to what expurgated edition she had, and the women discoursed as to the folly of giving an ordinary copy to a child.' Bryce 'supposed we should omit the story of Jael as having an immoral tendency'. Meta thought that Bryce displayed a 'curious conservatism about his religion in opposition to the radicalism of his other opinions'.[75] Pattison agreed with Bryce. 'No young mind is injured by having natural facts, naturally stated. What is injurious is approbation of immoral conduct such as that of Jael when done in the interest of the Church.'[76]

Meta went to a fête at the Botanicals 'like a fairyland' with Mark's sister-in-law, Margaret, to the Oxford and Cambridge match, and to hear the highly reputed Stopford Brooke preach 'not uninteresting but I felt as if he were thinking of Stopford not of Paul or Barnabas.'[77][i] It was a verdict in which Mark concurred; 'those kinds of sermons are all so—epideictic eloquence, the Greeks who knew, and invented the style, called it.'[78]

In July she moved on to stay with the Rev R. S. Tabor at Cheam 'where I shall have to play Lawn Tennis vigorously, poke up a lot of heavy girls, flirt hard with some amorous brothers, and talk kindly to a paralytic mother'.[79][k] She found, as she expected, the visit somewhat tiresome. The Tabors 'are very fond of me, rather fonder than is quite convenient'. They played lawn tennis energetically; but the family was philistine in its cultural attitudes, 'most uneducated', only the governess showing the least acquaintance with literature. The eldest girl, 35 years old, had recently married a man thirty years older than herself, Admiral Richards, 'a rough diamond and very weather-beaten and odd looking, with a queer wisp of black hair hanging

[i] Stopford Brooke (1832–1916), celebrated preacher, left the Church of England 1880.
[k] The Revd R. S. Tabor (1819–1909) Trinity College Cambridge, Curate of Enfield (1844–58), was Headmaster of Cheam School 1888–90; he was succeeded by his son A. S. Tabor in 1891, Eton and St. John's College, Cambridge (d. 1920).

over his eyes'. Meta had dined with the happy couple some weeks earlier and thought the admiral 'so spoony' while his wife was 'one of the primmest and stiffest of women'. Her husband's behaviour made her blush all the evening, so 'I considerately came away long before 10, knowing well what would happen directly my back was turned.'[80] Mark was charmed. 'Your account of your Admiral and his young wife is in your best manner. I am convinced you ought to write a novel, though you couldn't, in old maidish England, print "knowing so well what would happen" etc.' His wife's brothers, she thought, were 'appallingly selfish and also horribly spoony'.[81]

Returning to London, she went to a party at the home of Mark's artistic friend, Mrs Pfeiffer, but found most of the people there 'old and ugly'. 'We had tea under those trees, and Mr Pfeiffer sang 3 things to his guitar, a woman sang, and Mrs Blind recited "The Sisters", not at all well, and the piece was most unsuitable. One old lady strolled off her young daughters as quickly as politeness permitted ... I overheard one [of the guests] making the broadest possible remark.'[82][1] For all her vaunted unconventionality, Meta's prim spirit was somewhat ill at ease in Bohemian surroundings. When a Mrs Maclean asked her to do a recital, she replied that she confined her performances to Mothers' meetings. She was less taken with her hostess than Mark; she noted that she was not wearing 'her Greek dress' but 'only a plain white garb'. The proceedings seemed curiously reminiscent of Mrs Leo Hunter's soirées.

Mark had returned to Oxford, spending August there in his wife's company. Jane, the only one of his sisters whom Mrs Pattison could long tolerate, spent a few days with her brother: 'estimable, being honest, unpretending, but she is trying; taking no part in what goes on, and, if anyone is there, never speaking the whole evening'. 'She has the way', Mark added, 'which they all have of keeping aloof from all topics of interest, and never desiring to be better acquainted with you.' Jane was en route to Bath to visit her cousin, Philippa Meadows. Philippa had once been close to Mark and a regular correspondent, but she had taken to religion in a big way. She and her

[1] When Meta went to amateur theatricals at St. George's Hall, she could not help observing that the 'comic piece was vulgar, as usual.' It is very sad that even a well dressed audience ... always applauds love making, however badly done. Kissing is invariably followed by clapping. I don't know why'[83]

mother peregrinated from Tractarianism—they had deliberately
moved from Yorkshire to Hursley in Hampshire to take advantage
of Keble's guidance—to Romanism. Philippa Meadows was, in
Mark's opinion, 'a woman of wonderfully strong intellectual powers
gone in for the lowest form of superstition.'[84] Meta remembered that
Mark still possessed piles of letters from Philippa and she 'opined',
one of Meta's favourite verbs, that he was relieved that he had not, as
he had once seemed on the point of doing, followed her example. 'I
don't believe', she added realistically enough, 'you would long have
remained a Catholic . . . The popular theory is that you had made up
your mind to become a R.C. but that you lost a particular train and
next day you'd changed your mind! My own idea is that that religion
would never have suited your character.'[85] Mark was not to be drawn
on this point. It resurrected too many anguished memories, his
devotion to Newman, the spiritual crisis which very nearly led to his
going-over, the withdrawal from the brink and the intense disillusion
which followed. He was not in the mood to discuss his spiritual
history. For he was intent on leaving Oxford and seeking refreshment on the Continent, with his niece Jeannie as his chosen acolyte.

As so often with Mark's journeys, the start was flawed by ill
omens. A bout of headaches and the irritation of the bladder sent
him to seek the advice of Sir Andrew Clark, but Clark was diplo-
matically reassuring, alleging that such symptoms were due only to
gout and could be easily alleviated by a strict diet. So Mark pestered
Meta to buy him various pamphlets on vegetarianism. Then shortly
before Jeannie was due to arrive, to stay with his brother, Frank, at
Burwood Place, the open phaeton in which her sister, Mary was
travelling, was involved in a collision with a horse. Mary sustained a
kick on the back. The doctor confirmed that she was only suffering
from a severe bruise, but Mark was characteristically full of gloom. 'I
don't feel at all equal to the journey, and am not anything like in the
same healthy spirits as I was this time last year. *Nobody* cares or takes
any notice, but the difference to my feeling is great.'[86]

So the journey started. Mrs Pattison was to accompany them as far
as Calais, and then entrain for Paris while Mark, and the faithful
Jeannie, were to travel to Zurich by the night express. They were
fortunate enough to get the last available berths in the sleeping car.
'You can even go through in a sleeping car from Calais to Milan. It

only wants the Channel tunnel to enable me to write "from London to Milan"' 'Next berth to us, 2 girls and their brother, good-natured, laughing, empty, gave us one of their biscuits, I having neglected to lay in a stock of provisions in the belief that we should have, as last year, time in Calais which we hadn't. I said I was Elijah and the 2 girls the ravens! the only poetical allusion I could think of which they could have recognised. Dinner at Tergnier where I paid 3½ fr for impossible horse beef and poisonous soup.' On such journeys he normally ran into one or another of his fellow academics, but the only one he recognized was George Butler, who had been appointed recently to a canonry at Winchester (only worth, Pattison noted—he had an eye for worldly values—some £750 a year with a large house to maintain) who was on his way to join his wife who had gone to Villars for her health.

At Zurich the sun 'potent over the animal spirits all the time' shone and he was 'astonished to find' himself 'not only quite well, but actually better'. They went up the Uetlingberg by the 'climbing railway' and walked back, the lake glittering in the sunlight. He visited the library and examined the collection of Pfahlbauten antiquities in the museum, mainly of pile villages, 'very well-arranged and intelligently shewn'. From Zurich they took the train to Cham on the lake of Zug, supping in the public guest room of the village inn, 'a new experience for Joan [as Mark had now rechristened Jeannie], the inhabitants of the commune assembling, to smoke, drink beer, play cards'. Their rooms were clean if sparsely furnished—only Mark's had an easy chair. As the sun slowly sank in a cloudless sky, he sipped white wine (at 7d an imperial unit) while Joan read to him, and felt at peace with the world.[87]

In England it was wet and cold, so much so that Meta was obliged to light her bedroom fire to get rid of the damp and to dry off her wet things. It was unfortunately a presage of the future on the Continent. Mark and his young companion moved from the lake of Zug to the lake of Lucerne, choosing to stay at Beckenried, a little village on its southern side. 'The water washes the terrace wall, Gersau nearly facing; is across on the other side, a paradise of scenery. Out of the track of the tourists a quiet homely pension where are only Germans, the mild, inoffensive, humble, uninteresting Germans, not the swaggering heroes who go to the great places. The serpent which creeps in this paradise is the mist, stealing down the mountain sides, sure soon to turn to torrents of rain, as it did this morning.'[88]

From Beckenried they drove through the drenching mist in a four wheeler up to the alpine village of Engelberg, some three thousand feet high, where his friends, the Tollemaches, were staying. The weather continued damp and chilly, mist covered the mountains and, though the Tollemaches' rooms were warm and the talk was 'rich', Mark thirsted for the expected sun of the Italian lakes. Momentarily, on his return to the lakeside of Lucerne, the weather shifted and his spirits rose as the steamer made its way through the rugged slopes of the Gulf of Uri en route for a few days at Axenstein 'revelling in sunshine and intoxicating air'.

'Here' [at Axenstein] 'we fell in with various English—2 sisters of the name of Holdship, doing Switzerland cheaply by writing before-hand, and refusing any place which would not accept them "en pension" at 7 francs a day.' They came 'to our inn for the English Church, which they diligently attended both times—we made once'. Then they travelled through the recently opened St Gotthard tunnel, only to be greeted by rain, hail and snow as they made their way down the Val Levantina to Bellinzona and Locarno on Lake Maggiore. A shaft of sunlight burst on them as the boat neared Pallanza, but Milan was shrouded in cloud. Jeannie climbed to the roof of the cathedral while Mark penned a letter to Meta. He was not wholly displeased with Jeannie, but he was unenthusiastic. She had proved so far 'an intelligent companion, and not unworthy of the trouble I take over her. Otherwise, she is no use to me, never does anything for me. I do all, as I have nothing else to do, it is no hard-ship. How I wish it could have been you!'[89] The qualifications were ominous for the future relationship of uncle and niece.

Then it rained incessantly; rivers and lakes rose well above their normal level, vines, mulberries, orchards, and maize were all ruined by the deluge. Roads and bridges collapsed under the weight of water as debris crashed down the mountain sides. Mark and Jeannie arrived at Como to find that the market-place was flooded, so that access to the neighbouring houses could only be made by punt. 'The lake rose to the steps of our hotel, from which we stept, in torrents of rain, to take us off to the steamer. It was a drenching business both for us and the luggage which we feebly protected with our umbrellas, and when we were on board, the boatman demanded 3 francs for a boat already paid for in the bill—you know me too well to think for a moment that he got it.' Verona too was under water and 'we would not have got there if we had wished'. They moved from Bergamo to the lake of Garda, and still the rain poured relentlessly down and thick mist enveloped the dripping mountain sides. All colour disappeared from the most colourful of lakes. A neutral gloom absorbed the whole. 'I will have to come home without the idea of what an Italian lake can be. They might as well have been Highland lochs, and I who came to get sun, have seen less of him that I should have done in England. Then I have not been well a single day since I started. You will not wonder at my being out of spirits. The tour has been a failure, both for my purposes and for Jeannie. All I wish now is to get home, and go to bed. I got hold of a *Times* in Cadenabbia in which I saw that Pusey was failing.'[90][m]

This letter was written from Brescia on 19 September, but some three weeks were to elapse before they were able to return to England. They were to be weeks of acute pain for both of them. The bad weather had caused the Brenner Pass over which they had intended to return home to be closed; the Splugen and the Simplon passes had been similarly affected by damages to bridges and via-ducts. As Mark telegraphed for additional funds to be sent to Bolzano, hoping that the money could be brought from Bolzano to Trent where he was going to stay, he began writing a description of the recent bad weather for *The Times* (which appeared on 24 September). By the time he moved from Desenzano at the southern limit of lake Garda to Trent the weather was improving. He walked along the deep gorge through which the river Felsine made its fierce way, 'hewn down into the untold depths in the bowels of the rock by a pretty Trent maiden'. But as his spirits rose slightly, Jeannie was taken ill by faintness, palpitation, and diarrhoea.

This new development greatly alarmed Mark, always aware of his own precarious state of health and relying on Jeannie to be his support. Instead of being cared for he would have to care for some-one else. It was, to say the least, a most unenviable prospect. His return might be delayed indefinitely. The new term at Oxford was

[m] E. B. Pusey died 21 September 1882.

due to start in early October. The Rector of Lincoln College was stranded with a sick young girl in the South Tirol, isolated by the ravages of weather and the onset of illness from the outside world. Jeannie became hysterical, gasping out to a horrified Mark that she thought she was 'going'. Her conduct seemed to her uncle wholly reprehensible, even if she felt ill. 'As a remedy for the disorder of the bowels, she had ordered herself yesterday a mutton chop and a bottle of beer!'[91] She woke at one in the morning and rapped on Mark's door (he was in an adjoining room), demanding that he should procure a doctor straightway. Mark hedged. Then she asked for food. Gloomily Mark put on his dressing gown and gingerly made his way down to the hotel kitchen where he managed to beat up a raw egg in brandy. 'But no sooner was I laid down . . . than she knocked me up again, and her whims become so unreasonable that I really was afraid she was going off her head. This went on for nearly 4 hours in the dead of night.'[92] At seven the next morning she asked for coffee and a couple of eggs to be sent up, but would not eat them when they arrived. 'It is now clear to me that she has herself aggravated the palpitations by falling back upon herself, and thinking of nothing else.'

Mark's one feverish thought was to escape from this nightmare. 'Imprisoned I am, but not so much by the closing of the Brenner Pass, as by J[eannie]'s illness.' 'The question urgent now is, How and when shall I ever get her home?' 'Everything is topsy turvy here, the railway time tables useless, and the post arriving and departing at unknown hours. Then the impossibility of learning about the distant communications. Up as far as Brixen, and down as far as Vienna one can ascertain the state of the line and the roads; but to ask if the Simplon is open, you might as well ask if the Suez Canal is in working order.' But at least the sun was now shining, the hotel appeared well-managed, 'on the German system, a great addition to comfort, coming from the dirt and the neglect of Italians. Again the neighbourhood of Trent is most picturesque, and the walks various and in fine invigorating air'. Fortunately the other guests at the hotel proved to be modestly congenial: 'a Dr and Mrs Welch—and 2 spinsters travelling together—one Scotch, Miss Scherar, the other English, Miss Darwall, a cousin of our chaplain. They know nothing and know nobody, but notwithstanding are intelligent, and have been everywhere among the Dolomites, and in Italy, and remember with accuracy what they have seen, as they saw it, innocent though they are of the knowledge to be learned from books.'[93]

But it was Jeannie's continued prostration that gnawed at even a comparative happiness. 'I am at my wits end ... you will imagine how low I drop towards evening. This comes of taking a companion. I should have done better to have come alone.'[94] Eventually they got away, travelling once more by the Gotthard route. They spent a day in Lucerne, sunlit but autumnal, before on 11 October, as the term was starting Mark and his niece caught the 4.45 p.m. from Paddington to Oxford. It was a day after his birthday; but there were only cards from his sisters Fanny and Jane and the cigar case which poor Jeannie had purchased in Lucerne.

'So you're safely back, hurrah', Meta wrote at half-past eight on the evening of 12 October at the close of a long letter which she had begun on 1 September but which, for want of an address, she had been unable to send until Mark's return to England. Long as the letter was, its contents reinforced her initial judgement that she had 'nothing to write about. My days slip away in doing odds and ends of things for J[essie], amusing the children, reading to a woman near who is very ill, and getting a little exercise.'[95]

During Mark's absence abroad, Jessie's imminent departure for India was in the forefront of her mind, a mind exercised by all sorts of premonitions. Jessie looked 'very seedy and dreadfully worried. I don't believe she'll last long. C[ourtenay] has no idea of coddling her'; in fact Lady Ilbert did not die until 1924. Meta fussed about the children, for the nursery maid had been taken to a fever hospital with suspected scarlet fever, often a killing disease in the late nineteenth century. 'Lettice and little Jessie look very white, ill and unutterably grumpy.' To add to this the nurse whom Jessie wanted to take to India refused to go as she was about to get married, though on the eve of her marriage she was to be jilted; 'what brutes men can be!'[96] Forty-three boxes and trunks were packed and eventually Jessie and her children, accompanied by the grieving Meta, left for the ship, *Australia*. 'We all started from W[imbledon] at 8.40 on the 11th and were kept waiting hours at Gravesend in the cabin of the tender, as the steamer, instead of coming at 12, never appeared till 3. It was an awful shame and I'd have made a row in the papers had I time. There

were we minus food all those hours and feeling like a man waiting to
be hung in sight of the whole fatal apparatus. Fortunately the
children were good or I don't know how we could have kept up. The
rain was heavy and the whole thing most gloomy. The cabins looked
tiny, poor Jessie.'[97]

Meta was writing from Bewdley in Worcestershire where she was
making the first of her autumn visits, staying with a Mrs Bury whom
she had never before met personally but with whom she had come
into contact through a drawing club which Meta had once managed.
She sought as usual to entertain Mark with pen portraits of her hosts.
'She is about 50 and he over sixty but both look 10 years younger. She
seems a very kind person, has an odd habit of saying Yere for here,
flows on in her conversation rather endlessly, would be nice looking
were it not for black teeth. They are both fairly cultivated in art, have
a not very good Canaletto, two remarkable Dutch drawings, some
very valuable China. She has still more knowledge of music. Both of
them draw better than most. She has a certain amount of literary
knowledge, more than I expect to find in a remote place in a woman
of 50. He has a horrid habit of laughing, is a simple minded old
fellow, enjoys an obvious joke, feels rather important as a magistrate,
and has a slight rotundity of figure which so adds to dignity.'[98] She
became, however, somewhat bored as the incessant rain poured
down, and conversation fastened on domestic problems and the
numerous cats who roamed the house.

From Bewdley Meta moved to stay again with the Tomkinsons at
Willington Hall near Tarporley in Cheshire. Jim Tomkinson was a
wealthy Liberal with political ambitions.[n] His wife was a firm
supporter of the temperance movement. She had met them when she
was staying with her sister, Jessie, at 17 Hill Side, Wimbledon when
they came to play tennis and stayed to dinner. 'He is 42 but feels like
22 and I should like him much were he that age. He strikes me as
being enthusiastic about politics—is full of interesting information
on the Irish question. Both he and his wife have connections among

[n] James Tomkinson (1840–1910) contested W. Cheshire as a Liberal in 1881, the
Wirral division in 1885 and after several more efforts was eventually elected MP for
Crewe in 1900. He was married in 1871 to Emily Francis, daughter of Sir George Palmer,
baronet of Wanlys Hall. Apart from Willington Hall, Tarporley, he had a house at
Cromer and a London residence at 17 Bolton Street.

the Liberals. She is ... rather clever, very bright and has been the making of him.' They took Meta to visit Chester which she found 'singularly picturesque', even if she 'did not fall in love with the cathedral'. On their way back to Tarporley they gave a lift to a 'man who lives in Liverpool and is something in cotton, not a gentleman but quite presentable, very heavy face, square and ugly but intelligent. He also is a thoroughgoing Liberal. Like the others I meet he thinks Chamberlain and Dilke the coming men, thinks Dilke quite the cleverest but doubts about his bodily strength.'[99]

The allusion to Dilke might conceivably have raised a wry smile on Mark's part. It would have been fair to say that to find his wife still in residence at Oxford on his return from abroad was almost the crowning catastrophe in a catastrophic vacation. 'I have for 7 years past returned to have the house to myself from October to May. Now she is here; and her greeting, if it can be called one, was sufficiently repulsive. I felt a hatred for my home, and an impulse to rush to my solitary lodging in London. However yesterday, she came round, and whether stimulating cordiality or not I can't say, she has been not only gracious, but even sympathetic and I am more comfortable today, so dependent as I am on those I live with!'[100] She used her influence with Dilke to procure a Fishmongers' Exhibition, tenable at Oxford, for a Lincoln undergraduate; and Mark felt obliged to accept an invitation to dine with the great man.

The armistice was not, however, of long duration. Mark compared his wife's presence unfavourably with the company of the young girls who normally stayed at the Lodgings in the autumn. 'Now by Her being at home, that is cut off, and there are no more nice evening reads.' Mrs Pattison commented that on his return her husband 'would not speak to me nor even take my hand!' He was agonized by having to sit night after night through a three-course dinner. As always he may have engaged in some palpable exaggeration, for, in spite of her ordeal, Jeannie Stirke was still there, and read the newspaper in the drawing-room after dinner, Mrs Pattison making comments, 'very good these', Mark grudgingly admitted. 'Then langour and mutual aversion reigns for $\frac{1}{2}$ hour, till I escape downstairs to smoke.'[101]

Meta, pertinacious, grasped at Mark's reference to his wife's greater friendliness and raised again the possibility of her being

invited to Lincoln. That, said Mark, was a false hope and even if it
were not so it would be more than embarrassing to meet her in his
wife's presence. 'It is that look which comes into your face, whenever
it is turned towards me. It is to me the dearest look, as it speaks of the
truest love and devotion. But it is a look which the world, and the
women, cannot tolerate, would not tolerate, even if I were not a
married man. It is no use your saying you won't put it on; you can't
help it . . . So that your coming to Lincoln would only confirm Her
and everybody in their prejudice against you . . . She simply hates
me, and wishes me dead, is quite impatient at my dying so slowly. All
this while she poses as a martyr to my ill-humour, i.e. staying in
England, to the ruin of her health, solely that she may look after me,
is giving me all she can, except sacrificing her life . . . And I am glad of
any excuse to come up to town to escape the misery of my home!'[102]
Mark seemed caught inexorably in a Catch 22 situation out of which
he could only reap bleakness and desolation.

    Although Jeannie, or Joan, as he preferred to call her, was still at
the Lodgings, the experience of their unfortunate holiday still
rankled, even though on 20 October he could declare that the 'dear
child really seemed to want love, and I gave her what I could'. More
and more he missed the solace which Meta's presence at Oxford had
brought him two years ago. 'I think of those months when my every
thought was divined, and every wish, even those I didn't know of
myself, anticipated.'[103] Meta's thoughts travelled exactly along the
same lines. She had returned to Orsett Terrace to celebrate her birthday, though unremembered by her parents, on 9 November. 'I've
been going back all day to the blissful one in '80. How happy we or I
were. As you say, it never can come again. I am exactly 40 years
younger than you . . .'

    In spite of the recent reservations which he had voiced, prompted
by the realization that it must be now or never, Mark, incautiously,
raised with his wife the possibility of inviting Meta to Oxford. He
met with an instant rebuff. 'She is willing to invite you, on conditions
which I dare not accept for you.' It is not clear what were the conditions. But Mrs Pattison, a sophisticated and cultured woman,
concluded evidently that Meta was a designing hussy. Meta had left,
Mark told her, 'a very unfavourable impression upon her when she
met you at the Winkworths as did Mrs Ilbert, but then you see She

was predetermined to put a bad construction on all you said or did'.[104]

That was not, however, the end of the matter. Worse, much worse was to come. Spurred on by her husband's remonstrance, which demonstrated his deep-seated affection for Meta, she determined to try to break off or at least reduce the correspondence. She wrote to the Dean's wife, Mrs Granville Bradley, 'very indignant at the idea of my ever being in their house. She should feel disgraced and insulted, that you were always bringing up my devotion, could nothing be done to stop this hateful correspondence between us'.[105] She sent copies of a card written by Meta to Mark to the Bradleys at Westminster and threatened to send another to Meta's father. Mark thought that Mabel Bradley, Meta's cousin from whom Meta had obtained some of her information, had exaggerated the degree of malice displayed by Mrs Pattison. She had told Mark himself, he told Meta, 'and I do not doubt, truthfully, what she *did* say. Nothing of the kind that you report to me ... the misrepresentation was total. What she wrote to Mrs Granville Bradley was the same she had said to me, and which I reported to you'.[106]

Whatever the accuracy of the reports,—and Mark's comments to Meta were themselves somewhat brutal—'the truth is, you adopt such a suspicious attitude of mind, that you don't report what you hear in this business with your habitual accuracy', the embers of what in the summer had seemed a dying fire were stirred again. Charles Bradley was predictably very angry. He told Meta that he would forbid the correspondence altogether. 'He said I must not be surprised to find myself a beggar at his death.' Mark remonstrated that the letters were so harmless in content that they could reasonably be read by a third person. But Charles Bradley had had enough. Meta once again voiced the possibility of leaving home. 'It may all end in my leaving the house, and I don't see that I should be much worse off if I do. I can earn as much as other women, I suppose.'[107]

Mark's own reaction to this new crisis in their lives was strangely mute, though he admitted to being [on 19 November] 'dreadfully disturbed' by the letter which Charles Bradley had sent him. Everything seemed conspiring against his comfort. 'I am having a deal too much of people this term', he wrote of College affairs, 'my soul is being vulgarised, and my locks shorn—my mornings are too often broken in upon by business. T. Fowler's departure [to the presidency of Corpus] has thrown upon me much which he used to do.'[108] His wife's influence was all-pervasive, so that the study was the only place to which he could escape. '*She* has come forward this year, and voluntarily undertaken the management of House and servants, including the man [this was the new male servant, replacing the careless Hans, 'clever and adroit, but scamps his work, and a worse fault, viz., is too fond of beer']. She pays the wages, issues all orders, and administers the reproofs. I never interfere, and consequently much is done I don't like, and my fancies are not provided.' He was wearied by long dinners, wasted evenings, Thursday receptions from 8.30 to 10.30. 'I must appear in the drawing room for at least an hour, unless I should give myself the appearance of avoiding her, that being the only hour of the day at which we meet at all.'[109]

And now on top of all this was a new crisis. If his affection for Meta was strong, he always considered every problem first from his own point of view. He was terrified by the implications of a public scandal which could not be avoided if she carried out her threat to leave home. 'Only think of the esclandre that would arise upon such a feat on your part! And if you have no pity upon yourself, have a little for me! Think of the *coup de grâce* it would be to my quiet in my old age, if it were known you had left your father's roof on my account ... You have put yourself very seriously in the wrong by telling him, you had rather give him up than me.'[110]

Meta retorted that Mark had misunderstood her conversation with her father. 'I never should have been so unkind or foolish to have volunteered that I'd rather give him up than you. It was last May that he *forced* me to answer his question "If I said 'Give up writing to the Rector or leave my house' which should you do?" and I *had* to say that only a written request from your wife would make me cease writing. That he said meant that I cared most for you and of course I could not deny it.'[111]

Sandwiched between her father who was determined to bring the liaison, however innocent, to an end, and her lover, made too nervous by the possibility of public scandal to offer fight, Meta could only acquiesce. She would not, however, go down without spirit. When her father asked her, in the presence of her stepmother and

'Grannie', whether parents should give their daughters free board and clothes after they had reached the age of 22 or 23 as a *duty* or as a *pleasure*, she replied that it was a duty 'unless from her youth the girl had been told that she would have to work for herself and had been given a first rate education to enable her to do so comfortably ... Then he said "Then you don't feel grateful for my keeping you?" I of course couldn't say I did, though I added that I was grateful for lots of things, though not for mere board and clothing! He said I ought to be deeply grateful that I had not been commanded to accept some horrid clerkship on the railway when I was old enough ... Any other girl would have flounced out of the room in a passion, or cried, while I was quite civil and calm. As if his threatening to leave me no money could make me love him. I may have wept my eyes out but I still did not lose my temper.'[112]

The episode had made Mark very apprehensive. He was fond of Meta but his love was now passive rather than passionate. He did not love his wife, but he shivered at the prospect of a scandal. Moreover in the last resort it was to his wife that he would have to turn for his creature comforts. She had apparently detected, so at least she told Ellen Smith, that he seemed a little mellower, and was seeming to seek a better relationship during her stay in England during the autumn. Nor, for all his readiness to support movements for female liberation, would he really countenance open rebellion towards parents. He tried to justify his attitude by arguing that he had Meta's best interests at heart. Since she had no money and no skills, she simply could not leave home. Since she was a gentlewoman by birth, the number of jobs open to her was limited. He wrote to Meta in what, had she not been already very familiar with his rancorous style, might well have seemed harsh language. She would have to abide by her father's wishes. Charles Bradley had in fact written to the Rector, asking him to stop the correspondence and Mark had replied without bitterness 'distantly dignified, while not concealing what a cruel blow this is to me ... I had to submit to the inhibition but in such a way as not to give an absolute promise, never under any circumstances, to write to you again'.

'Dearest Meta', he sighed, 'we must submit for the present. All the world would say I was in the wrong if I did not obey, and you too. You must conform to his wishes. And what I want you to do is to conform cheerfully, and honourably, and instead of crying to begin a new life, to try to find your satisfaction in patiently doing your duty in the sphere open [to] you, whether that at home, or the new duties you have opened up, by your own energy, beyond your home. A very few years will see me dust, but go out into the world, and look round for younger and more vigorous spirits ... Courage dearest! It is harder for me than for you; at my age one cannot hope to form new friendships, but you will have many opportunities, find some man you can esteem, if not love ... Things will take a turn, who knows how soon! and I may be able, blamelessly, to write to you again, or even to kiss your dear cheek as I do now in dumb show. Bless you my own heart!'[113] It was doubtless well-meant, heart-meant, but it was craven and cowardly, explicable only in terms of Mark's own weariness and fading love. Even so, in the circumstances of their lives and the society in which they lived, they may well have felt justifiably that they had no other option.

Even Meta appeared to have been convinced that this was so. 'God only can know how almost unbearable this trial is and will be as long as it lasts ... Thank heaven we have never had a shadow of misunderstanding ever. I need not say another word. You know all I would say and how deeply grateful I am for all you have been to me ever since I knew you.'[114] So the pens were laid aside, and the postman ceased to bear their letters. Mark's life reverted to its routine, working without enthusiasm at the biography of Scaliger, attending meetings of the Bodleian curators and the Lawn Tennis Club; and in the evenings in the dim lamplight Jeannie read W. D. Howell's *The Undiscovered Country*. 'How is it', Mark commented after hearing it, 'that a man who can write a capital story, gets down so low as this unreadable rubbish.' The meetings with Meta and her long garrulous letters seemed simply a pleasant dream in the desert of his existence which had reverted, bereft of her soothing existence, to normality. One concrete thing he did. Towards the end of the year 1882, tired and ill, the Rector decided to add a codicil to his will, substituting a legacy of £5,000 for the benefaction he had earlier earmarked for her. In the circumstances it was perhaps the least he could reasonably do.

V

1883

WHEN his father ordered the young Edward Gibbon to abandon his courtship of Suzanne Curchod, he, it will be recalled, 'sighed like a lover but obeyed like a son.' Meta Bradley sighed deeply and desperately but she too obeyed like a daughter. Sighing, we may say, had become Mark Pattison's professional avocation, yet if at best life seemed a melancholy business, it was at the same time never wholly devoid of pleasurable sensations, the learned escape into the world of literature and philosophy, the occasional companionship of congenial people. And at its worst it was always preferable to the nihilism of death, death which like a triumphant athlete seemed daily to be gaining round. Meta had consoled his lonely spirit. She had comforted and soothed his wounded heart, albeit so many of the wounds were, as his wife correctly diagnosed, self-inflicted. She had sustained his inner vanity. He regarded her still with the deepest affection. But it could not be the passionate love, the limitless infatuation, of youth. He was too old, too self-regarding, too jaded, too remote. If there had been momentarily a strong desire for physical intimacy, age and distance brought some diminution of feeling.

His heartache for the separation so callously imposed by the redoubtable Charles Bradley would be less intense than that which Meta experienced. Meta was more like the daughter that he had never had than the wife he really wanted. Yet for Meta, withered and desiccated as Mark appeared, he was evidently something more than a mere father substitute. To call him her lover would be a misuse of language; but he was a kindred soul whom she found she could cherish as well as admire. He was the master, she the adoring disciple; it was a relationship which both of them wanted. He would remain for ever an image in her mind, the last romance of her life. She knew, given the forty years generation gap and the ill-health which Mark enjoyed, that there was an upper time limit to their relationship. Over it there was, as both them well realized, a lengthening shadow. If only because of the ration of time, the probable fracture in their relationship brought to her the greater grief. She carried on, though without her letters we do not know exactly what she did, the dull routine of her life in the company of an angry and ailing father in the tall house in Orsett Terrace.

Mark's life for the period of separation is the better documented. Between the end of November 1882 and April 1883 it too, however, seems at least on the surface to follow a well-trodden routine; the onerous round of College business lightened only by the College's decision to dispense henceforth with the annual audit day on 22 December 'one of the most wearisome in the whole year—thank God! a day thus added to my life'; attendance at learned societies in London and Oxford.[1] 'Jowett', he wrote on 16 February 1883 of a meeting of the Delegates of the Oxford University Press, 'proposed his scheme of Greek texts, the prospectus, a most unscholarly document . . . the conversation which ensued showed that you may be Regius Professor of Greek without knowing the most elementary conditions of the formation of the Greek text. But all the Delegacy are in such terror of the Vice Chancellor that they held their tongues and allowed me to go into the breach alone.'[2] Characteristically he believed that he had been deliberately punished for his stand by 'Jowett's myrmidons, Max Müller especially', by their refusing to consider for publication his Lincoln friend and pupil Althaus's edition of Schiller.

Earlier in February he had been greatly shocked by the death, at the early age of 56, of one of his few intimate Oxford friends, Ellen's brother, the mathematician Henry Smith, the Savilian Professor of Geometry. Smith was as brilliant as he was attractive. 'The most accomplished man', Pattison so described him, 'in the whole University—at once scientific and literary. 20 M.A.s—any 20—might have been taken, without making such a gap in the mind of the place . . . to me it is an irreparable loss.'[3] It was a verdict re-echoed by all his contemporaries. 'Among the world's celebrities it would be difficult', Lord Bowen commented, 'to find one who in gifts and nature was his superior.' 'One of the ablest men I ever met with', was Huxley's opinion, 'and the effect of his great powers was almost whimsically exaggerated by his extreme gentleness of manner and the playful way

in which his epigrams were scattered about. I think that he would
have been one of the greatest men of our time if he had added to his
wonderfully keen intellect and strangely varied and extensive knowledge the power of caring very strongly about the attainment of any
object.'

Henry Smith was more self-evidently Pattison's supporter than
his capable sister, Ellen, with whom he had lived since their mother
died in 1857. He was almost as good a classical scholar as a mathematician. He was a Liberal in politics, and had fought for a University seat in Parliament at the general election of 1878. The previous
year he had become one of the members of the Royal Commission
set up to investigate the University; at his nomination Sir Mount-
stuart Grant Duff alluded not merely to his 'very extraordinary
attainments' but also to his 'conciliatory character' which 'made him
perhaps the only man in Oxford who was without an enemy'.
Pattison felt his loss intensely, so much so that he took tea with Mrs
Percival so that he could talk about his dead friend, 'sympathetic to
the utmost limit of her nature, but so limited!'[4] His death at an early
age was to Pattison another unwelcome reminder of the common
enemy.

The Lodgings seemed less like a home than a cell, for Mrs Pattison
was still in Oxford. They preserved a screen of harmony; she accompanied him on his walks round the Parks. Jeannie Stirke went home
for Christmas—her sister Mary had not yet recovered fully from the
horse's kick—but returned, making the evenings less tedious by reading to him. On 1 February Helen Colvill came to stay, but the visit
was hardly a success. Her shyness and brusquesness grated, even if
she read poetry to him, and even tried her hand at Greek. 'Helen
Colvill is a failure ... She shirks me and shirks talking ... All her
faults, rudeness, abruptness of speech, secretiveness have gained on
her since I last saw her, hardened probably by the crushed life she
leads at home.'[5] Without Meta to boost her morale, Helen was petri-
fied by her host. Once more he found his hopes of a young friend
frustrated. The orange proved to have no juice, the flower never
blossomed. This had happened so many times in his life.

In the Spring 1883, on Sunday 4 March to be precise, Jeannie
Stirke began reading Rhoda Broughton's newly published novel,
Belinda, to him as they sat at lunch. Since the episode of the

anonymous letter, his relations with Rhoda had cooled, though in late October he had travelled up to London with his wife in her company, evoking the comment from Meta, 'So you came up with Rhoda! Has she then forgiven you? It will be a slight relief to me to hear that she is fairly pleasant to you again as I hated to have been even the remote cause of any of your amusements being curtailed, and she certainly did amuse you.'[6] Although on occasions he found Rhoda exasperating, yet Meta was right; Rhoda entertained him and still came round to the Lodgings to read German literature. But Rhoda had not forgotten or forgiven. She was a novelist by profession, if one of secondary rank, and she had the novelist's prospensity for memorizing the more idiosyncratic characteristics of her acquaintances and protraying them in her books. For such treatment Pattison was fair game. Mrs Humphry Ward, who knew him and Francis well, was to paint a vivid picture of him as Squire Wendover in *Robert Elsmere*.[a] George Eliot had very conceivably utilized some of his features in her portrait of Dr Casaubon in *Middlemarch*.[8]

There was no doubt whatsoever that Rhoda Broughton made him a central figure, forbidding and unattractive, in *Belinda*. She had not forgotten Miss Laffan's unfortunate *démarche*. Vindictively Professor Forth was Mark Pattison in a distorting mirror. He was portrayed as a desiccated pedant 'whose contempt for undergraduates in general is not to be equalled save by his aversion'; 'a slovenly middle-aged figure, clerical, if you judge by its coat; scholarly, if you decide by its spectacles.' The story told of two sisters, the younger of whom, Sarah, was a gay and nonchalant girl who had been originally engaged to Professor Forth but had broken off the engagement. Her elder sister, Belinda, was more serious-minded. She was an aloof and studious girl who had been engaged to one David Rivers, but David, worried by his father's bankruptcy, had

---

[a] Mrs Ward's description of Squire Wendover recalled Pattison's appearance forcibly: 'Mr Wendover was a man of middle height and loose bony frame ... all the lower half had a thin and shrunken look. But the shoulders, which had the scholar's stoop and the head were massive and squarely outlined ... The hair was reddish-grey, the eyes small but deep-set under fine brows, and the thin-lipped wrinkled mouth and long chin had a look of hard sarcastic strength. Generally the countenance was that of an old man, the furrows were deep, the skin brown and shrivelled. But the alertness and force of the man's whole expression showed that, if the body was beginning to fail, the mind was as fresh and masterful as ever.'[7] Compare John Sparrow's comment that Mrs Ward 'left the fullest and most sympathetic presentation of Pattison that has come down to us.' (*Idea of a University*, p. 22).

allowed his relationship with Belinda to cool. In reaction Belinda took to study under Professor James Forth. Forth fell in love and Belinda accepted his proposal. Thus far the novel might seem fairly remote from Pattison's own life story.

Yet Forth's marriage, which took place on 10 January (Pattison's, it will be recalled, was on 10 September), to Belinda bore an uneasy resemblance to Pattison's own. In his treatment of Belinda, her husband was inconsiderate, mean and pedantic. He was a hypochondriac oblivious of everyone's comfort save his own. 'The press of my occupations', Professor Forth tells his wife, 'and the condition of my health forbid my indulging in many amusements and enjoyments enjoyed by other persons, but from which I shall be compelled to require you as well as myself to abstain.' 'You forget', Belinda tells him, 'that I am young. If you had married a wife of your own age, it would have been different; but you must remember that I am at the beginning of life, and you at the end.' 'Is this', she asks herself, 'the man whose *mind* I have married? . . . this, whose soul is occupied by mean parsimonies, and economies of cheese-rinds and candle-ends?' She had learned, to her anguish, that the silence of Rivers, her former lover, had been motivated by his love for her, and that to try to recoup his shattered fortunes he had taken a job as a common labourer. Her love for him revived. She decided that she would leave her husband for her lover, but she was so troubled by her conscience that she returned before completing her journey, only to find that the professor had died before he knew that she had left him.

That Professor Forth was deliberately based on Pattison can hardly be doubted. '"I cannot see that there is any apology for a systematic neglect of all the more serious duties of life", he replied fretfully. . . . ill-humour rendering yet more pinched and captious his pinched pedant face. "I know", Belinda said, "I am not more than very moderately bright." "You have a good average intelligence", he answers drily, "it would be flattery to imply that you have more."' Such conversations surely took place between Pattison and Meta Bradley in the Lodgings on more than one occasion. The pursuit of learning was the pre-eminent object in Professor Forth's life. 'You must be aware that the whole tendency of my teaching is to show that the pursuit of knowledge is the only one that really and abundantly rewards the labour bestowed upon it.'

The book was replete with details which could only have come from a close observation of the Rector's habits. His meanness is stressed; he omits, for instance, several works of reference from his baggage because he will not pay the excess fare. He prefers to travel abroad by himself. He is the centre of a salon of admiring young ladies. 'You should have seen how they all sat at his feet', Sarah recalled, 'and hung on his words.' He met Belinda at the National Gallery, one of Pattison's favourite meeting-places for Meta. He dislikes the smell of flowers. Pattison would not have cut flowers in the house. He keeps the windows tightly closed. 'There is no doubt', Pattison told Meta later, 'that Professor Forth is meant for a degrading caricature of me—some superficial traits, leaving all that makes character and gives worth.'⁹

Pattison's comparatively mild reaction to what he might well have construed as a maleficent satire was surprising. He did not break off his outwardly friendly relations with Rhoda. When he called at her home on 30 April 1883 he had himself announced as 'Professor Forth'. 'Protests from her that she did not mean it—but!'¹⁰ In June Jeannie would again read the novel aloud to him in the evenings. Perhaps the portrait appealed to his sardonic sense of humour. Rhoda's own respect for him had been irretrivably lost by the episode of the anonymous letter, and by her own innate sympathy for Mrs Pattison. After the Rector's death she told his former pupil, Theodore Althaus, who had written a favourable portrait of his old master in *Temple Bar*, that 'your description of his appearance was a little over-coloured by friendship'.

As soon as the Hilary term at Oxford ended, Pattison decided to go abroad. May Laffan tried to induce him to join her in Sicily. Whether he or she thought that this was a serious project may be doubted, but she relished the idea. 'I *wish* we were going together to Palermo. In *her* last she [i.e. Mrs Pattison] spoke of your going south. I fancied and *hoped* you were going to her, poor dear puss. It would be so good to go along with you and take care of you. I would not be either fast or rollicky and I am a first-rate nurse, but its no use, dear. You know right well and you will have to mope off by yourself. *It would not be allowed* . . . unless you took me on the sly. Could that be done? I fear not. I'd give all the world to go with you, but, would it be safe? . . . Oh, to *talk* to you though, dear. What a murdering pity we cant go off into the South together.' Much as Mark liked Miss Laffan, her personality was too strong for her to be his ideal companion. She wondered whether she might meet him in Paris. 'What concern is it of anybody's that I go over to Paris and when there take the train for Marseilles or Lyons? Only we are not going to do *it* since you have made up your mind that I am too heady for you—you are a dear old goose.'[11] So to Paris Mark went, strolling in the sun 'without the drag of knowing that every hour of the day is appropriated to some wearisome engagement'. Then he moved to the south-west, visiting Nantes and La Rochelle, the château de Toufflon, Chauvigny, Chatelerault and Châtillon-sur-Indre before he returned to London on 12 April. While he was away one of the major barriers to his relationship with Meta had been at last removed through the death of her father, Charles Bradley.

Charles Bradley, who had been in failing health for some time, was by March 1883 in the throes of death. Death-beds had a peculiar attraction for the Victorians. Freed from the rotund phraseology with which the Georgians so complacently decked their memorial tablets, the Victorians tended to indulge in an orgy of sentiment. The onset of death, the protracted suffering, the incipient decay, the penitential solemnities, the unctions of religious faith, were memorialized by the friends and relatives of the deceased. Both Charles's brother, the Dean of Westminster, and Meta, have left detailed descriptions of his last days. 'Dear Charles', Granville wrote to Jessie on 3 April, 'had been ailing for some time; he took to his bed from 3 to 4 weeks before the end; but I was only anxious, not alarmed. Yesterday fortnight (Monday in Passion week) I went at 8.30 a.m. to ask Sir Andrew Clark about him. He looked very grave and said it was an infection of [the] liver region from which he could not recover, but that he might live a *year* or more. From that time I saw him daily . . . [grow] weaker. He was always rejoiced to see me. On that Monday when he said *if* I get well, I took his hand which I was holding and kissed it. He knew what it meant . . . He clearly got weaker though without pain and was always quite himself, talked cheerfully of all his concerns, *yours*, mine, Mimi's, the abbey, everything. On Good Friday I got up after preaching twice and met Jenner there. He confirmed Clark's diagnosis; said that "tapping" his side might give relief not cure. So I told dear Charles this last, and saw that he did not wish it ... I saw him of course everyday till the end. On the Wednesday he was very weak and very *tired*: extreme weariness was his main sensation; but he was perfectly clear; discussed a text in St. John; told me about his funeral etc. Talked of you Courtenay, Annie, Jack and Mimi—and said now send Annie to wash my mouth—goodbye, goodbye. I though him dying as he closed his eyes and looked like death, but he was not in pain. I kissed his hand and arm, as it lay on the pillow, blessed and thanked him and went to howl in his den. Then to Kensal Green to choose his grave. I thought it better for Annie to leave her alone with him; though I longed to stay. The Nurse was excellent. Meta most tender and attentive. He died the next morning.—We buried him yesterday ... The loss to you! the blank to me! but I would not or scarcely would bring him back unless to full health. Cheer up dear Jess. If he has passed away he is gone in full calmness, resignation and trust with little pain, surrounded by love; full of it himself, and oh how deeply lamented!'[12]

Another friend of Jessie's, Emma Bull of Elmhurst, sought to reassure her that she must not regret her own departure for India just before the critical time. 'He would have been the first to bid you look up and believe that it is not a blind chance that rules our lives. He did not talk much of the future life. What he said was just like himself "That land to which I am going, I don't know much about it. No one does I think but I think it is a land of peace, of peace and rest, I feel sure and of foregiveness, I hope!" I said "And of love". "*Certainly*", he said, "surely forgiveness *means* love." But it was clear to me he did not give himself much thought about it—to have won to the end of his pilgrimage and feel he had done his duty, and stuck to his post, was the great thing, the rest he clearly left in faith to the Master he had served. It was this which seemed to me so noble and so like himself.'[13]

Such encomiums were edifying but there was a darker side. Meta's attentions to her father, even if she had been slow in realizing his dangerous condition, were, the Dean admitted, quite admirable, 'all that was loving in good time'. That this was the case is plain from the long letter which she scrawled in his last days to her sister. He played his last game of backgammon with his wife on Good Friday. On Easter Sunday she asked her father if he had any message she could give Jessie. He replied 'Jessie knows my heart as well as anyone. I wrote to her some days ago, and to Charley.' He exclaimed: 'It is Easter Sunday—a beautiful day to go. What a Sunday I shall have! To go on Easter Sunday full of Easter hope. I hope you will do the same some day.' Meta played his favourite hymn tunes, and he dozed off murmuring the words. He rallied somewhat on Easter Monday and saw friends and relatives. The next day, a Tuesday, he summoned his solicitor, George Lake and, Meta reported to her sister, 'signed a codicil making straight some slight muddle concerning me, he told me'. Mary Toynbee and Emily acted as witnesses. Meta sponged his eyes and lips, made his head fragrant with eau-de-cologne and read out Jessie's last letter. Then he read the Indian news in *The Times*, the last thing he perused. 'He sent me down for that sheet and made me light him one of the candles in your candlesticks.' Although his limbs were now so swollen that he could hardly move, and his lips so parched that he could barely speak, his mind remained clear. 'Make her good', 'Send her away' he said to Meta.[14] Eventually he relapsed into unconsciousness, and died painlessly and peacefully at 10.30 a.m. on 29 March 1883. 'I have written', Meta told Jessie, 'for a cross for you ... I have ordered a wreath for the children to give him with their own money and some Star of Bethelem and azalias for them I have put inside near his face. Transom sent lots of camellias, which cover a great part of him and I have placed just on his throat a bunch of violets from the garden of your house.'

What Meta had not realized was that the 'slight muddle concerning me' was intended virtually to disinherit her. The codicil which her father had dictated shortly before his death reduced Meta's annuity to a mere £50 a year, which would be increased to £150 a year on his wife's death. Furthermore, in a note which he pencilled at 4.30 p.m. on the Wednesday before his death, he bequeathed two gold watches to Courtenay and Jessie, adding that 'Jessie was her own mother's daughter and also her father's too', and a silver watch to one of Taffy's children [was that a reference to Charley?], but there was nothing for Meta. 'Meta must be content with my forgiveness which she has fully and will some day feel she needs. She it is that has crushed me.'[15] It is difficult not to feel that there was an element of the sanctimonious in Charles Bradley's last hours. The basilisk had not lost its venom. Until Mrs Bradley died, Meta would still have to depend upon her goodwill for board and lodging. Unless Meta married, her wings were clipped effectively for all time. She must be brought to feel a sense of guilt. Charles Bradley stressed his affection and his forgiveness to show how much he felt she had erred in her duty to a loving father whom she had not properly understood. 'No doubt', as the Dean expressed it, 'her affairs cost him 1000 fold more suffering than years.'[16]

The root of the matter was her relationship with Mark, and the fear that her father and other relatives had that her father's death might lead to its renewal. 'She will, I certainly trust', Granville Bradley told Jessie, 'have no more to do with Mark Pattison who is I fear far too selfish to enter into her position.'[17] Meta lacked 'tact and insight into other people's feelings'. From Elmhurst Mrs Bull reported [on 7 June] to Jessie that she felt that Meta was not as forthcoming as she might be. She had 'already been made anxious'. 'At that sad time in April I did everything possible to show my affection for her, and I implored her both then and afterwards to come to me and talk over the past and future, hoping that then, when her heart was softened by all that has passed, I might be of use to her. Since then I have written, done all I can to shew my love for her and sympathy for her, and her letters are always affectionate and loving and as if she tried to be expansive but there is a tone about them which, I know not why, makes me unhappy and anxious, and now that you say she writes only commonplaces to you, I am doubly so, for it seems to me she has not *one* real friend, and my fear is that the Rector has cast to the winds promises and all besides and is getting hold of her again. On him I won't waste words, but I do long to save her.'[18]

How to save Meta? The writer argued strongly that Jessie should invite Meta out to India, and that her sister should, to express it crudely, exploit Meta's affection for her. 'She would feel she was doing something for you, and was not centred in herself, and her affection would be drawn out by the children.' She doubted whether Meta could live in any degree of amity with her stepmother. 'Whether she and A[nnie] will ever live happily together I have always doubted, and doubt still more now.' The Dean shared Mrs Bull's fears—'I tremble for her future poor dear girl'—but thought little of the projected Indian trip: 'she will with the best intentions be a tax on you'. Perhaps social work was the answer. 'Meta works *very* hard and is thoroughly well and usefully employed, not only in secretarial work, but in really looking after the poor.'[19]

Perhaps the Dean had an over-optimistic view. In fact Meta was confused, puzzled, and uncertain. Momentarily shaken by her father's death, ultimately it can only have been a relief. 'I don't believe', she was to recall, 'I could have borne the absolute silence much longer.'[20] Although Mark and Meta were still seldom to meet, Charles Bradley had been the principle obstacle to the continuance of their relationship. The correspondence at least could be resumed at its previous level, even if it superficially was now to be informative rather than deeply affectionate. Yet the mutual love which had brought them together in such strange harmony was partially re-fuelled by the letters which, at least on Meta's part, were now to pass almost daily between them.

Mark was immensely relieved by the turn of events. 'I don't suppose', he commented at the start of his summer trip to Yorkshire, 'confidence was ever more perfect between any two people than it is between us, though 40 years of life comes between us. It was entirely your doing. You conquered me. I should never have dreamed of setting myself to acquire your friendship as an equal. I should have continued to regard myself as in the paternal relation in which I stand to Joan and others.'[21] 'Yes', Meta replied the next day, 'I shall never cease to wonder over our strange and perfect friendship. If the ins and outs thereof could ever be known and understood by others, how much more interesting they would find it than any that I can come across in books! I never could have thought that such a difference of age would be as nothing, not the slightest bar to absolutely entire confidence. I have two feelings about it, one that it is so beautiful that all the world ought to know of it, another that it is too sacred for any one else to know of it.'[22]

Mark had been in Paris when he learned of Charles Bradley's death and the terms of the will, 'the cruel iniquity of your father's disposition of what he had to leave', first from Jeannie Stirke, then from Meta herself. He was appalled. 'I am so stunned not by the intelligence of the death, but by the cruelty with which you are treated, that I don't seem able to say anything rational, but keep crying out, "What will she do"-?' 'The best thing you can do is to marry an old man! . . . Dearest! what anxiety you must have had.'[23]

'Dearest! As long as I live, though that can't be long, you must remember that you have one friend, all whose thoughts turn towards you, and who whatever comes before him involuntarily asks himself what Meta would think of it!'[24]

He returned home, staying the night at his rooms in 12 Norris Street, Haymarket, so that on the following day, 13 April, after the lapse of so many months he might see Meta again; later Mrs Pattison scrawled out the note he made of his intention in his diary. Meta, by and large, took her fate philosophically. Although she realized that during her stepmother's lifetime she would be dependent on her goodwill, she hoped at Mrs Bradley's death, or unlikely re-marriage, for a larger and adequate annuity which would enable her to live an independent life. Although life with Annie Bradley was bound to be irksome, she could at least look forward to a round of visits, and her voluntary social work would absorb her energies. 'I should have thought', Mark observed a trifle sardonically, 'all this sanitary occupation could have been sufficient to have diverted your thoughts in a healthier channel.'[25]

Meta wondered whether she might spend some of her capital to get some enjoyment out of life while she was still young rather than wait for a decade or more for a better income. 'I am seriously think-ing of using the capital [of the settlement money] by degrees. You see £50 a year is not enough for me, and I would much rather have £100 a year for the next 12 years, supposing Mrs Bradley lives so long, and then make £150 suffice me after her death. That would be more sensible, I think, don't you, than being extremely uncomfortable from 30 to 40 for the sake of another £50 a year. Hitherto I have had from £35 to £40 a year for clothes and washing and cabs, everything in fact save travelling doctor and dentist. But there are lots of things which I must now pay for which I can't ask Mrs B[radley] to settle . . . I also mean to enjoy myself in the way of operas and theatres and concerts and taking in newspapers etc. I could do all I most want on £100 a year.'[26] In practice, however, she would be unwilling to sacri-fice long-term security for immediate gain.

Meta claimed that she was in better spirits in spite of the ordeal through which she had recently passed, but Mark was much alarmed by her pale and haggard face when they met again for the second time that year at the end of May, spending a morning dawdling with

Meta in Kensington Gardens. 'I was so sadly grieved to see you look so thin, worn and haggard on Thursday—quite unrecognisable—no longer the bright, hearty, vivacious being you were when I first met you. When I think further that I have been the cause of this unhappy change in you, I feel very guilty and remorseful. But I still feel that recovery is still in your power, if you will make the effort to throw off the illusion which at present possesses your imagination, and take once more the sound rational view of things you once did . . . I cannot but see that you are lapsing into an entirely unhealthy condition both of body and mind, and that the two are acting upon each other to the breakdown of both, in which you are sure to end. I would myself do *anything* to promote your recovery, short of being unkind to you, which I could never bring myself to be, you may be sure.'[27]

Meta indignantly repudiated the drift of Mark's comments. She reminded him that she had been much saddened by the recent death of Grace Toynbee's brother, Arnold. 'I perpetually have Arnold's face and figure before me. We saw so very much of them both last summer that I feel as if I had lost a brother almost. I don't think I have ever met a finer fellow, the papers have not lauded him one bit too much. The youngest Toynbee is spending a day here, poor boy. None of them come near Arnold.'[28] Her own looks were a reflection of her age and 'so much anxiety and real sorrow in parting with my only near relatives'. 'You forget', she reminded Mark, 'that I am *very* fond of the children. I am as much alone in the world as anyone could well be, and those partings take a great deal out of one. I wonder I am sane after all the worries I have had for the last few years! As for my mind it is quite "healthy", and I'm sure I take as "sound and rational view of things" as ever. You must know that I would do anything on earth to please you, but I can't make my face look young and fat! I may have been "bright and vivacious" when you first knew me, but I never was "hearty" . . .'. Mark's view of her was not in any case the opinion of all her friends. Mrs Charles 'says I look 10 years younger but I shan't expect you to endorse that sentiment'.[29] "Some one", she told Mark on 5 June, 'I lunched with the other day thought me looking very well! I quoted you, "My greatest friend says I look 10 years older than I am and haggard and ugly", and she said she wished she could face that deluded friend!'

Grey and worn as Meta appeared to Mark, the renewal of the

correspondence brought at least a restoration of confidence and
affection. Yet some ingredient was lacking to revitalize their intimacy to its fullest extent. Mark's age and increasing ill-health
appeared to dilute the intensity of his feeling. His letters were curt
and informative rather than passionate. Meta's too, discursive and
descriptive and if anything even longer than they had been, lacked
some basic ingredient which their occasional meetings in London
were insufficient to generate.

Shortly Meta was to begin her round of visits. She stayed with the
Toynbees at Pembury, near Tunbridge Wells, enjoying drives around
the Kentish countryside, the beeches in full bud; but Mary Toynbee,
still upset by the recent death of her brother, Arnold, was 'just a
bundle of nerves, can't sleep alone and won't go upstairs before I do,
so that I have to go to bed horribly early to please her, and can't read
in bed'.[30] From Pembury she moved to the Tabors' country house at
Hawkwell. The Reverend R. S. Tabor was her father's former friend
and pupil and Headmaster of Cheam School, with whom she had
stayed a few months earlier. 'He built this place in a moment of
aberration, and occupies it for about 3 months every year. Has 350
acres to farm, 4 gardeners who can't produce any flowers, can't
possibly leave the place to one of his children as the rest would be
paupers ... My great disappointment is that the milk is simply
horrid, and I was hoping to drink quarts daily!' As on her earlier visit,
she found the family jolly and sporty but totally lacking in intellectual interests, 'quite the most uninteresting family I know', though
she felt obliged to add that 'I am sort of fond of them all ... They
have absolutely no feeling for books, but they play lawn tennis
beautifully.'[31]

She returned to Orsett Terrace in early May. 'Thank heaven there
is no lack of useful work in London, which work occupies one's head
though not one's heart. The C.O.S. [Charity Organization Society]
are going to employ paid women as well as men agents. If I were hard
up it would just suit me and I it.'[32] Absorption in other people's
problems directed her mind away from her own. 'I found two ladies
to discuss the emigration of a family; had to half my dinner and bus it
to the Grosvenor Gallery Library. We began by chatting, then a man
read a paper on the subject of provision for old poor people ... Mr
Dick Grosvenor was great on friendly societies ... I nailed Mr Bond

for a debate on Progress and Poverty for my Workman's Club, and $\frac{1}{2}$ got another man, who is making Co-operative shops pay at Bermondsey.'[33] 'I am very cross too, for the family about whose emigration I have taken such trouble have changed their minds and decline to go.'[34] 'I went', she wrote two days later [27 May], 'to see Miss Marshall today with Rose Nicholls. What a very queer creature it is, and the people who also called were all characters ... Miss Marshall is certainly clever and as certainly vulgar. There was also a Mrs Perrier who loves talking, and it was very entertaining to see both of them trying to engross the talk, or rather, to do it all ... I had 2 hours Lawn Tennis but it was stupid as Adele Kensington can't play, also it rained.'[35]

In July she described how, with Margaret Pattison, she had gone to a social meeting in Bell Street. 'At 3.30 a troop of men and women came in till 6.30 and were read to, sung to, talked to, and generally amused and rested. Tea and good cake at 1d a cup and 2d a slice. Not a bad way of keeping the young men out of mischief and giving them some thoughts of higher things than beer, and the old folks thoroughly appreciate the flowers and picture books and magazines. Mrs Mallet recited not badly, and sometimes Clifford Harrison, Kegan Paul [whose publishing house had been damaged recently by fire, though without damage to Pattison's works], the Butcher girls have helped. I wonder whether such things go on in France. I always think a revolution may be staved off by such mixings of classes!'

Meta was continuously intrigued about Mark's early life. What made him the sort of man he became when she met him? He was himself intensely introspective, and wondered much about the development of his inner life. He was nostalgic in contemplation of the past, indulging in mnemonic recall and constantly turning over the pages of past letters and diaries. 'I found my diary [which he had lent Meta to read] in Norris St. [where he lodged with a Mrs Lynn when in London]. I was surprised to find it so interesting. I suspect you were too much occupied with your home troubles to have leisure to read it properly. The two things which seem to me most surprising about those years in looking back are 1. My own industry—while I seem to myself to be doing nothing and I see what a mass of reading I got through, doing a little every day—and the other what mental suffering my wife's selfish egoism caused me. I wonder if it does so still, though I have ceased to record the fact.'[36] 'I have come away from home', he added, 'this week chiefly because she is there, as I can't bear it better than I did when I used to diarise it.' But the diary entries are missing; every reference to his feelings for Meta or his wife were to be scrupulously obliterated, with very few exceptions after his death.

Meta had planted already the notion of a memoir. As early as 1881 Mark commented that Renan had done what she had suggested he might do in his *Souvenirs de Jeunesse*, 'highly interesting, bien q'un peu basillard?' 'I know', Meta had written in August 1881, 'you've often *thought* of an autobiography but I do wish you'd begin your history of a mind'. Early in May she began reading *Essays and Reviews* to which Pattison had contributed a chapter on the historical theology of the eighteenth century.[37] 'I find Temple very interesting and suggestive, but fail to find out what the critics objected to on the score of orthodoxy … What a long time ago it must seem to you. The education of the world has progressed rapidly in some ways! How Jowett's position has altered! I suppose he is now considered quite behind-hand by young Oxford, and I am sure he is grieved by the agnosticism which he doubtless helped on.'[38]

Mark was undoubtedly pleased at the interest that Meta was showing in his spiritual and mental evolution. 'Little as my share in it now represents my standpoint, it is a landmark in my mental development, but I am *always* secretly flattered whenever you shew your interest in my past, and you are the only person, I suppose, who does. Though I have drifted on, beyond my then self, there is some of my best work in that essay, and I have sometimes thought of re-writing the chapter with the added lights of 25 years, and in the setting which much enlarged ideas of the world would give it. I suppose no one would read it now, as it was only adventitious circumstances which gave the whole collection the vogue it had at the time.'[39] A few days later Meta commented that she had not yet read Pattison's own essay, but had moved on from Temple's, which 'would have surely escaped hostile remark in other company', to Jowett's. 'I can see even now how Jowett's must have shocked the stupid orthodox.'[40]

As was his custom, Pattison tried to escape from Oxford at the end of the Trinity term as soon as he reasonably could do so. 'Garden

and evening parties are raging all round. I never get to bed to nearly
12, which is destroying me by inches.'[41] And, again, as was his
custom, he made for the more bracing air of the Yorkshire dales.
Accompanied by Jeannie Stirke as far as Northallerton [where she
changed to take the branch line to Jervaulx] he arrived at Richmond
to find 'everything I could desire in my lodgings and landlady. The
rooms are low, and looking east, must be dark in winter. There is not
much prospect, but I do catch an inspiriting glance of the Hamble-
don Hills between two houses opposite.' The lodgings were only two
doors away from the house of his sister Sarah and her husband Dr
Richard Bowes, but they 'have taken flight at the report of my
arrival'.[42]

The dales performed their therapeutic task. The solace of Swaledale soothed him. 'I would not work for my living [he was referring
to his fishing] . . . The river dead low and very clear, difficult to catch
fish . . . though I beguiled four unwary souls.' His first evening he
played at tennis at the Smurthwaites' house, Prior House. For the
most part, however, the social life of Richmond was, as usual, a
vacuum and he lacked congenial company. 'The curate is an "angel",
i.e. a donkey with wings. The master of the grammar school is an
unsuccessful pedagogue, whose failure had cankered a naturally
crabbed and obtuse mind . . . I should think he is the only person in
the place who could translate a line of Virgil, though there is living
here the Senior Fellow of Christ's [Cambridge].' Yet he admitted that
'I am pretty content in my Patmos—the only drawback being that
my left eye is weak, and I fear the sight of it failing. Do write soon!'[43]

There were, however, more drawbacks than he admitted, reflected
in his own sisterhood. If Sarah and her husband were holidaying in
Switzerland, the devoted but tiresome Fanny came for a week's stay.
'It was a great trial to me. She is really attached to me in a way in
which none of the others are, not even Mary. But you can hardly
imagine how out of my world she is—shut up in a little world of her
own. Her icy reserve soon gets on my nerves—we seemed to have no
objects in common—she neither saw, nor heard nor understood anything, refused to take part in anything which was going on, had the
power of sitting for hours with her hands before her, and her mouth
open, doing nothing, thinking of nothing, never touched a book or
newspaper. I think I must myself have come away. I could not have

stood it any longer. She is gone, and I shall not live to see her again. When I ask myself if I wish to do so, I seem to myself a monster of egotism. Except *one* [i.e. Meta] Fanny is the only human being who has a personal affection for me.'[44]

Sister Jane was much more welcome. 'She remembers what she knows with more accuracy than any of us. Considering the secluded life she leads—her own choice—she manages to hear a great deal that is going on, but her way of telling you is peculiar. You must humour it, not interrupt by a question. If you should, she will take no notice of it. The effect will be that she will go some minutes back in her story and give an account of it.' Jane's understanding, he concluded, after an unusual confidential talk, 'is superior and her sense sound and impartial.' Sister Jane, it will be remembered, was Mark's contact with his cousin, Philippa Meadows, with whom she stayed at Bath. The mention of his cousin always aroused Mark's latent hostility to her faith. She was 'now wholly given over to the basest superstition and sacerdotalism. Except Jane, she never sees anyone inside her door, and never reads anything but the *Osservatore* and the *Univers*, two rabid ultramontane prints, which circulate among the converts. England is a hateful and despicable country, the English an odious people who foul every place where they set their foot etc. She would go off to Italy at once were it not that the English maid, on whom she is dependent, declines to leave the country.'[45]

Then there was Sister Mary, Mary Roberts, the wife of the Rector of Richmond, towards whom his attitude was ambivalent. He had so often thought her cold and aloof, but this time she had apparently given up a part of her holiday to be with him. 'Partly no doubt she felt it would not look well for all the sisters to be fled at the sound of my arrival, but partly also a real wish to have me, or what she imagines to be me.' While he recognized that in some respects Mary had a 'wider horizon than any of the others', in terms of human understanding she had astigmatic vision. 'She is absorbed in her own affairs, wants to hear about nothing else, and spends the time she is with you in lengthy narratives of parochial events.' 'Mary's finesse and manoeuvring are so incessant, that you never know when you have her. She is as false as "Sister Dora", only in Mary it takes the form of manoeuvring, instead of imaginative invention ... At the same time she is so kind and well intentioned that she is rather avoided than disliked.'[46] But he was obliged to admit that when he was unwell, Mary had been assiduous in her attentions.

Mark could never really forgive Sister Dora, who had died in 1878, and he was invariably unfair to her memory.[47] After becoming village schoolmistress at Little Woolston, near Bletchley, she had joined, to the indignation of her father (and the contempt of her brother) the sisterhood of the Good Samaritan at Coatham, near Redcar, taking the name of Sister Dora. In 1865 she was sent to Walsall to help in nursing at a small cottage hospital, and spent the remainder of her life in nursing in difficult and even dangerous conditions. In 1877, having resigned from the sisterhood, she took charge of the Municipal Epidemic Hospital at Walsall where the cases were generally smallpox. She fell ill with cancer and died on 24 December 1878. A memorial window was placed in the parish church and a statue was unveiled at Walsall in 1880. But Mark could not bring himself to approve the combination of religion and philanthropy which made her the centre of a minor cult. It savoured too much to him of the pretentious and the hypocritical.[b]

Although the Rector was fascinated, and at the same time repelled, by the social web of his native place, he felt, and complained of, the onset of ill health which prevented him from fishing or lawn tennis. 'I have had a fit of the old sort, lodging of gouty superfluities in the bowel, ... I get no good sleep, can't eat, and have no strength or energy about me.'[48] The attack subsided but in early July he decided to return to Oxford. His friends and relatives were so used to complaints about ill health that they were unlikely to take this recent bout seriously. He made no allusion to the event, but he may also have been a little upset by the news of his friend, May Laffan's forthcoming marriage. Meta had been told by Claude Montefiore. 'You always told me she would never marry, so you must have been surprised. Claude thinks that she cares for this man? As her home will probably be in London I'm afraid that her interesting letters to you will cease or arrive seldom.' The prediction seems in part to have been true. May Laffan married Walter Noel-Harvey, Professor of

---

[b] On hearing of her death he wrote (26 Dec. 1878): 'Only 14 months ago I saw her at Birmingham, full of life and energy, a striking contrast to myself faded, worn away to nothing, and yet here I am! I shall not go to her funeral, as I should be sadly out of place among those "sisters" and long-coated hypocrites.'

Chemistry at the Royal College of Science in Dublin, in July. He was, as May told the Rector, 'as hard-working and clever as he can be'. 'I am sure you will be astonished, and I am too, for I had made up my mind to live and die a rolling stone.' In some sense May Laffan's marriage may well have weakened the bonds of their friendship.

While Mark was in Yorkshire, Meta industriously gathered together a *mélange* of gossip, information, and enquiry to entertain him. 'Well, I made myself useful at the National Health Society on *Monday*, talked a little to your Mrs T. Taylor, who has a curious habit of saying "What say?!" Did you notice anything queer about her clothes? . . . *Tuesday* I spent as usual on committees and worked very hard. *Wednesday* much the same until the evening, when I went with Harry Toynbee and a girl to the Lyceum, and saw the Lyons Mail. *Thurs*. I had all the morning in my district struggling with Convalescent Homes. In the afternoon I wrote my weekly budget—6 sheets to Jessie. Then Fanny Campbell and I went to the Court and saw Danischeffs, both piece and players indifferent. Today I've spent the whole morning at a committee. Saw Grace Frankland for a few minutes after lunch. Percy's lecture at the National Health Society . . . was a great success, although it was 2s 6d a day . . . That young man will get on in the world . . . *Sat*. Pall Mall art. Mrs Carlyle. I am much enamoured of her style. Its far above my best!' 'A very pious girl, but full of good sense and intelligence', who taught at the Home and Colonial Society had suggested to Meta that she might like to try her hand at teaching.[49] Mark was definitely discouraging. 'I don't think you would like teaching, and have great doubts if you would teach with effect.'[50]

With Lewis Campbell and his wife, Meta went to hear Jowett preach at Westminster Abbey. 'I was disappointed by the Master's sermon, but he said some things I was glad to hear said in such a place. His voice was very much used up, and he drank freely.'[51] As they reached the Abbey they had seen Pattison's friends, Claude and Charlotte Montefiore, getting out of their carriage. 'I didn't look at them as I know that Charlotte has talked most nastily about you and me.' Mark criticized the implied innuendo: 'Of *me* I can't believe it, of you she was under no obligation to speak other than she chose, but thinking ill of Leonard's memory would prevent her of thinking ill of any of his friends.'

Meta provided glimpses of social life, of lunch with Mrs Percival, the wife of the President of Trinity College, Oxford, 'very down-right', and her daughter, 'an amiable, gentle creature, wanting in power all round.'[c] The talk turned on Queen Victoria's son, Prince Leopold, which led Meta to ask whether the Prince visited the Lodgings much when he was studying at Oxford.[52][d] 'Leopold', Mark replied, 'liked to be at Lincoln. I am sure it was not any desire to cultivate *my* society. So what it could be? It was because L[eopold] was coming down to commem[oration] this year that Mrs Mark Pattison insisted on staying for it, in spite of my wish to shut up the house as a protest against these so galled "gaieties" which place the University in a false light in the eyes of the country. My silent protest was neutralised by her staying through the entertainment, taking a party to lunch in the College Hall, going to the ball, and even into the theatre, a thing which when we were first married I could on no account induce her to do. All this was to get a little notice from a princeling such as Leopold—and to rivalize with Mrs Liddell! She is paid for it by an invitation from Constance Flower (Rothschild) to a highly select evening party at 7 Hyde Park Terrace where the Prince is to be.'[54] Earlier she had besought her husband's participation in purchase of a birthday present for the Prince; but the Rector had kept a discreet silence.

On 28 June 1883 Meta went to stay at Marlborough with her aunt, Mrs Bull, 'most excellent company, bright, clever, amusing, original, interested in anything'. She found Mr Bull less attractive: 'obstinate and disagreeable to boot . . . simply swallowed up in conscientiously doing his work.' 'The marriage always seems to me to have the saddest throwing pearls before swine. There are 2 nice bright little girls, 12 and 15, and there is a charming German holiday governess. She is quite a lady, so unlike most Germans, and intelligent and lively. Our meals are rather a trial, most unappetising and all windows shut. I have my mornings quite alone, but have simply wasted the last 2 in just bearing those headaches with closed eyes.'

[c] Mrs Percival was the wife of John Percival, first Headmaster of Clifton College, President of Trinity College, Oxford 1879–87, later Headmaster of Rugby and Bishop of Hereford.
[d] Prince Leopold, Duke of Albany (1853–84), fourth and youngest son of Queen Victoria, entered Christ Church 1873, given an hon. DCL 1876.[53]

Among the visitors to the house there was a Miss Jebb, the sister of the classical scholar, R. C. Jebb. 'Well-cut features, very like a man's, thick, short white hair, very tall and striking and dresses vilely . . . She is about 35, I fancy, has a tricycle, and a suit of dual garments which she offered to rig me up in, but it is far too hot for tricycling!'[55]

Back at Orsett Terrace, she attended a Charity Organisation Society meeting where she talked with Octavia Hill,[e] and next day was at Fanny Kensington's 'at home' where, *inter alia*, she conversed with Vernon Lee,[f] 'ugly and angular, a curious contrast to her friend, Mary Robinson', and with Mrs Donald Crawford, 'very bright and friendly', who invited her to lunch.[56] 'I like studying with her, and she is always very friendly to *me*. She is a curious mixture of worldliness by education, and straightforwardness by nature. She flirts by night and is most energetic at the east end by day. I ventured to ask what her mother [Mrs Eustace Smith] thought of the latter! She argued that it was no business of hers! I shouldn't think Donald saw much of her.'[57]

Would they ever contrive to stay together again? It was a thought which recurred to both of them constantly. Earlier in the year Mark had hazarded, though with little confidence, the possibility of her accompanying him on a continental tour. In June she hinted that a friend of hers, presumably one of the Tabors, might lend her a house at Cheam, 'an hour from town, capital tennis ground, pretty walks, shady trees. Do you smoke me? About the only sentence I have carried away from Swift!' Mark thought the project a fantasy. 'It can make little difference to either of us, as I cannot anywhere in the United Kingdom stay in the same house with you!'[58] So, apart from the occasional, brief meeting in town, letters still remained the principal means of communication, 'the only letters', as Mark put it, 'I get which satisfy my thirst for love'.[59] 'The thing you dangle before me of the house at Cheam seems too good, but all I can see, the same invisible hindrance which keeps us from meeting in Piccadilly, will operate at Cheam as well.'

[e] Octavia Hill (1838–1912), philanthropist, influenced by Christian Socialists and John Ruskin, concerned with housing reform and other charitable measures; co-founder of the National Trust.

[f] Vernon Lee, pen-name of Violet Paget (1856–1935), author. She was a prim-looking little woman with round-lensed spectacles who indulged in passionate female friendships; though her lesbian tendencies seem to have stopped short of physical intimacy.

Oxford, to which Mark returned at the end of his stay in Yorkshire, was embowered in the calm of the long vacation, 'the only limit to what one can read is power of brain and eye, and I sadly admit a diminishing quantity of both'. It was so serene and peaceful that he even resented his excursions to town. 'How I hate this rush of existence! I was all the morning writing letters, then down to Cannon St. to the ½ yearly meeting of the London and County Bank. Then to lunch at Pyms with West [the former bursar of Lincoln] to talk over the report and Chairman's speech.'[g] After lunch he went to 'advise my Muse Mrs Pfeiffer, as to the publication of her poems . . . She read the new poem, which is very good. By the time I got back to Pall Mall I was quite done. I find myself very weak, have not picked up properly since my bout of sickness last week.'

Later in the month he designed to join his brother Frank and his wife, Margaret, in a tour of the Tyrol, but, as so often happened on the eve of his proposed journeys, fate intervened with a chill which looked as if it might lead to a postponement of the venture. 'Tour in Tyrol abandoned altogether', he wrote despairingly on the 13 August. Not for the first time he had cried 'wolf' too soon. His next letter to Meta was written from Coblenz nine days later. He had taken a berth in the *Baron Ozy*, then moored in St. Katherine's Wharf, 'as steady all night as the drawing-room floor and a full moon to light us', subsequently disembarking at Antwerp and travelling to Coblenz, then a thirty-two hour journey. He lodged at the Bellevue Hotel, 'just overlooking the Rhein Bridge, the old bridge of boats which has been there since the days of Germanicus'. He was well-satisfied with the cuisine, strolled about the town, up the Ehrenbreitstein; there were 'no people of whom I can make anything, but I haven't much tried'. But he felt happy, 'wishing I was to stop for good in Coblenz'. For light reading he had taken two of Ouida's novels, *Dogs of Flanders*

[g] West was an astute financier who served the College and his own fortunes well. It was said that when there was a suit pending against the London and County Bank which had reduced its stock to a very low ebb, West realized all his investments, assiduously attended the court and when he inferred that the case would go in the bank's favour, hired a cab and bought the Bank's stock when it was at its lowest figure. In the course of a sermon he had said that Judas Iscariot was to be severely criticized for his 'unbusinesslike conduct in accepting such inadequate remuneration as thirty pieces of silver'. He left a very substantial fortune but nothing to the College of which he had been a fellow for 52 years.

and *Sprigs of Lilac*, 'both pathetic little stories, with well imagined plots, full of variety, but spoiled in the telling, instead of being left to the natural pathos of the events, smeared over with false, theatrical, pathos and made ridiculous instead of affecting'.

He was serene but withal solitary and just a little sad. 'It is a sorrowful pilgrimage to be making, with the sense that it is the last. Every object, all the familiar places, the foreign sights and sounds, to be bidding a farewell to. I seem only to have come here to take leave. Even the old Rhein, when I quit him this evening, I shall have to say to him "Good-bye for ever."'[60] He seems to have become habituated fatalistically to the belief that he was approaching the end, though how far at this moment this was simply a reflection of his native pessimism and how far a symptom of a real decline in health it is impossible to know.

He would not linger long in Coblenz. He journeyed thirteen hours to Munich, only to find to his irritation that Frank and his party had moved on the previous day. 'If they had cared about meeting me, I think they would have waited another day.'[61] All his native suspicions about his companions were aroused. But he spent a restful night and walked about Munich in its summer evening garb to attend a performance in a suburban theatre of a comedy *Deutsche Treue*, 'a regular comedy, no clowns, no buffoons, no ballet girls, no intrigue, no one in love with anyone except the girl he afterwards marries—a Philistine respectability in a 6d threatre which measures the distance between Germany and France and Italy'.

From Munich he moved to Innsbruck to await the arrival of his brother, Frank. His decision to stay there turned out to be a happy one, for the sun shone brilliantly on the old town. 'The rush of tourists into the town was such that I thought myself lucky to have a room at all. The very landings were made up with mattresses and on Sunday at dinner 80 people, all English or Americans, sat down.' 'I crept for a couple of hours in the morning to sit in the Hofgarten, and drink some Pilsener, but all the rest of the day I have lain upon the bed, without energy to write or hardly read.' The 'absolute insensibility' of the summer heat gave way to the delight of an after-dinner stroll beside the rushing waters of the river Inn and a walk up the wooded slopes of the mountain-side. At Laus, at two thousand feet, he had a 'decent *déjeuner* at a little inn, and a good-looking maid to chaff'. On his return he found Frank and his party who had been delayed by 'adventures in the Zillerthal'.[62]

Thence over the Brenner, so different from his expedition the previous year, to Bruneck and the Pusterthal, in sight of the Dolomites, though not yet among them. They stayed first at a simple inn, and then at a 'brand new railway hotel with all the appliances and pretensions of such mushroom monsters black-coated waiters and other nuisances'. But there was rushing water, the watershed between the Danube and the Po, invigorating air and endless walks in the surrounding hills. 'Nothing can beat this air, and the Pusterthal is very like Wensleydale, at this point.' He took his fellow companions philosophically and perhaps more tolerantly than was his wont, commenting that the 'irrelevancy of the suggestions [as to travel plans] which occasionally proceed from some members of the board remind me of a College meeting'. Frank seemed rather unwell, 'indifferent to everything, eats hardly anything, and drinks neither wine nor beer'; but since a few days later he set off on a walk of 28 miles he must have been pretty fit.

Apart from Frank's wife, Margaret, a kindly but rather stupid woman, the other member of the party was a daughter of Mark's old friend David Horndon, who was then in his 79th year but hale and hearty. Miss Horndon 'is an absolute blank—anything more addle-brained than Margaret I never met with—she can't give attention enough to anything to understand or to remember it, yet all the arrangements of the party reside in her, and it is she who gets it under way, though not till late in the day, as they are not good at getting up.' The company was not intellectually stimulating, but when Mark remembered his experiences with Jeannie Stirke the previous year, he thanked his stars that 'no matter what material your companions may be composed of, it is a great resource to be one of a party, and not single'.[63]

From Toblach to Landro to Cortina d'Ampezzo, Margaret and Mark travelling in a carriage with the luggage, Frank and Miss Horndon walking; 'the pass of Monte Cadini between Landro and Cortina' 'one of the finest things I have seen in the Alps'. There was a small cloud over the horizon, for Mark began to feel unwell. 'You mustn't be ill at Cortina, for its resources are nil.' He felt his distance in terms of human sympathy from his fellow travellers. 'How I do

wish you were here!' he wrote feelingly to Meta. 'Why am I not
permitted to conduct you and M[ary] T[oynbee] over the beauties of
Wensleydale. No Dolomite has for me the charm which the mountain limestone of Scarthwick and Addlesborough have'.[64] Yet even
his complaints evaporated temporarily in the charm of the mountain
drive which they made over the Kreuzberg—Frank stoutly walking
the first thirty miles or so—through the heart of the Dolomites to
San Stefano, all in exhilarating, shimmering, Alpine sunshine. 'It
really was a most successful little expedition, only that I was as usual,
very unwell.'

Mark then left his brother to spend a few days by himself at Meran
[Merano]. The little maid who had waited on him at the *Aquila* hotel
at Cortina had recommended a small hostelry, the *Erherzog Rainer*,
which he found excellent. Meran rejoiced his heart, in its picturesque
situation, 'the comfort of the visitors is considered in ways unknown
to us in England'. 'I think in horror of the savage barbarism and
extortion of a Buxton or Bournemouth lodging, and here seats in
every direction, where you may sit till 8 or 9 without any perceptible
difference in the atmosphere, and grapes 4d a pound.' He left reluctantly and sadly: 'I conclude at Meran my last tour abroad.' He
confessed, though it was an evanescent mood, that he felt 'wonderfully better ... than when I passed through Innsbruck in going'.[65]
The optimistic feeling soon passed. 'At Meran I felt very well, but the
journey home, 6 days and nights, have entirely done away with all
the good I hope to get'.[66] He arrived back on 24 September 'after a
very bad passage' over the Channel. 'It is certain that this is my last
tour abroad. I don't say I may not, if I live till Christmas, go to Paris,
but never again on a long excursion.'

Meta meanwhile had been revelling in the sights of the North
Riding, saddened only by the fact that her obvious and loving guide
was some thousand miles away in the Tyrol. She had been invited to
join the Toynbees in Ilkley and then move on to the Lewis Campbells who had taken a house in the village of Askrigg in Wensleydale.[67] 'Do you know Askrigg?' she had naïvely asked Mark, to which
he replied sharply 'You are certainly losing your wits! ... It is in my
native dale on the banks of my own Yure!'[68] 'I didn't think I had it in
me to feel so excited as I did as I got near your country.' 'Instead of
reading "Uncle Silas" I looked out of the window and thought of

"Uncle Mark".' With Mary Toynbee for company she explored the beauties of Wharfedale, went to Otley and up the Cheven—'the river low, very thick brown in some places, just the colour for fishing, I should think'—a trip marred only by mist and the somewhat awkward companionship of a middle-aged solicitor, a Mr Byrne, who had an alarming spasmodic laugh, 'very uninteresting and inferior'. Unfortunately he was stung by wasps on both his feet. How he achieved this curious feat, no pun intended, Meta did not record. Had he taken off his boots and stockings? In spite of this mishap, he treated his companions to 'huge basins of tea and sponge cakes' before they made their way over the moors, covered with purple ling, to visit Fountains Abbey.

At the centre of the household Mrs Toynbee, 'very grumbly', presided.[h] 'Poor wretch she can hardly move alone. She can't get off the camp stool [from which she liked to sketch] without a hand, and a strong one too!' She exploited her frailty, was almost unduly demanding. Either Meta or Mary had to be in attendance, carrying her camp stool and drawing materials. 'I spent ages this morning in getting Mrs Toynbee to a church to sketch there. She stops between every few limps, tells you some interesting fact such as "I felt so ill yesterday I had to take brandy" (this is in a murmur) or "Mary is so silly she quite upsets me".'[69] Whereas Mrs Toynbee rarely attended church in London, in Ilkley, whatever the weather, she went twice on Sunday and insisted that the girls should go at least once. Meta was not best pleased, but she conceded that the vicar, a Mr Attlee, 'really preached decently', and found him and his curate 'good company, not a scrap stuck up'. She added, however, perhaps for Mark's benefit, 'I do dislike the tone of those parsons. They speak in such a superior, condescending way that it rubs me up the wrong way to go to church.'

Even if the rain continued to sheet down and the mist obscured the landscape, it was a relief to join the Campbells at Askrigg. 'What an old-fashioned place Askrigg is', she exclaimed, 'I am deeply in love with it already. We have a house just opposite the Post Office. Most primitive, no bedroom carpets, next to no furniture in any room. The landlady took Lewis a year ago when he and Jowett were here with

[h] Mrs Toynbee, widow of Joseph Toynbee (1815–66), née Harriet Holmes, mother of Arnold, Grace, Mary Toynbee and Rachel Falk.

a reading party. We dined at 2 and at 3 walked to Mill Gill, Galley
Hall, Bainbridge where we separated, Fanny and Lewis going home,
and the girls and I walking up the moors until we see Semer Water,
then under Addlesboro. We lost our way and had to tramp across the
trackless swampy moor, and climb 5 high walls before we got down
to Worton and home. We were late for tea, alas! Evening was spent in
games with the children and a chat afterwards. The girls 17 and 15,
and the boy 13 ... Very childish and delightfully bright and talkative
and frank and eager.'

Then there were visits to Aysgarth Falls, up Nab End, and the
Butter Tubs Pass in drizzle and mist which made the luxury of a
warm fire doubly welcome. Next day the drizzle turned into a steady
downpour, so that they had to stay at home and listen to Nathaniel
Hawthorne being read out loud. 'How weird and eerie he is, and how
vividly he makes you picture every scene.' Then they went to Richmond, travelling by train from Hawes to Leyburn, since the trap
which they had engaged to take them to Muker never turned up.

For Meta, Richmond was naturally a veritable shrine, St. Mark its
patron. 'I nearly shouted as we saw the woods of Marske. I wonder
whether you drive that way for your fishing sometimes. We put up at
the King's Head ... I gazed on the sometime lawn tennis ground ...
Then we walked to Easby and saw the chapel and ruins ... I wonder
whether you often church it there, or whether duty detains you at
Roberts. What heavenly strolls we might have together in those
woods ... While the others pored over photos I rushed along as
many side streets as I had time for. It is the most picturesque place
I've seen for a long time. I did wish I knew some of your main
lodgings. At 4 we had a high tea of ham and eggs and coffee. After
which I had 20 minutes for another tear with a girl. We fled across the
river so I saw the castle from that side. How fascinating the houses
down by the bridge are, and that walk round the river looked most
tempting ... I longed for another hour, but the Campbells always get
to the station too early, and would start at 5. We waited over an hour
at Leyburn. We drove back the same way as the fidgetty old dear
Lewis was nervous about the old hilly road. The sunset was lovely
and was succeeded by a bright moon and stars. F[anny Campbell]
said as we drove to Richmond, "It's a pity the old gentleman isn't
there".'

The weather soon caved in again. Meta wrote her letters while the others were in church. They whiled away the time by reading Walter Besant's recent life of Edward Palmer and by playing paper games 'which I must teach you'. Then, fortunately, the mists lifted and they tramped up Hardraw Fell and over the Butter Tubs to Muker. Meta liked Swaledale with its steep sides and stern charm better than Wensleydale. So to Napper Hall, 'sad to see a historic place turned into a farm', and to Whitfield Gill, 'a tremendous scramble holding on by our eyelids in a vain attempt to reach the bottom . . . very filthy and tired', before in a 'very uncomfy dog cart' they made Walldale, Bishopdale and home.

Meta asked whether she might call on the Stirkes at Grazing Nook. Jeannie met her at Finghall with a pony trap. She found Mary in rather better shape than she had expected, 'only paler, as bright as ever. She is allowed to fidget, can use her arms . . . She is lifted from sofa to bed . . . They hope to get her down before the warm weather is over . . . The danger of spinal inflammation seems over, and now this is only muscular weakness, paralysis, which I fancy Dr Bowes thinks can be cured directly she can be galvanised.' After playing tennis on a misty, wet and dark evening, Meta stayed the night, gossiping with Jeannie in the mid-night hours, exchanging news of Uncle Mark. The long-suffering Jeannie drove Meta to Jervaulx where she caught the train to York, climbed the Minster and lunched on mutton, potatoes and bread, all for a shilling.[70]

Her Askrigg visit was over, but she went back to Ilkley where she had an aunt, Mrs Burke, her mother's sister. Her aunt, still beautiful with charming manners, reminded Meta of her mother who, she admitted, was less good looking 'but far surpassed my Aunt in mental and moral worth'. The household was a dull one. Since Mrs Burke could not bear artificial light, it was impossible to read until they went to bed (which they normally did at 9.0 p.m.). 'We are not all en rapport as they are very evangelical, narrowminded and wholly unread. Conferences, Moody and Sankey, Captain this and Miss that are household words.' 'All their instincts are so essentially conservative (in every day trifles even) as mine are liberal, and I had to keep an unpleasantly close watch over my tongue. If "devil" [Mark's favourite swear word] had escaped I can't think what would have happened! She says I don't wear enough clothes, and I can't persuade her that 2 woollen garments are much warmer than 3 calico ones. To wear flannel knickerbockers instead of a d. petticoat she thinks indelicate, to be friends with a Roman Catholic she thinks too dreadful to conceive possible. Woman doctors are only second to the most degraded of their sex etc.'[71]

The weather continued overcast and wet, and with some relief she left to join her friends, the Tomkinsons, at Willington Hall, Tarporley. 'This scenery is so unlike Yorkshire, a very broad well cultivated plain, with Beeston and Peckforton just breaking the level, and dim distant hills on one side, while Delamere Forest studs the country on the other side.' Willington Hall's comparative luxury was pleasing after the spartan lodgings at Askrigg and the angularities of her relatives at Ilkley. 'Everything is so comfy not to say luxurious. There's a very large hall in which one chiefly lives, sofas, piano, easy chairs so easy, tables covered with all the latest good papers and books, endless sorts of writing paper, and lovely ink and pens. My room in which I'm writing contains all that heart, or rather body, could desire. Talk at dinner chiefly on strikes and politics. Our party is small, as the only grown up guest is an American, sister-in-law of a certain age, say 50 I guess. She is not much of a person, uneducated and underbred though well meaning doubtless. Altogether a sore trial to my very refined hostess, whose people are among the upper ten, as are likewise those of mine host.' 'Life in this sort of house is *bien autre chose* to what it is in a small London house, where shillings are a consideration. Even if one hasn't time to read it is pleasant to have piles of new books and mags on the tables . . . if you wake early you have but to ring 7 "downstairs" bell — some delicious, fragrant creamy tea soothes your restlessness; breakfast brings really good coffee and heralds a morning during which you please yourself by reading writing and picking flowers for an old woman . . . Luncheon means 4 children, who capture you for stories till 2.30 . . . Jem.[Tomkinson] is most keen on politics and not clever enough to object to female discussion . . . His wife is a very bright, clever, dear little woman, who would suit you for a few meals, especially if she were clad in one of her gorgeous garments.'[72]

Meta enjoyed riding her hostess's hunter, 'an unusually beautiful dark brown thoroughbred mare'. 'The roads were soft, and the Chester high road has yards of good grass for miles on both sides of it, so we had any amount of galops and canters, and our steeds were fast trotters as well as easy canters ... Why does one feel so unusually contented, even happy on horseback?' On her return from visiting her friend, Rachel Falk, at Whitegate, she lost her way. 'It was 3, so we ought to have been hungry having had nothing since 9 ... I had a lovely, boiling, big bath, and then trifled with a partridge's fat limb.' 'Lord Tollemache's daughter and daughter-in-law called and they had to be taken round the garden. A return visit was called for, to Lord Tollemache's 'Gothick' castle at Peckforton.[i] 'It is built on the top of a hill covered with trees, and the wild rock and heather come up to the very doors. Inside the place is severely plain. Most of the rooms have'nt paper, just the sandstone, which is only slightly red ...'[73] Her praise of Willington Hall was so unusually unqualified that Mark ventured to remark that 'It is far too warm a home to lose, or to be content with a week's stay. In those peoples' circumstances life is a different thing from life lived in holes and hutches like ours.'[74] It might be questionable whether the Rector's Lodgings or even 25 Orsett Terrace could properly be so described, but doubtless they paled into significance by contrast with the luxury of Willington Hall and the grandeur of Peckforton Castle. But the Tomkinsons were soon to leave for town and in early October, on the eve of Mark's seventieth birthday, Meta returned to town.

The Michaelmas term at Oxford had opened for Mark in a queasy fashion, and it became more so as growing ill health cast a sinister and lengthening shadow over the future. His patience became easily exhausted. 'Church Congress going on at Reading,' he commented in his diary for 4 October, '... lofty pretensions of the clergy, assuming more and more every year—one can remember the humble and despised place they held 25 years ago. Now they aspire not only to regulate their own personal matters, but to dictate all social policy.' Twelve days later [16 October] there was a meeting to choose a man to look after the Senior Common Room. 'The taste of the fellows', he observed, 'for the inferior in everything asserted itself, and they chose the most inferior man they could find—a goggle-eyed baboon who can't speak English.'

[i] Lord Tollemache (1805–90) MP for South Cheshire 1841–68, and West Cheshire 1868–72; created first baron 1876.

His wife's return to Oxford on 29 September added to his frustration, for 'I shall have no more studious evenings or teas, but be
expected to wear a black coat and sit up for a 7 o'clock dinner'.[75] But
he found time to prepare a lecture to be given at Bedford College on
his birthday—'so I shall lose my birthday plum pudding'—which all
his friends, Gertrude Tuckwell ('how swell Gertrude was—not at all
like a poor parson's daughter'), the Kensingtons, the Pauls ('Nancy
looked quite fat') and the devoted Meta assiduously attended.[76]

Meta was worried by the obvious fatigue which he showed
towards the end of the lecture. His friends were so used to his
hypochondria that they tended to shrug off the ominous signs of
physical deterioration. There was too the worry that his relations
with Meta since her father's death evoked among his friends at
Oxford. He had to tell Miss Smith that her father's will had not been
the result of the 'clamor about our friendship'. Unfortunately he had
now learned that there was some substance to the charge, and, in fair-
ness to Miss Smith, he felt he should correct his original statement.
'It will be important to have the true facts known as the justification
of a legacy, which though not large, is more than public opinion
would allow me to leave under other circumstances.'[77] But Meta
objected to Mark's proposal and grumblingly Mark acquiesced.

Towards the end of October, Mrs Pattison herself became
seriously ill with sinal neuralgia, 'intense pain, no sleep for 3 nights
and only by injecting morphia—doctor 3 times a day, nurse all
night'.[78] On medical advice she gave up the idea of wintering in
England and decided to return to Draguignan until the following
spring. In normal circumstances his wife's departure would have
given Mark cause for rejoicing. Now that he felt so low, he felt somehow abandoned. 'Very bad night', he commented in his diary for 19
October, 'nothing seems to be able to move my inside.' There were
occasions on which his life seemed centred around his bowels.
'Thoroughly done up', he told Meta three days later, 'life on the sofa,
a useless log most of the day, yet so worn down by 9 p.m. that I crawl
off to bed. House shut up, no one admitted except on business, into
the ground floor. I drag myself out into the air twice a day, but am
glad to creep back to my sofa after half an hour's walk.'

Fortunately Jeannie Stirke had returned to the Lodgings, but after
the débâcle of the summer holiday in 1882, she had never fully

regained her uncle's unqualified affection. 'She is more self-asserting than ever and patronises everybody in a laughable way ... Joan writes my letters and takes me out to walk, but is otherwise of no use in the house.' His main prop had become the housemaid, Ellen, who 'has even by her patience and goodness softened the mistress, whose face has hitherto been as flint against her'.[79] 'My illness', he wrote five days later, 'is getting serious ... Thinking my time would be but short now, I wrote all the morning at reminiscences of my life.'[80]

This was the first real reference to the project which Meta had been encouraging him to undertake, and which had been gradually maturing in his mind, the writing of a memoir. It was the one thing which somehow seemed momentarily to deflect his attention from his other troubles. He now had genuinely to force himself to fulfil the few obligations which he could not escape. When the College Chapter Day came round on 6 November, he went to chapel to read prayers at 8 a.m. as the statutes laid down, then had breakfast with the fellows and took the chair at the subsequent College meeting which lasted until 4.30 p.m. when he left exhausted; 'could not dine with the chapter and lay on sofa'[81] while Jeannie read Hayward's life of Goethe. He could not prevent thoughts of Meta breaking in. As he lay on his sofa he sent her his good wishes on her 30th birthday. 'Dear! I send you a birthday gift—probably my last! I am not sure that I ought to do so, as it is only tormenting your secret scheme of taking your capital—an unprincipled way of life whether adopted by a state or individual! I was wishing you were by me to calm my fever pulse, and irritated nerves.' 'You poor Rector', Meta replied, 'what a day you had on the 6th. Of course you needed me to read you to sleep and spoil you hard.' 'This malady', he wrote in his diary on her birthday, 'has now a firm grip of me, and is not likely to let go. This is my dear Meta Bradley's birthday. Wrote out memoirs and have got 75 pages done ... Took up Amiel's Journal for second time of reading—arranged books with the feeling of being soon to part with them for ever.'[82] Two days later, 'I feel myself going and everything wears a serious, solemn aspect to my mind.'

Although she was well used to Mark's complaints about his health, Meta was much distressed by this new development nor did she know what precise importance to attach to it. Time and time again he had spoken in the gloomiest terms about his health, and had

emphasized the shortness of the time left to him. She had wasted her
commiseration too often in earlier days. Uncertain therefore as to
the true nature of his illness, Meta decided that she should write as
cheerfully as possible. A stream of prattle, a diary of her daily doings,
came from her pen as she endeavoured to hold his interest, as she did
with some success, and to divert his attention from his ills which it
proved impossible to do. She described a lunch at home at which her
deaf stepmother competed with a deaf clerical brother, rambling on
at 'cross-purposes'. 'Once he asked after an old Aunt, and Mrs
Bradley said "She's in the Infirmary", thinking he referred to a
servant! and there was no one to laugh with'.[83] She spent a Saturday
afternoon 'playing games in Kensington Gardens with 70 children
from Gertrude Tuckwell's district! When they arrived they were so
tired that we sat on logs and told stories ... I was equal to the
occasion and invented a thrilling tale of shipwreck which quite fixed
all their eyes and even amused me!'

Meta was still very much concerned with the fate of her sister and
family in India, apprehensive of their health and worried by the
problems which a bill, in the drafting of which Courtenay Ilbert
played a leading part, had created. This bill was designed to remove
the disability from which Indian magistrates suffered, preventing
them from trying British offenders. While it was introduced largely
for administrative convenience, so that Indians in the Civil Service
might be placed on a similar footing to that of their British colleagues
in judicial questions as they were already in their executive authority,
it was greeted by the British residents with hostility. Meta was much
interested to meet one of Jessie's protégés, 'a very clever Mahomedan
Syed Mahomed, who is one of the few of his creed high up in the
I.C.S., a judge in the High Court ... This young man would not go to
the Ilbert bill meeting as he is in Government employ. He made one
point which does not seem to have struck anyone here re. the Ilbert
bill. For years the English have made accusations against natives
before native magistrates and no one has suggested that the native
magistrates have been swayed by race partiality ... Syed Mahomed
said that Courtenay was very popular among the natives—his
sincerity was so thoroughly recognised.' They met again at the Yates
Thompsons. 'Syed Mahomed says we never *conquered* India, and that
we keep it by the consent of the people. When he was a boy ... he

was taught and took for granted that we were only the servants of
the Mogul ... I imagine that he is always cool and self-possessed and
would stand up politically to any one ... I'm afraid the English in
India are most rude and nasty to the natives still. I had hoped that
gradually a better spirit had been introduced but Syed Mahomed
told me some disgraceful instances of rudeness.'[84]

The bill provoked a great outcry in India against the viceroy, Lord
Ripon, and Ilbert himself, led by Griffith Evans, a member of the
Legislative Council and a former member of Lincoln College.
Although Ilbert had anticipated the criticism and had warned the
viceroy of its likelihood, Lord Ripon was much aroused by the
hostile onslaught he had evoked. Jessie was very worried about
Courtenay 'lest bullets as well as hisses follow him and Lord Ripon'.
'We can evidently form no idea here of the dangerous state the
Europeans in India are in', Meta told Mark, after talking with a
Major Conway Gordon who had just returned from Simla. 'Major
Conway Gordon was at a theatre last year during which a skit on
Lord Ripon was played, and at the end the whole audience stood up
and shouted "Rule Britannia" for ages, and were in such a state of
excitement that they would infallibly have looted Government
House had anyone suggested it.' In the upshot a compromise was
arrived at by which British offenders tried by an Indian magistrate
were permitted the safeguard of a British jury, a virtual surrender of
the principle of racial equality inherent in the original bill. Mark
observed when Meta told him that her 'amatory curate' had never
heard of the Ilbert Bill that it was incredible that 'there should be
clergy living in London, so low down in the scale of humanity as
never to have heard of the Ilbert Bill'. Yet although he sympathized
with its liberal objectives, and on 1 August actually attended a
meeting in support of the bill, Meta commented that he did not
really care much about India. Truth to tell, Indian affairs, like Meta's
detailed descriptions of the Charity Organization Society, were
remote from his interests, only tediously bearable because Meta
wrote about them.

Meta had immersed herself in social work, and talked blithely
about the Charity Organization Society, in part at least to keep at
bay the inexorable decay by which Mark was seemingly steadily
absorbed. 'Our curate was very pugnacious and kept us ages

disputing over a principle on which we have worked for years i.e.
if a man drinks it is useless, and wrong to help his wife.' 'Still
more monstrous', Meta added, 'a sober man who keeps his wife
without assistance sees that sobriety and thrift don't pay.'[85] Such
were principles to which Mark could give a warm approval. 'If
a man drinks his wife ought not to have money given her—he is
sure to get it out of her.'[86] Meta had 'tea with a sick friend, evening
spent in interviewing an out of work man, writing to a possible
employer'.[87]

So she tried to maintain a brave front, but the grim possibilities of
his illness kept creeping in, intensifying the native depression which
life at Orsett Terrace and the wearying companionship of her deaf
and loquacious stepmother evoked: 'very cross and miserable, and
had to drink brandy at dinner to keep me going at all'.[88] In
anticipation of worse to come, she drew up a list of books which she
thought Mark might like to give her: 'all George Eliot in good type,
binding immaterial, Keats, Clough, a good selection of Sonnets, Epic
of Hades, Earthly Paradise, something of Rossetti's and Swinburne's
and your Casaubon if it's not very ruinous. I am also open to
Thackeray and Miss Austen and something of Carlyle's and
Ruskins's.'[89]

It was a tall order with which Mark felt that at least in the immediate future he could not fully comply. 'You can't buy the Casaubon,
it is out of print, but I will send you one.'[90] But he had some hesitation about dispersing his library to the extent that Meta had somewhat naïvely suggested. Moreover he was irritated that Meta had
thoughtlessly, and not for the first time, addressed her letter to him
directly at Oxford rather than sending it to the Athenaeum. 'Of
course she opened it.'[91] If Mrs Pattison considered the contents, as
she doubtless did, she must have felt further humiliated.

Then Mark came to London to consult his doctor, Sir Andrew
Clark, who diagnosed his complaint as 'palpitation of the heart', and
laid down a dietary regime. He took the opportunity which a
London visit offered of meeting Meta at the National Gallery. He
had now decided that the time had come to end the tenancy of the
rooms which he had leased for seventeen or so years from a Mrs
Lynn at Norris Street, Haymarket. At first Mrs Lynn refused to
believe that he was not going to come again and kept the rooms

vacant for some weeks. 'She daily expected to hear that you were coming up for a night.' For Mark it was another effective, even traumatic, break with the past, 'the first nail of the coffin', he thought, as he returned to Oxford laden with parcels and wreathed in wraps and furs. 'Your face haunts me', Meta sighed, 'and I can't tell you how deeply I long to hear you are mending, however slowly.'

On 15 November Mrs Pattison was considered well enough to undertake the journey to the South of France. When she bade Mark goodbye, she was surprised, even disconcerted, at his unusual show of emotion as he kissed her hands with tears in his eyes.[92] He was left to ruminate alone in the solitude of the Lodgings in a state of steadily deteriorating weakness which neither Sir Andrew Clark nor his Oxford physician, Dr Tuckwell, could properly diagnose. 'Dr Tuckwell tells only what he thinks expedient. That little', he commented, 'reads like a sentence of death'.

Flustered and dismayed by the turn of events, Meta's reaction only served to irritate. Her suggestion that Mark might consign some of the gifts he designed for her to her great friend, Daisy Woods, evoked a swift response: 'your tact was much at fault when you proposed I should send things to Daisy's. They have both cut me, and the house, [and] are almost the only people in Oxford who have never called to enquire.' Tact was not indeed Meta's strong point. She questioned Andrew Clark's diagnosis. He had been proved wrong before, but the instances she cited could hardly be regarded as consoling to a dying man. 'One was John Mylne [the husband of Juliet Kensington.] A fortnight before he died (when the local Doctor said there wasn't a ghost of a chance for him) Andrew Clark said he should start shortly for Colorado and that he wasn't dying. 2. A cousin of mine Andrew, he said was at the last gasp—this was 2 or 3 summers ago. He is now in New Zealand perfectly well. 3. Another relative of mine he treated for simple indigestion whereas he had a very complicated set of the malaria order picked up abroad. 4. A girl I know well died suddenly this year 24 hours after he had said she was perfectly satisfactory. 5. He said my father would live over the summer and in less than a week he was dead.'[93]

Mark showed his exasperation. 'You've never written me such a rather grumpy letter before! It is a little comfort on the whole as I am sure you wouldn't have done so had you really thought it would be the last! I don't mind sneers when they fall from your lips, but on paper they somehow hurt!' Querulously Mark reproved her. 'You have evidently not realized how ill I am. The sooner you make plain to yourself that the heart complaint is mortal, and may carry me off any day, the less we shall be at cross purposes in our letters . . .'[94] It was ironical that medical evidence showed later that his heart was relatively sound.

Upset, Meta sought to be reassuring. 'We must both comfort ourselves with the reflection that you've been very unwell often before.' Such sentiments were in part intended to salve her own failing hope. 'My life without you', she wrote on 17 November, 'would be too desolate. You *must* get well. You are the only person I know intimately who has never irritated me—somehow your queer ways and your faults never annoy me as other peoples' little peculiarities do! It is strange, as you are not at all my ideal personified!' Perhaps the wording could have been more elegant, but there was no doubt of the dog-like devotion.

Mark relented and in a letter which he dictated to Jeannie he sought to make amends for his brusqueness. 'It is indeed extremely hard that I can't have you with me at the supreme moment when you would have been the very ministering angel of Scott, and all for what, nothing more than the malignant gossip of your Aunt Granville and two or three old cats. I think it is very magnanimous of you to say that we have never had a disagreement as I have upon my conscience several outbreaks of anger against you, and I think you have said, or written, that on such an occasion, I was "unutterably cross". But you forgive me, dear Meta, don't you?'[95]

He had by now become an invalid. Of that there could be no doubt. 'It is quite true', he wrote to Mrs Hertz on 30 November, 'that I am very ill indeed. I cannot conceal from myself that I am dying, and that I shall never see you again. My regret at leaving the world touches many points, one is the variety of schemes left incomplete or not even begun, the thoughts that I shall carry away with me without ever having had the opportunity of communicating them . . . It would be affectation to pretend that I am not deeply depressed at the prospect of leaving the world. I daresay you never guessed from the tone of my conversation how deeply I was attached, after all, to the medium in which I lived.'[96]

As he lay, convinced that he was dying, his attitude to his visitors was as ambivalent as it had always been. When the classical scholar, Robinson Ellis, came, he overstayed his welcome, but he confessed none the less that his 'unflagging interest in scholarship' was a 'refreshment in this arid desert of shop-dons'.[97] Mrs Hertz, touched by his recent letter, asked if she might come. Pattison at first demurred. 'A deliberate adieu' would be simply 'an aggravation of a situation already sufficiently sad'. Then he relented if she would stay longer than a day.[98] Curiously the visit turned out to be immensely successful. She cheered him, 'most sympathetic, rational and comfortable', showing an unstinted interest in his writing, so much so that he dictated some of his memoirs to her, and she 'made me tell her many other unwritten passages of my life which I have never told to anyone'.[99] The day ended somewhat austerely if appropriately with a reading of Browning's *Grammarian's Funeral*. Pattison, though himself President of the Browning Society, could only express his astonishment 'that such doggerel should in these days pass as poetry'.[100]

For Ellen Smith's constant devotion, even if she was pre-eminently the watch-dog of his wife, he had unqualified admiration; 'the only thing I complain of is that when she comes she does not stay long enough'. It was strange that Bywater, the classical scholar with whom he liked to smoke and one of the most frequent visitors to the Lodgings, was a less welcome guest, appearing, close friend that he was, unable to generate the warm sympathy which had flowed from Mrs Hertz, herself an acquaintance rather than an intimate friend. 'What can be the nature of the mysterious spiritual outflow, which can come to me from a comparative stranger like Mrs Hertz and cannot come to me from one who is after you the best friend I have, say if you like the best man friend.'[101]

Apart from the effort to survive, two other objects engaged his mind above all others in the sad winter months of 1883, the distribution of mementoes that she would treasure to Meta, and the composition of his memoirs. 'I am thinking of what little articles', he told her, 'I can save for you as a souvenir out of the wreckage, as nothing will be given you after the breath is out of my body.'[102] Meta's tears dripped on the pages of the letter with which she replied, but she did not hesitate to express her preferences. 'I'd like

anything and everything belonging to you—those ash trays, your
favourite chair in the studio, the machine for stamping your books,
any books you'd like to give me, any rubbishing odds and ends
which no one else could value. I should like one of the kneehole
tables at which I've written for you so many hours, and your studio
safe, and all the books we read together, your favourites, such as
Dante, and those many poetry books with extracts, all of Men of
Letters series so many bits of which I've read you and *Moths* and Miss
Laffan's books, Hildebrand which we read but I've forgotten which
set of essays they were, and wasn't there a book of Japp's on German
literature, especially a book in the study containing several of your
early essays. I think it is near that stamping machine. If the Ruskin's
aren't too valuable I should like some, and Browning and Disraeli
and Lytton and Carlisle [sic] and Macaulay and anything else you
often read.'[103]

Mark immediately dispatched a parcel of books which included a
copy of his *Casaubon*. 'It is too hard', Meta commented, 'that those
perfect days can never return … I'm almost glad that you can't
possibly realize what I'm suffering … If I live the longest I shall have
bitter remorseful feeling that I could have done more or felt more for
you than I have. If Mrs Grundy had only consented what wouldn't I
have done for you those 3 years.'[104]

Mark began sorting out press cuttings, articles which he had
written or which related to him, so that they could be pasted into a
large scrap book for Meta. She went round to his London lodgings
and collected his fishing-rod, 'now of no consequence, as I shall
never see the Swale again'. On 12 December 1883 he sent her another
parcel, 'containing some precious things, the packet of your own
letters to date, my first account book, my earliest Students' Diary,
my own copy of Pope's Essays and Satires, bound in one volume and
Leonard Montefiore's papers privately printed. Lastly George Eliot's
Essays never collected in this country, in an American edition'.[105] A
week before Christmas he sent a further package, 'The most precious
part of its contents that unique volume in which I had bound
together my essays. I put this into you hands because I believe there
is no one else who will either prize it, or take care of it as you will do.
I am sure you see that it is on no account to be reprinted, and I hope
you will have sufficient value for it not to lend it as girls are so fond

of doing with their books. The rest of the box contains hardly any-thing but novels—as I am sure you will never read anything else the rest of your life.'[106]

'The essays', Meta wrote in thanking him, 'I value most of all ... Your own paper, and your Endowment of Research, and George Eliot's Essays, and in fact every single book will you know be prized ... I should much like your Brownings, his and hers. The only doubt I have is whether I could ever bear to read poetry again. Every line would remind me of our reads ... It seems incredible that we have only known each other a few years. To me it seems if you had always been my best, kindest, dearest, most intimate friend. To you, of course, our friendship has only been an episode, a soothing, comfort-ing one I know, but to me it has been pretty nearly the whole book.'[107]

On Christmas Eve Mark told her that he had sent her a collection of vignettes and postcards which he had brought together on visits to parts of England and the Continent; but he could not send her the Browning for which she has asked as 'as that is one of the books she [i.e. his wife] is likely to wish to keep'. 'I sent you up today a "Christmas box" full of those little worthless odds and ends which you have named as wishing to have as souvenirs'.[108] 'No one', Meta replied, 'could ever have had such a Xmas present as that boxfull, so exquisitely painful and yet so precious. I still have a tiny bottle of scent which you gave me that Xmas day we spent together!'[109] 'You would hardly believe', Mark answered, 'what an amount of thought and effort of recollection it cost me, to bring all those little nothings together and what a pleasure I took in thinking how you would appreciate such little worthless objects ... I must draw your atten-tion particularly to the piece of soap which I brought from Paris in April. I had to pass Houbegan's shop every evening on my way home to the avenue Friedland and the beautiful order of the interior visible from the street was at last too much for me and I went in, not knowing what I went in for, except to enjoy the luxurious étalage of all imaginable perfumes and cosmetics, I ransomed myself by soap.'[110]

But what engaged his attention beyond all else, managing at least momentarily to turn his thoughts away from the dismal prospect of the future to time past recollected, some memories sweet, some sour,

was the composition of his memoir. It took him through his boyhood at Hauxwell to his life as an undergraduate at Oriel College,
Oxford, his close association with Newman and his friends in the
Tractarian movement, his part in the revival of academic standards at
Lincoln and support for reform in the University, and ended with
the disastrous defeat in the rectorial election of 1851 which had left
so indelible a mark on his mind and so wounded his spirit. His was to
be the story of a crippled soul, told, however, with such clarity and
insight that it was to be, though recognized as such only by a few
connoisseurs, a minor classic of English literature.

He was engaged in a task which would have defeated a man in
better health; but his spiritual or intellectual narcissism led him to
triumph over adversity. Introspective, over-sensitive, egocentric, he
found in the contemplation of his mental and spiritual development
a theme of absorbing interest which gave him a way of escape from
the stark routine of the sick-room. Jeannie dragged out boxes full of
diaries and past correspondence, read them out to him and acted as
his amanuensis. Meta had already tried to sort out his early letters
when she stayed at Lincoln three years previously. Mark came to the
conclusion that all this material should be deposited in the Bodleian
Library at his death, and that no one should have access to it at the
earliest before 1910 or possibly 1920.

By 6 December 1893 he had reached his days at Oriel. 'I want to
understand', Meta commented, 'how the you of Oriel grew into the
you of Lincoln. I should have liked to have seen Newman's letters to
you, also George Eliot's and Lewis's . . . I understand you perfectly as
you are, but I do long to know more of your younger days. When I
was staying with you I implored you to begin a short memoir, if only
for me.'[111] 'There were', he replied, 'no interesting letters from
Newman', 'I have told you often but you have never realised it, that I
was not *in* the conspiracy! being a generation too young', and only a
formal correspondence with George Eliot. 'I am losing my zest even
in literature which for 70 years has been my passion and support. I
read next to nothing, and if it was not for the desire I feel to complete
my Memoirs I should have the blank of nothing to live for . . . The
Memoirs . . . are addressed to you so that whether they are printed or
not, you will see them.'[112]

Given the circumstances of his life, he made striking progress.

'I have done with photos', he replied to a request of Meta's, 'and am giving the few ounces of blood which remain in my body and brain to the written photo of myself which I pompously call my "Memoir".'[113] By Christmas Eve he had finished it down to his proposed terminal date. 'It only comes down to 1861', he told Mrs Hertz, 'the time of my Rectorship is too recent and people still living makes it too dangerous ground.' He was, however, wondering about its publication, for to keep the manuscript interred in the Bodleian Library for the next thirty years would deprive the memoirs of 'even the little interest that may belong to them now'. He was fearful that what he had written would be edited, perhaps more especially anxious that they should be free from possible re-writing by his wife. 'I cannot allow them to be corrected expurgated or altered in one title from the text as I leave it, and I have no friend whom I can trust to print them as they stand.'[114]

Meta may have been hurt that Mark should not instantly have decided to entrust the publication to her. She offered to ensure that she would supervise their publication without the smallest possible change. 'I should deeply value this opportunity of doing something for you. I don't see how my doing it could do you any harm as only the publisher need know. In any difficulty that might arise I could rely on Mr Milner's help and advice . . . You must know, my dearest friend, that my chief pleasure has been and *will always be* to think that I am doing what you would wish.'[115] Fond as he was of Meta, Mark yet knew Meta's intellectual limitations and was basically unconvinced of her judgement in such matters. Rather to her surprise, he did not leap at once to her suggestion. 'You must remember', she wrote a little plaintively, 'that I'm not a helpless, dilatory fool, but a very energetic, capable young person.'[116] Meantime he had made arrangements with Macmillans, though he was as yet undecided as to whether the manuscript should be published or simply printed for private circulation.[117]

Much as Meta tried to maintain a cheerful countenance, chattering about the dinners she attended, the problems of the Charity Organization Society, even the best way to fit draught excluders to her rooms, she could not banish the sad thought of Mark's gaunt face and weakening body. She read *Belinda* but thought it dull. 'The plot goes for nothing—the Professor is simply impossible, the girls aren't

interesting nor amusing, and the lover doesn't love. As for the Professor being like you! except in a matter of coats and galoshes, and a
long nose, your worst enemy couldn't trace any resemblance. He's a
mean, heartless puppet, and that you are certainly not.'[118] It was a
loyal gesture, but even the victim realized that the portrait, satirical
as it was, had a superficial likeness.

She talked with friends about the Rector, and to Mark's delight,
evidently persuaded Fanny Kensington to spend a few days with him
at Oxford. She made one desperate effort to come herself, but Mark
barred this absolutely. The experience would be too searing, too
heart-breaking. Earlier in the winter, Mrs Percival, the wife of the
President of Trinity College, had actually asked Meta to stay with
her for a week in Oxford. She accepted the invitation gladly, even
though she realized that it would be impolitic of her to call at the
Lodgings during her stay. 'Of course Aunt Marian [Bradley] will be
rabid, but who cares? not even her husband and girls! I suppose I
shan't see you and I can't see my old home for the happiest 2 months
of my life.'[119]

Meta's tactless scrawl was intercepted and read by Mark's wife
before she left for Provence. As Mark predicted, the consequence
would be that 'she stops your visit to Mrs Percival'.[120] Mrs Percival
had had to use all her tact to rectify the situation. 'Strong representations' had been made to her by 'several persons whose judgement we
are bound to respect . . . My husband and I feel we have as a matter of
duty no choice in the matter . . . It would revive so much gossiping
talk and cause so much pain that [it] would not be right either to Mrs
Pattison, who as you probably know is abroad, or to the Rector, or
to yourself.'[121] Meta accepted the withdrawal of the invitation
meekly, outwardly sympathizing with Mrs Percival for having had to
write 'such an uncomfortable letter'. She was sorry that she could
not come, and 'particularly glad of an opportunity of showing that I
am not in the least ashamed of my deeply valued friendship with the
Rector, all the more so as I much fear that his rapidly increasing
weakness will soon make that friendship only a memory of which I
shall always be proud'. Conventional courtesies sustained, Mrs
Percival thanked Meta for her 'very kind letter and appreciation of
my very difficult and unpleasant position', but she didn't take her up
on an invitation to call on her in London.[122]

Mark's increasing illness indeed made her all the more determined to break through the barriers which prevented her from even calling at the Lodgings to enquire after him. She sought to engage Mrs Bradley's support. That elderly lady appeared more scatter-brained than ever, having set fire to her cap. 'It had been pulled off and extinguished by the servant! I know she'll come to a violent end. She is quite the most recklessly careless person I know.' The Hereford Georges—he had been a fellow of New College—asked both Meta and her stepmother to stay. 'Think, dear', Meta pressed Mark, 'how very useful I should be. I could read for ever, and you used to say that you liked my reading! . . . And then I daresay you could bear a little affectionate teasing such as no one else gives you . . . You needn't think I shall make a fool of myself! I haven't had all these years of trouble for nothing, and you shan't say good-bye to me, only good-night. There is no need for either of us to refer to what we have been to each other.'[123]

Mark was in no mood either for a little affectionate teasing or for an embarrassing farewell. 'There is not the least prospect of my recovery, and the only question now is how long Tuckwell, at a guinea a day, can enable me to hang on.'[124] 'Of course nothing can hurt me', he said à propos her visit to the Georges, 'but your appearance on the Oxford scene would immediately set going the tongues of all the old cats in that place. They have nothing much to clack on just now, and they would greatly like a good opportunity for a Christmas caterwauling . . . I have told you over and over again what I think of those dying interviews and leave takings. They are odious ceremonial . . . Love friendship and affection cannot feed themselves upon ceremonial kisses and hand-shakings.'[125]

Meta was obliged, if reluctantly, to acquiesce in his wishes. 'Our friendship has certainly not been fed on "kisses and handshakings" (chiefly on letters!) and I don't want to be with you because its' the thing, but solely because I want to know exactly what you're think-ing and feeling every hour.'[126] The Rector was very much upset when his well-intentioned brother, Frank and his wife, made an unheralded visit.

He professed, as he had done throughout his life, to prefer a solitary existence, even though at its core there had been always an aching feeling of loneliness. He was much touched by a gift of 'cut' flowers, hyacinths, camellias which normally he would not tolerate, from Rose Nicholls; 'was it not a brave thing of her to do, to remember me at this moment in such a way, seeing how very little I have seen of her?' Surprisingly he was revivified by a bottle of beef essence which Mrs Bradley sent (and on which characteristically he reprimanded Meta for not having paid the correct postage). Yet he could only live from day to day. Meta sent him a potted plant, a primula, for Christmas. 'My reason is offended by the want of propriety of making presents to a dying man, who has already more things to part with than he likes to leave behind, and does not wish to have the leaving this world made more difficult to him.' But he became reconciled to the gift as a symbol of Meta's affection.

So sombrely the year came to an end and Meta scribbled her New Year letter at 11.00 p.m. on New Year's Eve. 'This very hour 3 years ago we were in the studio together, not going to bed as usual at "10 o'clockie" but staying up to 11 as a last great treat to me. How vividly I recall it. If I live another 30 years (which heaven forbid) I shall remember it as well. Xmas evening and this evening we did the same. I distinctly remember saying on the first occasion that I did wish I could die that moment while I was so perfectly happy. You were half touched, half shocked . . . Oh, my dear, you *must* get better. If you don't I shall always suspect that you might have pulled through had you had me at your side to scold, swear at, bedevil, and care for, that might have soothed, or coaxed, or teased you, each in turn, into living. My one desire is to have you to write to still next December 31, or to saunter with you through fields of asphodel in some brighter clime. But our souls are so unalike that I can't imagine the possibility of our meeting in any other stage of being unless indeed true affection counts. Whatever my lot there may be, the thing I must be ever proudest of is that I was your friend (as well as you mine) and perchance the desire to show that I was in some degree worthy of your regard may help me in many a strait. Certainly I have altered since we first met, and I think you have a little. You've given up saying "no one cares" . . . the things we tell each other most certainly would not interest our other friends. Our letters would be invaluable in 1983 as shewing the life of this age.'[127]

1884 The Last Days

NOTHING in the New Year of 1884 could dissipate the scenario of gloom which, like the dense yellow fogs of the winter, enveloped the Lodgings at Lincoln College and Meta's room in Orsett Terrace. The Rector appeared to be no worse, even temporarily a little better, since he was able occasionally to pace slowly up and down the gallery room of the Lodgings and even take the fresh air in a hired brougham or be pushed in a covered bath chair around the Oxford Parks. When Daisy Woods went to London, she made a kindly gesture by placing her own brougham, complete with coachman, at his disposal. Although he had no real reason to distrust Daisy's sincerity, his dislike of her as the daughter and suspected ally of his arch enemy, Mrs Granville Bradley, made him chary of accepting the offer. 'Of course', he snapped at Meta, 'I know that Daisy *was* your great friend. What I doubted, and still doubt, is her remaining so under the altered circumstances both of herself and her family.'[1] 'If I once have a friend', Meta replied with some asperity, 'our souls are grappled for age, and Daisy and Mab. don't exactly pin their faith on their mother's judgement.'[2]

This was an issue on which he and Meta would never see eye to eye. 'Dear little woman, she looks so frail', Meta commented.[3] When Mark learned that Daisy had called on Meta at London, he expressed querulous surprise that Meta should not have related the conversation which took place between them, supposing it turned on his own friendship with her. He had no wish to be beholden to Daisy. When Meta remonstrated ever so slightly at his carping, he replied with irritation, 'I don't like using other people's horses. I don't think anyone who knows what horses are ever does. I believe you think a horse a kind of flesh steam engine which cannot damage.'[4] It was the sort of hurtful remark, the more poignant since Meta liked nothing better than to ride a good horse, which his illness evoked, but one instinctively natural to his disposition to which Meta by now was

quite hardened. He had, however, little or no time for her friend,
Daisy. Daisy had waited six weeks before she called after his health.
When she came 'she was restless and wanting to go all the time ... I
was trying to open the oyster with the point of a knife, and the oyster
determined I should not, so that I was more alienated from her than
ever.'[5]

He still managed to punctuate his long tedious days by reading. It
was both a habit and a necessary escape from the realities of existence. But his concentration lapsed after half an hour. Mental weariness constituted therefore an added burden. 'I regret the waste of
time as it would be an excellent opportunity for reading.'[6] He
perused Sophocles' *Antigone* in the original and found that it gave
him greater satisfaction than on his earlier reading of the play.
Perhaps its sense of impending doom and the inexorability of fate
touched a personal chord. Theodore de Banville's *Souvenirs*
impressed him as a fine example of the French feuilleton, exemplify-
ing the richness of the French language.

Meta could only throw herself into her social work to forget her
depression. Her committee work had produced a new acquaintance,
Mrs Stewart Headlam, the wife of the radical clergyman and philanthropist.[a] Mrs Headlam was 'very plain, with an ugly, rasping,
mannish voice, very downright, decidedly emancipated ... She
dresses vilely but evidently has lots of money as she rides and drives a
dog-cart'.[7] They drove to a place near Hampstead in it 'and didn't we
just get wet'. For a short space Meta found solace in Mrs Headlam's
friendship. There were other diversions. She visited Mrs Althaus,
whom the Bradleys had befriended twenty years earlier, the mother
of Pattison's favourite pupil, T. F. Althaus. She told Meta how dreadfully upset her son had been by Mark's illness. 'Fancy his coming
from Brighton solely to see you, not like many young men and he is
very poor. It must be *almost* worth while to be ill to have proofs of so
many people's affectionate interest.' With characteristic bluntness,
she added, 'When you next make a codicil you might do worse than
leave him a trifle'. Mark rose to the bait. 'I don't know what you
mean by Althaus being very poor. Sir Nathaniel has guaranteed him

---

[a] Mrs Stewart Headlam wife of Stewart Headlam (d.1924), Christian Socialist and
curate of St. Michael's, Shoreditch 1881–4.

a fair income for a certain number of years.' Less characteristically he heeded Meta's advice. Her friends, the Tomkinsons of Willington Hall, aware of her depression, took her out to dinner at the Grand (five shillings a head) and followed it up by a visit to the theatre to see *A Scrap of Paper* which 'absolutely forced' her 'to laugh'. When, however, her mind was diverted from the thought of Mark, she felt a sense of guilt. 'I can't enjoy this sort of thing one bit', she had written before the play, 'but I suppose I ought to go! There is a queer mixture of the puritan and sybarite in one's composition still! The more I see of other people the more unlike them I feel, perhaps that's why we feel as we do towards each other.'

But then it was back to social work, to the Charity Organization Society, arranging tea for a hundred girls. As the singers who were to entertain them were late in arriving, the girls became unruly, and Meta 'hopped on to a chair and asked them a lot of sort of sanitary riddles such as "What should you do if a person gets a bone stuck in her throat" or "a bead up its nose" etc', which surprisingly held their attention—at least Meta thought it did—save for a few 'loud guffaws until the singers arrived'.[8] 'We chiefly discussed', she wrote of another meeting held at the Grosvenor Gallery ('such a queer-looking lot, evening and morning clothes mixed, which is always ugly, some people very antediluvian, one very pretty girl not at all Charity Organization Society style'), 'parish and sanitation, and Henry George. I am thankful the latter has alienated the liberals and most radicals by his own non-compensation. His influence is strong enough as it is among the ignorant, who dream foresooth that the nationalisation of lands will give them each a snug cottage, a horse, a pig, a cow, with very little labour.' Hardly surprisingly, on her return home, she turned for bedside reading to a birthday present intended for Lettice, R. L. Stevenson's *Treasure Island*, which she perused with immense enjoyment.

She told Mark that the Charity Organization Society had sent her a very interesting case, that of a lady, who was a widow with six children; 'eldest deaf! I sent her off with such a huge bundle of old clothes, school books etc. She's the sort its some pleasure and real use to help, energetic and bright.' The next day, a Friday, she made her 'first inspection of some unsanitary houses' and dined at the

Garretts where she met Mrs Garrett Anderson whom,[b] to her surprise, she discovered was a practising lady doctor.[9] With a large sanitary deputation, some 50 to 60 men, 3 or 4 women, she waited on Sir Charles Dilke, but failed to be impressed. 'Of course his speech was very able but while others were speaking his eyes roved in such an underhand non-straightforward way. I felt as if he wouldn't look anyone in the face. I should have thought from his appearance and manner that he would be courteous enough but formal and depressing in private life.'[10] 'Your perçu', Mark responded, 'has a certain amount of truth.'[11]

The news from India about Jessie and her family lowered Meta's spirits further. 'Olive', her niece, 'is very ill with probably typhoid, and she and a trained nurse were just starting from Simla. Jessie unluckily had her carriage upset 2 weeks before and can't use one knee . . . If our sweet little Olive dies either Helen Ilbert or I simply *must* go to Simla at once. Helen would love to go and I should hate it but if she absolutely can't I see no way of escape. It will go near to breaking my heart to put such a distance between us, and I shan't have a moment's peace till I hear from Helen.'[12] Fortunately Helen agreed to go if it proved necessary.

Mark thought that Meta should have greeted the opportunity to visit India. 'What an extremely foolish girl you are! To have had such a chance of seeing India free of expense, and to have let Helen Ilbert mop it up! I have scarcely patience to write about it. How your want of sense in this matter has made you sink in my estimation. The silly childishness of preferring to stick in London over committees when such an opening to your mind and experience was before you!' To this heavy-handed humour, Meta meekly replied that no one had suggested paying her expenses. 'Of course I should spend nothing while there, but the mere outfit would cost most of my income for a year, to say nothing of the voyage. How you can understand me so little as to imagine I would willingly go *now* shows me how far you are from realising many things about me. If you *won't* understand I

[b] Elizabeth Garrett Anderson (1836–1911), opened dispensary for women and children which developed into the New Hospital for Women 1866 and became senior physician there 1866–92. Did much to improve status of women, and for long was the only female member of the B.M.A. See Joe Manton, *Elizabeth Garrett Anderson* (London, 1965).

know that its useless to try to make you. The mere possibility of its
being my distinct duty kept me awake hours and hours. There are
evidently feelings and motives undreamed of by your philosophy! I
always suspected that I understood you better than you did me, and
now I'm sure of it.'[13] The news from Simla continued to be on the
depressing side, for though Olive had an intermittent fever rather
than typhoid, Jessie had an infected knee and Lettice was in bed with
suspected scarlet fever.

So the shadows deepened. The flowering primula which Meta had
sent Mark as a Christmas present lasted a month before it drooped
and died. While it lasted he found some pleasure in its colour, a soft
spot in that dark house, for it recalled Meta to him.[14] He sent Meta
the diary of the tour which he had made of Germany in 1858 as well
as the *Meditations* of Marcus Aurelius, expressing the hope that she
might read them 'when you shall have gathered to settle out of the
blighty style of life you seem to be leading now'.[15] Accompanying the
Meditations there was a quotation from Schopenhauer: 'The animal
knows nothing of death till it actually comes to him. Man
consciously approaches his death every hour, and this gives life itself
a doubtful aspect in the eyes of one who has not perceived that
constant annihilation is the character of life throughout.'[16] 'The
monotony of the life I am now leading', he wrote a week later, 15
January 1884, 'is absolutely necessary for me, and my nerves could
not bear even the little shocks of ordinary society. But its cast iron
regularity tends to crush the spirits, and when I am not able to read
as often happens I sink down very low.'[17]

Shortly after the New Year he was very much moved to receive a
note from his old mentor, Cardinal Newman, 'in the most affectionate terms offering to come and see me'. He had only seen
Newman on two occasions in recent years, in October 1877 when
they had 'an affecting interview', and Newman suggested that he
should write down some of his memories—'gave me his blessing
when I left'—and on 26 February 1878 when he dined at Trinity. He
was flattered by the Cardinal's concern, doubtful as to the emotional
upset such a visit might cause.

He, eighty-three years of age, would have made the journey from
Birmingham to Oxford & back merely to see me for half-an-hour. You

may suppose how I was upset by this proposal and the perplexity I was in as to what to reply. I felt that my state was too weak to bear the agitation of the interview and still more of the suspense of expecting him. I wrote explaining this to him at the same time in a way to make him feel how great the loss was to which my weak state compelled me to submit, and I said that I felt his persistent affection for me all the more as he must have known that I had travelled very far in a direction quite opposite to that which I was once in 1845, sharing with him. He took my letter in an excellent spirit, repeated his offer to come to me when I get stronger, but guarded himself from the sort of suggestion my words had conveyed that his toleration as a Catholic was exceptional and individual to himself. Nothing that has happened during my illness has moved me so much as this renewal of correspondence with my old master after a very long interval. I have never seen or written to him since the Cardinalate which I view as degrading much like Tennyson's belordment. And I had been just giving an account in my Memoirs of the steps by which I had passed beyond him leaving him as it were wallowing in his fanaticism. I feel it hard hearted now to let that page stand and yet it is the simple truth.'[18]

'Dear Rector', Meta responded, 'I can well imagine all that it was to you, and how many recollections it stirred up within you. I wonder whether you will see him when you're stronger, and whether the interview would not give you more pain than pleasure.'

Intellectual integrity appeared to triumph over the bonds of friendship, but in spite of Pattison's response, the aged Cardinal came, giving but the briefest intimation of his intention, for he was in no doubt well aware of Pattison's suspicious nature. He came partly out of a sense of duty but partly also of a feeling of remote affection. He recalled the warm intimacies which had cooled steadily in the past three decades; but the haze of age may well have made the conversations and religious exercises of Littlemore the more precious. There had, after all, been a time when Mark had seemed a disciple, if never the beloved disciple, and Newman the master. It may have been impossible to rekindle the warmth but he could satisfy the conscience. Did Newman believe, as the Rector thought, that he was a lost soul, a searcher after truth who might yet be brought to the true faith before his confrontation by the great reaper? Newman was a priest who might still have supposed that the dying embers could be refired. It is difficult, however, to believe that this was his motive force in travelling to Oxford. The Cardinal's act was the expression of his deeply affectionate nature. As the brougham from the station drew up outside the College Lodge, the Rector was to turn back the pages of his life and wait for the master whose beliefs he could no longer share.

'After he had accepted, or acquiesced in being put off for the reasons I gave, on the Wednesday morning I got a note saying he would be here at 12 o'clock. I need not say how flurried I was by this, for other reasons, but also how my invalid routine of hours was upset. He came at 12 and left at 2.15 to return to Birmingham and out of that short time had to be taken lunch. The interview was most affecting. I was dreadfully agitated, distressed even. On the one hand I felt what a proof of affection he was giving, to one who had travelled so far from what he regarded as all important. On the other I felt that it was not all personal regard which brought him but the hope, however slight, that I might still be got over in my last moments. And I could not tell in what proportion these two motives might have influenced N[ewman] to undertake a fatiguing journey. The conversation at first turned on old times and recollections. It gradually slid into religious discourse, when I found as I expected, that he had not realised the enormous distance at which I had left behindhand the standpoint of 1845. More than that he did not seem to apprehend more than any ordinary Catholic would have done, that there is such a space to travel, or that one can look back upon the ideas of those days as the ideas of childish ignorance. Of course I could not set about trying to put things in this light to a man of 84, let alone a Cardinal. On the other hand I did not feel it right to leave him under the illusion in which he evidently was that I was still hesitating about my road and doubting as we were in 1845 as to where the true church was to be found. In this dilemma, having to be true and on the other hand having to avoid the futile attempt to explain to him what it was evident could not be explained, I was in great embarrassment as to how to express myself. N[ewman] did not of course attempt the vulgar arts of conversion, nor was there anything like clerical cant or affectation of unction like a parson's talk by a death bed. He dwelt upon his own personal experience since he had been reconciled to the Church, the secret comfort and support which had been given him in the way of supernatural grace under many great trials, that he had never been deserted by such help for a moment; that his soul had found sweet peace and rest in the bosom of the Church. Then we got for a moment, but only for a moment on more controversial matter. Here he had nothing to say, but the old argument of the *Apologia* which I need not repeat to you. I said in answer three hypotheses each less probable than the one before it. After I had said this I regretted it, but was relieved to find that he had not taken the scope of the remark, so it passed harmless. We very soon changed the conversation, he allowing me to ask several questions about Oriel before I became a member of it. This last conversation I should have liked to have prolonged as it interested me much more than the other but I felt that that was not what he had come for and was therefore shy of pursuing it.[19]

In early February Mrs Pattison was sufficiently alarmed by the reports of her husband's health to decide that she should return home to supervise the nursing. She had long been considering this, for while her affection for Mark had been more or less eroded, yet she was always moved by a sense of dedication and duty. She could not conceal from her friends her poor view of her husband's moral qualities. 'I can't get to the point', she told Ellen Smith on 4 December, 'at which I can conceive of the life as a whole or with any touch of great or true humanity in it. It seems an *unspent* life, neither enjoyed nor used, insufficient in purpose and result, and this makes me feel embarrassed when he talks to me in terror of the end.' Yet his growing weakness awakened her sympathy. The spinal neuralgia which affected her eyes and made writing difficult had made it impractical to take this step at an earlier date. Moreover the Rector's own attitude towards her still acted as a positive deterrent. She had recently had a bequest, no more than a few hundred pounds, from her mother. The Rector was named one of her mother's executors. He wrote to her, agreeing to transfer the sum but reminding her that as her husband he had a 'moral right' to the bequest. It was a good illustration of the double standard by which he sometimes acted; the warm supporter of woman's rights was at heart a Victorian pater-familias.

Then the news from England became increasingly unfavourable. 'I believe I am right', Francis had written to Ellen Smith, 'in begging to be allowed to return ... When I am with him, he has (*of late*) invariably softened and had even seemed to cling to me expressing vexation that Jenny persisted in coming in on "our last evening together" ... To mine the day before yesterday came an answer "I now give way to your wishes and will say not a word more as to the prudence of your prolonging your stay in the south. I withdraw my opposition to your return." To this I have replied that I will start next week—the week after I shall be at Lincoln College. The die is cast.

I hope, but with *deep* anxiety, that I have chosen well *for him*. If I were not convinced of *this*, I should say I ought not to come. I believe I bring "quiet" with me . . . Tell Orson too, that I can honestly say my chief motive *is* "consideration for the Rector".'[20]

Ellen Smith demurred. She thought that Mrs Pattison was wrong to return. 'Your letter which was brought to me as I went to the station yesterday was a great blow', Mrs Pattison was writing from Paris, 'Encouraged by you and hoping against hope I have gone on striving for years for the relation which you always prophesied might be possible.' 'Your prophecy began to realize itself last summer and though I have given way to fits of impatience and said impatient things to you, yet I was at heart beginning to see things as you wished me to see them.'[21] 'As to the Rector's requesting me not to return etc. you must remember *this* is how he has behaved each time *Jenny* has left the house—against whom he can hardly even fancy he has a grudge, and also *this* is how his father behaved each time a daughter was absent from Hauxwell . . . His last letter but one was full of that tender sentiment he makes so captivating and expressed the wish for me in the house that you had led me to expect he was forming. I instantly replied in the spirit with all the sympathy and pity that I sincerely felt—told him I was better and asked Dr T[uckwell] to tell him I might safely return so as to remove from his mind the only fear he expressed—that of having 2 invalids in the house. In reply, he has written a letter which made me almost sick— an *evil* letter, in his worst mood, forbidding etc. homecoming with a wonderfully clever and cunning mixture of truth and lies. *Something* has been at work meantime or *some one*—he refers to friends "who may not come near him"??? Of course I intend to return very shortly . . . if he persists in objecting I think of informing only Mr Bywater yourself and Dr T[uckwell] of the date at which I shall leave.'[22]

The Rector was in fact divided in his own mind. He did not love his wife nor she him. Nothing could eliminate the bitterness which he felt at the way in which she had helped to sever his connection with Meta. Her return must put paid to any but a limited correspondence with Meta since she might well have to be his sole amanuensis. Nor could there be any hope of meeting Meta in London if his health improved sufficiently to enable him to make the journey there. On the other hand, Mrs Pattison was a competent and efficient woman

who could ensure, if she set her mind to it, that he was made comfortable. He was depressed by the lack of real attention which his
sister Fanny and his niece Jeannie Stirke, both of whom were staying
in the Lodgings, were giving him. Fanny was well-meaning but
utterly incompetent and 'counted for nothing'. Jeannie had sunk still
further in her uncle's estimation. He thought her lazy and inefficient.
She lolled by the fire in an easy chair in the mornings and spent the
afternoon visiting her friends. 'I was not *bored* by Jeannie Stirke but
disgusted at her for her indifference and neglect of me. The cause
came out at last, she was too busy angling for a husband, and now she
has hooked him, she can snap her fingers at me.' Jeannie was to
marry Charles Newton Robinson on 9 April 1884.

So Mrs Pattison returned, with the 'best professions' to which it
would be wrong 'to turn a deaf ear to', though he still could not
persuade himself of 'her genuineness'. 'This, you will say, is like my
cynical scepticism—time will shew.' Hastily he decided to return
Meta's letters to her. 'I think it safer . . . to place them in your hands
as she will have all my keys and access to my lock-up. Sorry I am to
part with them, they contain so much of your life.' His wife's professional competence restored 'order and discipline in the house', he
secured a new amanuensis to undertake his correspondence, and his
morale and even his physical well-being seemed to improve. 'In
December I was resigned to die, not liking it, but resigned to the
inevitable. I gave up reading the papers, asking for any news, in fact
shut out the external world. Now lately that I seem miraculously
returned to life', he was writing on 22 February 1884, 'I certainly do
prefer it even though it is wholly this sofa and wheel-chair life, in the
middle of books, to any other life which I can imagine possible for
me anywhere else. Mrs Mark Pattison's return has made a much
greater difference in favour of my wellbeing than you imagine. You
know I looked forward with fear to what might come of it; now it
has turned out, quite contrary to all my expectations, to be the very
best thing that has happened to me.'[23] How far Meta appreciated his
sentiments we do not know.

The improvement was, of course, relative and, though he was
unaware of what it forboded, it was countered by a new symptom, a
dull pain in the region of the stomach. In January Mrs Thursfield had
offered to find him a lodging in London or even to put him up at her

house in Montague Place; but '*I* am still far from the time when I may hope to be able to be removed!' But by early March, he felt strong enough to contemplate a move to London; a change of scene might be itself a spur to improvement. His wife took a house in London, 33 Gloucester Place, Portman Square, 'the rent ruinous, but we shall have the whole house to ourselves except the rooms which the landlady and her daughter occupy themselves'. 'You cannot tell', he wrote to Meta, 'how weary I am of my confinement, three months fixed in the same room, on the same sofa; it will be a relief to me to change the look-out even though it is only the greengrocer's shop in Crawford Street.'[24]

Meta was greatly cheered. 'Fancy your coming up perhaps in less than 2 weeks', she ruminated when she first heard of his plans, 'of course you'll come some morning—have a rest and talk and lunch, and then I'll read you to sleep.'[25] This was certainly not on Mrs Pattison's prescribed programme. Mark responded warily: 'Of course I shall come to see you as soon as I am settled in our lodgings, but certainly not to lunch. You evidently know not how minutely particular I have to be in my diet. Besides Mrs C[harles] B[radley] [who was very deaf] when ordinary talking fatigues me and to have to raise my voice above a very low key gives me positive pain.'[26] Mark, aware that this might be their last meeting, hoped that he could arrange one to which his wife would not object. Mrs Bradley left her card at 33 Gloucester Place (though at first Mrs Pattison failed to inform her husband that she had done so), so providing him with an excuse for calling at 25 Orsett Terrace, for it would be impossible for Meta to visit his lodgings. He could only walk a short distance, and that on the level. Normally he hired a chair from the chair stand in Montague Place to take him round the park. After lunch he had to rest, and Mrs Pattison expected him to take tea with her at 4.0. The time for visiting Orsett Terrace could at best be short.

They arranged to meet on 30 March. 'You must not order tea for me ... You may give me seltzer water, if you have it.'[27] It is unclear why the visit went wrong, but it looks as if Mrs Pattison insisted on accompanying her husband and was dismayed and angry to find '"her" Carlyle's Dante lying on your drawing-room table'. Mark felt obliged to write, in his own hand, asking Meta to return it. 'She vows she will never look at it again as it has lost all interest for her, but I will at least offer it to her.'[28] So Meta could carry away from his last visit to London, indeed their last meeting, only the memory of his sad face 'so white and weary'.

In spite of the welcome change of scene, London had not brought any really marked improvement in his health. 'The monotony of my life is depressing, 11 hours spent in bed to get some 6 hours sleep out of it.'[29] Stephen Gwynn has left a graphic description of seeing the Rector make his weary way round the Oxford Parks accompanied by his wife, 'drawn in a bath chair by a shambling menial, lying more like a corpse than any living thing I have ever seen. And yet there was a singular vitality behind that parchment covered face, something powerful and repellent. Beside him walked his wife, small, erect, and ultra Parisian, all in black with a black parasol. Her presence conveyed detachment from her convoy with an emphasis that absence alone could never have given.'[30] Although he had among his recent visitors, a number of old friends, Stebbing, Thursfield, Althaus, the time for 'gardening' his soul was restricted. Yet, as he said, habit was too strong to forgo the pleasure of reading. 'In vain I ask myself "Why should I read or know this or that?" . . . I generally have 2 hours reading in the morning, sometimes a third hour before dinner when my visitors have left me.'

At Eastertime Meta made an expedition to Ely with some acquaintances, the Mastermans.'[31] At Cambridge they stayed in a 'dear old fashioned hotel, the University Arms, and doesn't always smell of cabbage as ours did at Ely. But the coffee is as bad as at those places where we tried it during our few walks.'[32] Even Meta was persuaded to attend the chapel service at King's (where it came home to her that she had never attended a service in Lincoln College chapel when she stayed with the Rector). As she mopped her eyes, she realized that the trip had failed to distract her from her woes. 'Work is one's only remedy.'

So she went back to the inconsequential routine of London life. A visit from Mrs Donald Crawford led her to comment that 'she is so wholly unlike the girls I know, so frankly reveals the absolutely worldly lines on which she was brought up. We wound up with her views on matrimony, evidently she never cared a bit for Donald and didn't realize how extremely unpleasant, to put it mildly, it would be to live with a person one didn't love. She had found such a life very liveable, I suppose, with her parents and sisters, and didn't know how wholly different it must be with a husband. Poor Donald! I think I pity him most. I was always brought up to take for granted that one would only marry for love. For at least 20 years no other possibility ever crossed my mind and then only in novels. To calculate, as her set evidently do, that if one refused the first or second man one mightn't have another chance and that on the whole one had better say yes, seems to me too horrid. It is better to be too romantic than to have no spark of romance.'[33] Meta's words formed a prophetic prelude to an act which Mark would never live to see but which was to involve his wife very directly. He did not in fact agree wholly with Meta's comments on marriage. 'I find', he said, 'the *mariage de convenance* may lead to very good results.'[34]

Then from Australia came news of her brother, Charley's, suicide. His death and its sequel had all the elements of paradox seemingly implicit in the Bradley household. He had only a limited success as a stock farmer, but his natural family grew. With four sons and three daughters he had enough to do to make both ends meet. In ailing health his father forgave Charles his misdemeanours more easily than he did Meta. 'Charles', his brother, the Dean, commented, 'said but little to me about him in his illness. What he did say was pleasant and cheerful ... It was through me that the last trouble about poor Charley in England came to him [for Granville had been then Head-master of Marlborough], and I was always shy of talking for that reason ... But he made me feel that he had been much comforted about him of late.'[35] His father's death consequently greatly eased his financial situation.

He was, however, an ill man, suffering from an illness which, it was rumoured, was venereal in origin. Jessie's husband, Courtenay Ilbert, learned that he needed surgery, and sent £100 to help. He emerged from hospital, but the disease recurred. Depressed by the pain and the ill-omened future, he went and shot himself.

At the time of his operation, in April 1882, he had considered the future, and wrote a letter for his children. He assured the two elder, Charley and Willie, that his father (who was then still alive) would continue to send them £50 a year 'which will keep you until the cattle and horses increase'. His estate at Myrtlebrook would be ultimately divided between all of them. Strangely oblivious of his own past, he declared that if any of them married without their mother's consent, they would 'forfeit all share of anything that I possess'. Charley's love for his 'wife', irregularly matched as they had been, shone through the letter. 'To all of you', he concluded, 'I would say never forget to take care of your Mother, never forget to say your prayers, and ask God to help, and protect you, and never under any circumstances break your word, and remember that however you may prosper in life and however rich you may become, all that you have is but lent you by God and that you will have to account for your use of it.'

As illness racked his body, did he feel remorse for the past? Or was it that early training, inherited rigidity, withstood the liberating force of early rebellion? On 16 February 1884, he revised his will. Startlingly it recalled his father's ultimate testament. He disinherited his two elder sons, Charley and Willie, 'because the first has chosen to go away on his own account and the second has today gravely misconducted himself and will, I think, soon follow his brother's example'. Nor, he added, should 'they be encouraged to be about the place'. The early rebel had at the onset of middle age become the disciplined conservative. If his two other sons, Frederick or Frank, wished to marry, they must marry with their mother's consent; if they did not, or if they married a Roman Catholic or 'grossly misconducted themselves', then they would forfeit all share in the property. The property itself, worth perhaps £3000, to which their mother would have a major share, would not go far to sustain even the two brothers, and their three sisters, Nellie, Minnie, and Bessie. In death as in life Charles Bradley lacked the hallmark of success.[36]

On Meta his death made relatively little impact.[c] She had not seen him since she was a little girl. Jessie who had kept more in touch was more affected. 'My brother is very ill, so I've just heard in a roundabout way. If he died I believe Jessie would be finished off quite. I hardly remember him but she was very devoted to him. Of course he didn't care for her and adored me.' 'I was dreadfully shocked by the news', Dean Bradley wrote on 6 June 1884, apologizing for writing to her 'on Hotel-paper which forgive' But Charles's death caused only

[c] 'Have just heard that my brother is dead—only the fact, nothing more. I have a cousin in Australia who will shortly send me details. Jessie was so very fond of Charley. Of course I was too young 20 years ago to care much, but there are complications in his affairs which make this very trying and worrying to say the least.' Compare Jessie

the smallest of ripples in Orsett Terrace. Obsessed by Mark's intensifying weakness, she could only experience a 'sort of frozen insensibility'.[37]

Diversions there had to be from the encompassing bleakness. It
was a glorious Spring, abundant with fresh life and colour. As Mark
was wheeled round the Parks, his tired eyes were refreshed by the
blaze of pink May and the yellow fronds of Laburnum. Meta was less
fortunate when a friend rowed her up the river from Windsor to
Staines, the day was overcast, the river sluggish, restful but 'more the
peace of death than of life'.[38]

Her friend Mrs Stewart Headlam continued to fascinate her,
almost obstreperous in her masculinity. Meta was attracted by such
mannish self-confidence, puzzled as to its source. 'Last night Mrs
Headlam came back with me after our Committee, and we had a long
confab. over your last 2 cigarettes! How a cigarette helps conversation! A puff fills in a pause in the most trouble-easing way. We agree
in many vital points and I daresay we shall contrive to see something
of each other . . . I don't believe a man would like her, but she seems
enough like a man for a woman to find her a capital friend.'[39] 'She is
absolutely untrammelled by prejudices and conventionalities and is
agreeable to discuss subjects with. She's as hard as nails, and if she
ever had any feelings or even sentiments life must have knocked
them out of her. But she is extremely efficient in this sanitary work,
and is in fact a very good fellow! I gave what's called a "Cocoa
Concert" last night, in a very low part of Notting Hill, which signi-
fies that you get in for one penny, and in return have 2 hours amusement and one cup of cocoa and a slice of cake.'

She returned with Mrs Headlam, walking to her home across
Kensington Park. 'I had a smoke and chat alone with Mrs Headlam
after dinner and like her very much.' 'It's very odd', she added somewhat naïvely, at least to the twentieth-century reader, 'She has a
woman friend who lives with her, does her housekeeping etc. etc.,
goes abroad with her, rides with her. They lived together before Mrs
Stewart Headlam married, and she told Stewart she wouldn't marry

Ilbert's comment to Courtenay in July 1882, 'Just as Papa and Charlie were getting on so
amiably, she [Meta] writes to Charlie that Papa won't let him come home because of the
expense . . . Charlie writes in a puzzled way to me and to Meta, takes up the tale and says
all nasty and completely untrue things about Papa.' [ex inf. Mrs Mary Bennett].

him unless his friend could stay with her.'[40] 'I like', Mark replied, 'the account you give of Mrs Headlam. What a rare thing freedom from prejudice is in the world.'[41]

Home life was tedious and troublesome, for Mrs Bradley was ill-tempered as well as deaf. She had come to feel that the maintenance of the house was too expensive, so to Meta's other worries was added the possibility of losing her home. 'I can very well live in 2 rooms in town and she in the country. So I could had I the wherewithal but £70 or £80 won't board one!'[42] 'I suppose still there will be compensating advantages in living quite alone. It is odd that one can feel absolutely indifferent towards a person with whom one has lived for nearly 20 years.' Mrs Bradley subsequently caused a great commotion when warming something by the fire by placing the lamp down in such a way that it caught the tassels of the mantelpiece on fire. She then tried to douse the flames with a flannel petticoat, in the process nearly setting fire to herself as well. 'I daresay this will decide her to leave this house in the autumn and either go abroad or take a little country house. She is in a wildly excited state and can't live in London.'[43]

In mid-May Mrs Pattison, strained by the tiring impact of her husband's condition, on her doctor's advice, went to spend a few days with her friend, Theresa Earle, at Woodlands, Cobham, Surrey. 'There is no hope', she told her friend Eugene Müntz, 'and yet one has to go on as if there were'. She was sustained by glimpses of light at the end of the long, dark tunnel. Among Mrs Earle's guests on 13 May there was Sir Charles Dilke. It seems most probable that it was on that day, the 'blessed 13th', that she promised that she would marry Dilke when her husband died.[44]

In the middle of June she decided that it would be good for Mark's morale, if not for his physical well-being, if he could be moved to his native county. Nothing had ever proved a better physical and spiritual tonic than the sights and sounds of the North Riding. It was a physical impossibility to take him to rural Wensleydale, so they leased a house in Harrogate, No. 8 The Oval; it was newly built, had every convenience, was well-drained and stood high and detached. The rent was 10 guineas a week which Pattison thought ruinously high. Harrogate had another advantage, for it was a spa where the patient could drink the waters, which Mark's doctors thought or at

least said might arrest the progress of disease. So he was to take four
ounces of chloride of iron water each morning. Chairs could be hired
to take him to the wells at 1 s. 3 d. an hour on weekdays and 1 s. 6 d. on
Sundays. The Rector appeared indifferent to the move. By now he
was no more than a passive spectator to what went on around him.
Mrs Pattison went to put the house in order, the cook followed;
Mark with a nurse made the journey in 7½ hours with a change at
Birmingham.

In general he was convinced that he was slowly sinking. 'One day I
fancy myself stronger, another day weaker. I have given up hope, and
now only wish the end to close in as peaceful a way as may be', he
wrote shortly before he made the journey, 'that I may cease to be a
burden both to my friends, and to myself. I am very weak, cannot
walk for more than 5 minutes at a time, and have no digestion. I take
no pleasure or interest in anything I do, or see, or hear ... Be
yourself'—he told Meta—'and go bravely on. It is quite silly giving
up, because an old man of 70 is about to die.'[45]

A fortnight's experience of Harrogate had not improved his
condition. 'After the heat of the day was past', he wrote on 29 June
1884, 'we had an open carriage, and drove a round of 3 hours through
a piece of real Yorkshire scenery, which, however, now instead of
soothing my irritated nerves, only brings with it the poignant, bitter
regret for the days when I could ramble at will through endless
ranges of the same character. Everything now with me is the "past"
and the bitterness of reminiscence is an emotion I was not prepared
for. Nothing in the present gives me any satisfaction, arouses any
interest.'[46] This was Mark's last letter, or at least last surviving, letter
to Meta.

The furies were closing in. 'What is the use, I ask, of storing a
memory which is ready to perish, with more facts? Instinct, the
"amor innatus habendi", drives me to accumulate material I can
never use. The fact is, I cannot, I am impelled by an invisible force, to
be always refilling the vessel of the Danaides.' As prostration and
weakness took over more and more, so the solace even of reading
failed, though even at Harrogate, as the last entry in his diary demonstrated, the habit was too strong to fail absolutely, 'Vambery's
Travels ... Jane's Siege of London, Werner's Gastenlaubenbluthen and
Goethe's Iphigenie.'[47] Indeed, two days before his death, his wife

heard him mutter, 'Could you read Te mensorem?' She couldn't at
first understand to what he was alluding, but then it came to her that
it was a line from an ode of Horace: 'Te maris et terrae numeroque
carentis arenae mensorem cohibent Archyta.' 'I got a Horace', she
told Ellen Smith, 'and he followed but *I* had to guide *him* all
through—a strange reversal.'[48]

Whatever neglect he may have felt he had suffered in the past at his
wife's hands, in these sultry summer days she was indefatigable in the
care with which she nursed her dying husband. 'C'est l'exil ici', she
wrote sadly to Müntz, but she laboured on, bringing some morsel of
comfort. 'He is so piteous ... Will you be surprised to hear that he
can hardly bear me out of his sight, that he hardly ever asks me to do
a thing without a "darling" or "dear love", that he is all gentleness to
me. He says today that my "independence" was too much if one was
well, but ill it was the one perfect thing, that he did not wish for, nor
the doctor suggest a thing, but it was there the next moment without
a question asked. I can't write on like this. It upsets me too much and
one has to keep *bright* with him.'[49] She tried as far as it was humanly
possible to distract the dying mind. 'The only answer I find to the
despairing cry is to say that some part of each day can yet be used by
us in talk of interest and suggest subjects. *This* is my nursing;—the
doctor says to save him thus from *mental distress* is *the* great mercy.
God grant I may be able to give it to the last. I asked him if there was
anyone whom he would like to stay here. He refused impatiently ...
I said as gently as possible "Is there *anyone*, I will ask anyone, no
matter who, to come." He replied first "No-one you would like." I
said "My dear soul that is not what I am thinking of. I want and
would like to have *anyone* whose presence would be a pleasure to
you."'[50] The allusion to Meta Bradley was not lost on Mark. Yet in a
sense she too had become the past. He had no wish to see her in the
no man's land in which he was now placed. 'You do not', he reassured his wife, 'know what you are yourself. You are *all*-sufficing.
You do not know how good you are to me. You are my comfort and
consolation, the only one I want.' But with some return of his native
asperity, he had observed a few days earlier, 'How good you are to
me, if you had always been like this, what a reminiscence!' Affected
as she was, Mrs Pattison could not be dishonest, "My dear soul, no
one could be for anyone *like this* for long, do you not see that it takes

all my intelligence and all my strength fixed on the one thought of you to be like this." I then went slowly over the calls and objects of a life like mine and of the struggle against ill-health which had affected much of its best years and then added "Let us both give thanks rather that now in your hardest need I am here able and ready to watch over you and smooth all that is most painful and distressing to give you constant help in your direst need."[51] The triumph, as it seemed, over Meta's hold on her husband's affections must have given her great secret satisfaction.

The days were interminably wearisome. His wife sat by him from eight to twelve in the morning and from 12.30 to 2.30 p.m. She then took a break until tea-time, a half an hour for dinner and finally retired at 10.0. Mary Stirke came to help. His brother, Frank, his sister, Mary Roberts, his friend Bywater made calls. A letter from the Vice-Chancellor 'gave him limited pleasure'. 'He has gone steadily from ill to worse the whole time', Francis Pattison wrote on 6 July. 'It is difficult to command oneself perfectly I find, and yet the one thing one can do.'[52] 'Believe', she wrote again two days later, 'the change for the worse advances *a little* every day; have not dared to put him in a chair since Saturday when it was piteous to see him look on sky and field as if he knew it was Goodbye. He *is* so piteous. Did you understand that I meant *that* was what made self-command hard.'[53] But a few days later he showed interest in the publication of his Memoirs, 'much interested today in dictating directions as to the editing of his "Memoirs" which he wishes to be done *wholly* by myself. He talked of the misery of dying, of its helplessness, and that none could aid but stopped "only *you*—you do sensibly lessen the misery of dying, you sensibly lessen it".'[54]

The arrival of his sister Fanny, so devoted and yet so incapable of showing feeling, brought distress without comfort. 'I have had an *awful* ten days', Francis Pattison wrote, 'the worst that can overtake me is past with the removal this morning of "Sister Frances" whose condition was such as to cause me gravest anxiety . . . She distressed him, so I had to keep her away from him as much as possible, and this seemed cruel for she is passionately devoted to him, but *wholly* incapable of showing it in any way. She crawled all about the house, a shapeless speechless, black body of anguish eaten up with heartache at her own inability to be anything to him. To console and encourage *her* was my work the moment I left *him*, and at last I found her entertaining the most fantastic ideas awake all night with them etc. Fortunately the family discovered all this and took the matter into their own hands. I believe the brother sent for the eldest sister who came yesterday and took her away this morning. I now have Mary Stirke installed as my aide de camp.'[55] It was a move which the Rector appreciated, so the coolness which had once developed between them evaporated.

The Rector remained mentally alert, though there was a slow diminution in his mental powers. 'My poor Rector and I have a great deal of solemn talk at intervals when it is not too much for either of us', she wrote on 15 July. 'He is full of interest in these small arrangements—details of life—where I am to go, what I am to sell etc. etc. ... have amused and occupied him when nothing else would'. 'When conscious', she told Ellen Smith, 'I gave him this quotation from Landor "I have seen too much wrong in life to believe that anything right can happen to me now."'[56]

The question of the eternal verities was so deeply inbuilt into his spiritual life that he preferred in general to keep it silent and unregarded. Yet once in these last days he cast the veil aside. They were only 'broken utterances' but spoken with a 'passion which showed the intensity of belief', or at least that was how Mrs Pattison interpreted it. Intelligence lay at the root of being.

The true philosopher is so oppressed by the consciousness of the vast space around him that he is always modest but he possesses in the life of the soul the worthiest thing of all worthies. That is the idea to which we give the name of God.

God in the Baconian or Positivist scheme means the First Cause but the Baconian and Positivist view is, how has the intelligence increased the sum of what Lucretius calls the 'commoda vitae'.

Newman and the Lives of the Saints first put before me the idea of the life of the soul, but that view may be called the *Idea corruptrix* of the true, for it contains as a balance to its renunciations and its asceticism the set off of future reward payment by results.

To the philosopher God means the highest conceivable value, it is the thing per se, it is intellect. Whether it belongs to an individual or is a different essence like ... we don't know.

Aristotle thought it was a portion of a diffused essence escaping. What becomes of it we don't know. Of its physical nature we are absolutely ignorant. All the philosopher can do in life is to bear in mind its moral value as a possession is transcendent. If ever you have realised its existence, lay hold of it, never let it go—the life of the soul will give you joy beyond all other joys, if you have ever known it let nothing carry you away from it, but the world will be too strong for you. Remember that the momentary visitations of being are worth any objects of ambition—moments of realisation of self, if self it is. There is no such joy as this, hold it if you . . . have seen your way to it, keep it fast.

The positivists get no further than Bacon, no further than the idea of 'fruit' of the conquest of nature by the intelligence—apprehending its relations—all *that* is only the substratum or basis of the grand development of thought which provides not only for my seventy years of life, but for the past and present, which pervades all things.

The greater part of mankind have no mind, or circumstances have not developed it. Yet the whole of this ideal order of intellect is only a scaffolding on which is built up the grand conception of the universe as a totality governed by fixed laws. The true slavery is that of the "doers" to the free idle philosopher who lives not to do, or enjoy, but to know.

True knowledge is connected with consciousness of itself, this joy in the realisation of self—the beatific vision—Can I transfer that part of speculative seeing, of intuition, unaided by discursive perception or the sensitive faculties? Should I feel 'I' reduced to that?[57]

So, through the haze of illness and excruciating pain, Mark perceived in dim outline the *camera obscura* of the verities of his existence.

The slowing down of the mental process was in some respect a comfort. 'I think it is, on the whole, less painful, as he grows weaker and the mind is less active. The dreadful days were those in which one had to try to hold his attention from morning to night to keep him from preying on himself.'[58] There were, however, times when the old Adam would out. 'There is much that is dreadfully painful', Francis wrote on 26 July, 'in the persistence of his cruel misconceptions of the conduct of those who have loved him best. His last half hour of clear head was spent in dictating a leter calculated to wound most deeply his sister Eleanor in answer to an appeal for one "last word in memory, at least, of all she once had been to him." Dr Oliver thought one should disobey. Mary agreed with me that I had no right to withhold the letter though it will be she thinks a never to be forgotten blow to her aunt, so it has been sent. This is but *one* out of daily similar occurrences *which* put one on a rack . . .'[59]

If there had been little actual pain at the start, he was now suffer-ing intensely, for he was dying, not as the doctors assumed of leukaemia, but of cancer of the stomach. He could take no more than iced soda-water and a spoonful of beef-tea, tea or cocoa. 'The terrible smell and the retching are horribly offensive', she told Rose Tuck-well . . . 'we are now keeping him under opiates (nepenthe) so it is easier for us all.' But opiates were insufficient to soften the torture. 'The nurses say they never saw anything like it—the always un-controllable temper, the rage, the pathos, the abject fits of terror, the immense vitality. I have been 72 hours without a sound sleep and we are all worn out. Poor Mary said just now "It is as he has been all his life only we think it so dreadful *because* he is dying." At 5 this morning'—she was writing on the 30 July—'the morphine passed off and then till the doctor came nurse and I stood for 4 hours witness-ing the terrible fits of terror with shrieks which went through the house and trying to ease and calm. Let not my last days be like his! The moral misery is awful.'[60]

On his last night his wife read to him the 'Ode on Eton College', Mark commenting on it 'with all his old aptness, pregnancy and refinement'.[61] Then he turned to dictate a cruel, farewell letter to his sister Eleanor. He relapsed into unconsciousness, did not wake with the morning light and died at 1.25 p.m. on 31 July, 1884. 'I am approached', he had written to his friend, Lionel Tollemache, 'very near the "famulae Manes et domus exilis Plutonia."' Now the curtain had fallen, and the agonized spirit was quiet. 'The chief Oxford event to tell', Mrs Johnson wrote to Jessie on 1 August, 'is the death of the poor old Rector whereby indeed the place loses a character, and a student which it has not the like of. I feel his death may remove a source of anxiety from you. It is very sad when a man's intellectual work is the best thing to be said of him—you know how little I ever liked the poor old gentleman, how angry I felt with him . . . and he has now gone to his God and we will keep silence.'

Aftermath

THE personal tragedy of the Rector's declining years had helped to set in train a series of consequences which, as in a Greek tragedy, had to be worked out before the tale was ended. Exhausted by her gruelling experience, Mrs Pattison left the house that they had rented at 8 Oval Place and moved to the Granby Hotel. 'My head', she told Ellen Smith on 2 August, 'still suffers from the incessant strain of the last six weeks and sleep will not come back rightly either to the nurse or myself for sometime to come. Last night even I started up on the point of springing from my bed hearing him shriek quite plainly . . .'[1] She did not take as her companion Mary Stirke, as Mark had wished, but her friend, Venetia Grant Duff, close to Charles Dilke, whom Mark had once described as a 'very unpleasant' woman.

The funeral was strictly private as, according to Mrs Pattison, Mark had himself enjoined. 'NO ONE is to come to the funeral except his near relatives and myself. I could not face it with an unknown troop and we are agreed *I* ought to go (I understand him to wish it). All is in accordance with his express wish to be "as quietly as possible" and to be "here". We discussed it fully, but when I went to the cemetery it was so hideously inappropriate, so unlike his idea of "lying in his own moor air in his own country" that I enquired and found a bit of ground on Harlow Moor in a country graveyard where the hills he loved will look for ever on his grave.'[2]

Mrs Pattison's decision was criticized by Ellen Smith. She certainly gave offence by failing to invite his Oxford friends. 'Francis has made some mortal enemies by her action and she has not too many friends just now', she commented to Ingram Bywater. 'So many wished to show affection and respect by going down to Harrogate and they naturally feel aggrieved at the one person who felt neither trying to forbid their coming. I was so sorry.'[3] Bywater had advised Warde Fowler, the fellow of Lincoln closest to Pattison, that the funeral was to be strictly private. 'I confess', he told Mrs Pattison, 'I would gladly have made even a much longer journey in order to be present.'[4] It is possible that Mark may have expressed such a wish, feeling that a Christian burial service was something of a meaningless pretense, a mocking apex to a failed faith. Yet in other ways he was a conventional Victorian. Although he did not believe in the proprieties, he held them dear. It is difficult to suppose that he would not have wished his friends, acquaintances, and critics to pay their respects at the last rites. Mrs Pattison's position was, however, understandable. She wished to close the book as soon as possible, to rid herself of her husband's remains as quietly and conveniently as possible, preferably not under the gaze of prying and even hostile eyes.

So, Mark Pattison was laid to rest in St. Peter's cemetery, Harlow Hill, Harrogate. Mrs Pattison superintended 'the making of the tomb about which he gave me the most minute directions'; it was a plain stone slab with a simple inscription. In 1927, Mrs Braithwaite Batty, a daughter of his friend, Henry Stebbing, gave money so that the grave should be kept in good order, a responsibility that the College has only sporadically fulfilled.[5] The post-mortem revealed that the Rector had died of 'extensive cancer in the small curvature of the stomach extending in various nodules into the liver. Every other organ heart included *perfectly healthy*, the heart murmurs due only to a little calcereous deposit ... The constitution iron.'[6]

Her task completed, Mrs Pattison returned to Oxford to recuperate. 'I was *very* ill at first, but chiefly my brain had given out from the continuous strain ... the doctor advised 3 weeks rest and iron water.'[7] She had to vacate the Lodgings, moving the greater part of the furniture to the house that Dilke was building at Pyrford near Woking, one of the four houses that he eventually owned and occupied.[a] For the time being she lived in a small furnished house, the Lodge, at Headington where she set about preparing her husband's memoirs for publication.

Pattison had died a relatively wealthy man. His will was proved

[a] i.e. 76 Sloane Street, Dockett Eddy on the river near Chertsey which Dilke had had built, and ten miles away a small cottage which Lady Dilke transformed into a country house, Pyrford Rough, as well as their French home, La Sainte Campagne near Toulon.

at £45,561, the bulk of which went to his widow.[b] There was, however, a legacy of £5,000, made by a codicil signed on 25 February 1884, left to Meta Bradley. Its disposal brought about on Mrs Pattison's part a recurrence of the ill-feeling which she had stifled during the last months of his illness. She had believed that she had come out the victor in the battle of wills and affections; but in the very hour of her triumph, so to speak, she discovered that she had been deceived. Indeed she held that she had been misled by her erring husband. At the time of making the codicil he had explained his need to consult his solicitor by informing her that he wished to reduce the legacies of £1000 each which he had left to Mary and Jeannie Stirke to increase what was due to come to her. Mrs Pattison commented 'I have divided £2000 between Jenny and Mary.' 'On his death-bed he told me there were no other legacies and he so *positively* assured me of this *without my putting any question* to him adding that except those nothing was left away from me that I felt myself justified in telling his brother [Frank] we might hope the legacy to which he felt so strong an objection [i.e. to Meta] had been cancelled. This was not the case. It is inexpressibly painful to think he was deliberately lying and to have these hideous thoughts to keep us company to his grave.'[9] What he had actually done, she supposed, 'was to add the £2000 taken from them to Miss Bradley's £3000 which he then raised to £5000'. A woman scorned, though the bequest was no more than a minimal part of the total, Mrs Pattison reacted, even over-reacted angrily.

For Mark his bequest to Meta was an act of generosity, taken not merely as a sign of his affection but in the full knowledge of the harsh treatment accorded to her by her father, and of the inadequate income on which she would have to live, supposing she never married, for the remainder of her life. As early as October 1879 he had contemplated 'leaving £5000 away from F[rancis].' In 1880 he revoked the legacy of £1000 which he had intended for Lincoln to provide for Meta. In December 1882 he had executed a further codicil to give her a more sufficient legacy, apparently informing his

[b] 'I cannot tell you precisely my circumstances ... I believe we shall swear under £52,000. There is nothing to keep out of the papers after payment of the legacies, everything was left absolutely "to my dear wife Francis-Emilia".'[8]

wife that he had done so. It was surely a small recompense for the affection that Meta had lavished on him.

If Mrs Pattison's reaction was ungenerous, the Bradleys proved as unsympathetic. They tried to bring pressure on Meta to give it back. 'Mrs Charles Bradley has been to ask the [Frank] Pattisons whether they would take a "more lenient view were the money returned"', Mrs Mark Pattison recounted to Ellen Smith. 'On Mrs [Frank] Pattison's indignantly repudiating the possibility Mrs Bradley explained that Miss Bradley declined to part with a sixpence but the family were making it up amongst themselves to give back to us.'[10] With unusual acumen, Meta had availed herself of the earliest possibility of obtaining the legacy; it was sent by the solicitor, Mr Robinson, on the very day that he advised her of it.

Mrs Pattison's view of Meta Bradley as a schemer bent on winning her husband's affections was further reinforced by reading his diary, 'making a very distressing discovery in the locked tin box which leads me to think he perhaps had good reason for telling me "it was his duty to provide for her"'.[11] 'I took the bold step of placing *all* keys in my brother-in-law's hands and authorizing him to do as he chose at Lincoln College till my return. *He* examined the Diaries the *worst* and then wrote me a letter hoping that *I* had all the others as they "were not fit to be in unworthy hands".'[12] Mrs Pattison was once more outraged by evidence of her husband's love for Meta; she was embarrassed by reference to its physical manifestation, though it seems reasonable to doubt whether this had ever gone beyond petting and kissing. Three weeks after the Rector's death, she learned that Meta had written a letter to *The Academy*, and she determined to bring out her big guns. 'The Miss Bradley affair is more serious that we had supposed. She has already begun threatening in *The Academy* to publish a letter. We are taking measures to let the family know that we have in our hands *evidence* of grave indiscretion of which we shall make use unless she keeps perfectly quiet.'[13] But no big guns were called for. Meta's letter was more like a damp squib. It commented simply on the obituary notice in the paper, adding that the writer possessed a letter with a 'slight sketch of his interview with Newman, in a letter addressed to me soon after that pathetic incident, that she might one day publish.' The letter was signed simply 'B'.[14]

The problem presented by the *Memoirs* constituted a matter of greater moment. Mrs Pattison, with the probable complicity of Frank Pattison who had been entrusted with the examination of the diaries, had excised or scratched out practically every reference to Meta Bradley in them, however innocuous. But Meta was indelibly associated with her husband's memoirs. It was she who had originally planted the idea of his writing an account of his early life, had industriously watered and tended the young plant, giving every encouragement and showing every interest in what he was writing. Mark had already secured a promise from Macmillans to print the book.[15] It was inconceivable that the book should be withheld, more especially as its contents were, from the point of view of both Mrs Pattison and Meta Bradley, entirely indifferent. But 'the Memoirs', Mark had told Meta 'are addressed to you'. It is possible that they were actually dedicated to her. In Mrs Pattison's present mood this was an unthinkable course. 'These "Memoirs"' she was to explain in the foreword, 'were originally entitled by the writer "Recollections of my Life", but when he gave his last directions concerning them he directed that they should be called Memoirs. He was asked whether they were dedicated to an old and valued friend of his early life, and replied, "They are not dedicated to anyone; you will see for yourself, when you come to read them, that they are not fit to be dedicated to anyone." A provisional dedication, which was found in the MS has been withdrawn by the same authority as that whereby the title has been changed.' Meta could only bite her lips at this disingenuous explanation. Some other minor changes were made in the manuscript, but the events were too remote to demand any radical alteration. Mrs Thursfield helped Mrs Pattison to correct the proofs.[16]

When the *Memoirs* were launched on the world in 1885, they met with a mixed reception. Although the Victorians not infrequently abandoned accepted formalities in private life, even the most critical among them sought to sustain a conventional public image. Ten years were to elapse before the Victorian world was scandalized by the case of Oscar Wilde. Victorian readers would be offended by revelations which cast doubt on conventional moral values. Pattison's memoirs were in no sense scandalous, but they were an implied criticism of established religious beliefs, more especially of Tractarianism which had by 1884, in contributing richly to the revival of Anglican spirituality, acquired respectability. Even worse was the lack of commitment, the negative tone, which the *Memoirs* reflected. The Victorians esteemed success, moral endeavour, strong convictions. 'The earlier part of the volume', a reviewer in the *Spectator* commented, 'has interested us very deeply; but the interest of the whole is like the story of a wreck told without the reader being aware that in a wreck it is to end.' The same writer found the 'later half of this volume . . . painful reading, not only for its picture of the pettinesses and spite of collegiate life at Oxford, but for the impression it leaves upon us that Mr Pattison in throwing off the moral restraints of all pure theology over the inner life, gave himself up to the indolent melancholy and the vivid moroseness which the disappointment of legitimate hopes had engendered in him, without making even the slightest moral struggle to turn his own wounded feelings into the sources of a nobler life than any he had lived before.'[17] 'The shadows indeed prevail', was the verdict of the *Oxford Magazine*, 'like its writer's face, it seldom brightens into gaiety, and is almost always keen, deliberate, self-possessed.' 'Remembering', the writer commented, 'that we are reading the life of a man whose most salient characteristic was an almost unintermittent desire to go forward we can partly understand why the history of Oxford should be treated in it with hardly a trace of gratitude or affection, and why we so often miss the resource and self-respect with which we should expect a man like Pattison to handle his own mental history . . . It is indeed a history of human error in half a century of Oxford life, cutting mercilessly to the canker at the core and laying aside almost unnoticed the more fruitful parts of each generation's work.'[18] John Morley in *Macmillan's Magazine* paid tribute to Pattison's scholarship. 'He was essentially a bookman, but of that high type . . . which explores through books the voyages of the human heart, the chequered fortunes of great human conceptions.' At the core the *Memoirs* revealed deep moral flaws: 'the stamp of moral defaillance was set upon his brow from the beginning.'[19] Gladstone was more just, ranking the *Memoirs* as 'among the most tragic and memorable books of the nineteenth century'.

The *Memoirs* encapsulated a past that had become history. Meta Bradley, never more than on the periphery of Mrs Pattison's real life, went out of it altogther. An intimate understanding had been forged already with Sir Charles Dilke, almost certainly finalized when they met at Mrs Earle's on 13 May, 1884. So even the recent past began to appear a wintry fog, leaving only here and there patches of raw mist. But she could not have foreseen the storm clouds gathering over-head. 'The day the Rector's death was announced', Ellen Smith informed Ingram Bywater, 'there was betting in London on who she would marry and how soon! What beasts people must be!'[20] In November Dilke told Joseph Chamberlain of his plans, but the news was kept from the general public.

To pass the period which Victorian custom supposed to be seemly between death and re-marriage, Mrs Pattison proposed to stay as a guest of Grant Duff and his wife, Venetia—her real names were Anna Julie—at Madras of which Grant Duff had been governor since 1881. After an enjoyable journey—'interesting companions, perfect weather, perfect comfort', 'arriving late caught the governor at the station surrounded by guards and officers and rajahs ... received a bouquet ... in royal state "progressed" up here [Government House, Madras] in all the state and none of the cares of grandeur.'[21] The governor was a gruff—that was the nickname by which he was known—rather unprepossessing man, not overly faithful to his wife. Mrs Pattison's affection for Venetia Duff may have been promoted by their partial experience of married life. So she moved to the sunlit gardens of the government house at Ootacamund in the Nilgiri hills, a house modelled by the former governor, the last Duke of Buckingham, on his palatial mansion at Stowe, where she was soon enveloped in the panoply and intrigue of imperial rule. 'The air braces one till the exhilaration is almost too much for everyday peaceful propriety. You want to dance, to sing, to shout with joy for nothing except it *is* so delicious to be alive.' It was an atmosphere transparently light years away from pain-ridden Harrogate, fog-streamed London, and the melancholy gloom of Oxford; she would, she told Sir Charles, readily accompany him to Cambridge—he was a graduate of Trinity Hall—but 'I don't think I should ever go to the (other) place which I devoutly hope I may never see again'.

It was hardly surprising that after such a sense of release that she should wonder about the wisdom of another marriage. Her affection for Charles Dilke had, however, become a part of her 'in *spite* of the terror of this and obligation which the past has left upon me'. 'You used to have,' Dilke wrote back reassuringly, 'terrors at the delay and now that the days draw shorter you have terrors at the tie.'[22]

If Mrs Pattison had achieved a serene composure, Charles Dilke was menaced. Deeply involved in political life, strongly ambitious, talked of as a possible successor to Gladstone, he had become the target of anonymous letters. 'I think', he wrote to Mrs Pattison, 'they'll try some plot to poison our happiness. They can't, of course, but they might give us a deal of worry.' This, in the light of future events, was a fair understatement. Some at least of the letters were probably written by Mrs Eustace Smith, who had been his mistress in 1868 and again after his first wife's death until, after reaching some sort of understanding with Mrs Pattison, he brought the affair to an end in 1875. Mrs Smith was an unstable woman, often at loggerheads with her brood of children and not averse to sending letters under the cloak of anonymity criticizing their morals to their various husbands. Her daughter, Maye, had been married to Charles's brother, Ashton, who died young. Another, Helen, was married to a rich stockbroker, the brother of the positivist, Frederick Harrison. Her fourth daughter, Virginia, was the wife of Donald Crawford, the former fellow of Lincoln College, a serious minded Scottish lawyer, Liberal candidate for North Lanarkshire, a man much older than his wife and apparently already tired of her infidelities, since he had engaged a detective to keep track on her activities and was himself envisaging a possible re-marriage.

It was on Friday 17 July, that Donald Crawford, agitated by the receipt of a seond anonymous letter accusing his wife of being Dilke's mistress, put the question to her in their bedroom: 'Virginia, it is true that you have defiled my bed? I have been a faithful husband to you.' She replied: 'Yes, it is true, it is time that you should know the truth. You have always been on the wrong track, suspecting people who are innocent, and you have never suspected the person who is guilty.' 'I never', Donald replied, 'suspected anybody except Captain Forster'. 'It was not Captain Forster. The man who ruined me was Charles Dilke. He seduced me six months after our marriage three and a half years ago and I was his mistress ever since.' On at least one occasion she was to assert that they had been joined in bed by one of Dilke's servants, Fanny Gray.

The news of Virgina Crawford's confession and of her husband's decision to name Dilke as co-respondent was carried to Dilke two days later by a mutual friend of both parties, Christina Rogerson. Christina Rogerson was yet another of the hysterical, unstable women who seemed to abound in the case. She was well-known in London society; Henry James depicted her as the worldly but attractive Lady Davenant in *A London Life*. Her brother, Charles, was Donald Crawford's solicitor, and she was a bosom friend of Virginia Crawford, conniving at her love affair with Captain Forster. Equally she was a close friend of the Dilke family, more especially of Dilke's uncle who lived also at 76 Sloane Street. She may have been his mistress and almost certainly was for a time Dilke's. She had been married to a wealthy Scottish landowner, much older than herself, whom she did not love and who had died in 1884.

She saw herself as a possible candidate for Dilke's hand. 'Meanwhile', Henry James wrote, 'another London lady whom I won't name, with whom for years his relations have been concomitant with his relations with Mrs Pattison, and whose husband died, has had every expectation that he was on the point of marrying *her*. This is a very brief sketch of the situation, which is queer, and dramatic and disagreeable. Dilke's private life won't (I imagine) bear looking into, and the vengeful Crawford will do his best to lay it bare. He will probably not succeed, and Dilke's political reputation, with the great "middle class", will weather the storm. But he will have been frightened almost to death. For a man who has had such a passion for keeping up appearances and appealing to the staid middle class, he has, in reality, been strangely, incredibly reckless. His long, double liaison with Mrs Pattison and the other lady, of a nature to make it a duty of honour to marry *both* (!!) when they should become free, and the death of each husband at the same time—with the public watching to see *which* he *would* marry—and the meanwhile "going on" with poor little Mrs Crawford, who is a kind of infant—the whole thing is a theme for the novelist—or at least for *a* novelist.'[23] Dilke himself alleged that 'the conspiracy comes from a woman who wanted me to marry her', adding 'but this is guess work'. Yet was it? Mrs Rogerson was a very likely candidate for the authorship of the recent anonymous letters. It must have been with very mixed feelings indeed that she summoned Dilke to her house in near-by Hans Place to tell him Crawford's decision.

It was shattering beyond belief. The implications for his political career would be enormous and catastrophic. 'Such a charge', he confided to his diary, 'even if disproved which is not easy against perjured evidence picked up with care is fatal to supreme usefulness in politics . . . I prefer therefore to at once contemplate leaving public life for ever.' But what of his future happiness? How would Mrs Pattison react to a tale of sordidness whose depths could not be surely plumbed? Since letters took at least a month to reach India, he persuaded his friend, Joseph Chamberlain, to telegraph briefly to Grant Duff, explaining what had happened, requesting him to pass on the news. 'Dear, dear love', she had written on 11 June 1885, 'I'm getting so well again, I don't know myself. I DO love you so and I will be lovely dear when you get me [word expunged]—my darling, please I *do* so love.' Shortly after this she had fallen victim to a mild attack of typhoid and was still confined to bed when the news reached her. But she had no hesitation. She at once cabled *The Times* to announce her engagement to Sir Charles Dilke. The notice appeared in the engagement column on 18 August 1886. 'To day', Sir Charles told Miss Smith, 'I had telegrams saying she should at once proclaim our engagement and saying the story was absurd on the face of it.'

'A thousand thanks', Mrs Pattison herself wrote to Ellen Smith on 10 September 1885, 'for your kind letter and offer to meet me with Sir Charles. I am in robust health — distinguished for the first time in my life by a total absence of nerves, and feel able to take a good grip of all that is before me. The first shock of finding such accusations possible was of course very terrible—*most* terrible to know the agony *which* was inflicted on him, but I feel confident that the strength which has been given to him for many years past in which he has sought the highest life will not desert him now. Men's justice may be deceived or fail us for a time, but I am confident that the truth of his nature and life will evidently make itself plain. The perfect confidence in his honour and innocence which is so widely shown by those whom one most heartily respects is already a great boon.'[24]

The marriage was to take place by special licence at St. Luke's Church, Chelsea, on 3 October. Mrs Pattison's brother, Colonel Strong, was not well enough to attend. 'Mr [Frank] Pattison will "give me away" ... My only grief is for him for his [Dilke's] bitter suffering ... I have to keep quite cool, never shed a tear, never be depressed and hide even my anger for fear of his breaking down. The service is 12.30. We *ask* no one to be present but Miss Dilke, my brother and sister, the Pattisons, but many have volunteered.'[25] 'What a beautiful service it was!', Lady Dilke wrote the next day from the Oatlands Park Hotel, 'and this morning we have just come back from church where we received the Communion together and felt as if it were a part of yesterday. Did you think of us when you read the Psalms this morning. They seemed chosen for *us*? One thing only vexed us yesterday—you not coming up to Burwood Place [the home of the Frank Pattisons] after. We were crammed of course, in their tiny rooms, but any *crush* would have been better than not seeing you my dear, dear Ellen.'[26]

The case of *Crawford v. Crawford* was heard before Mr Justice Butt on 12 February 1886. It resulted in a verdict which by the quirks of English law was legally possible but historically paradoxical. The case against Dilke was dismissed: 'the unsworn statement of a person in the position of Mrs Crawford is not entitled or even considered in a Court of Justice as against the person with whom she is alleged to have committed adultery.' Yet the judge accepted the fact of adultery and granted Crawford a divorce. This was in conformity with the law which allowed that a wife's confession to her husband constituted evidence of her guilt but did not thereby necessarily mean that the co-respondent whom she had named was himself guilty. As Roy Jenkins has put it 'the verdict appeared to be that Mrs Crawford had committed adultery with Dilke, but that he had not done so with her'.[27]

Dilke, who had not given evidence, was at first pleased with the verdict, but his pleasure was to be short-lived. The case was taken up by the militant puritanical journalist, W. T. Stead, who had a salacious taste in sexual matters, in the *Pall Mall Gazette* of which he had been editor since 1883 in succession to John Morley. He wished to promote the circulation of his newspaper and thought that Dilke could act as a lever against Chamberlain for whom as a politician he had a particular detestation. He hounded the unfortunate Dilke relentlessly and mercilessly. He had failed to go into the witness box to clear his name. He had let down his constituents at Chelsea; the moral dimensions of the case were obvious to all.

In the face of such criticism Dilke decided that the only effective way to clear his name was to invoke the intervention of the Queen's Proctor in the hope that he would upset the verdict of 12 February. This was to prove an ill-advised move. Dilke had supposed incorrectly that he would still be a party to the case and that his counsel could submit witnesses to cross-examination. But he learned to his dismay that he could only be called as a witness and that the only counsel with the right of cross-examination were the counsel for Donald Crawford and the Queen's Proctor. Furthermore the Queen's Proctor, Sir Augustus Stephenson, from the start revealed a stiff hostility to Dilke. Crawford was represented by a redoubtable QC, Henry Matthews, brusque and penetrating, whereas Dilke's interests were represented by the counsel briefed by the Queen's Proctor, Sir Walter Phillimore who lacked his opponent's skill. Where Mrs Crawford was a crisp and confident witness (and the most skilful of liars), Dilke was evasive, unsure, and long-winded. The verdict was a foregone conclusion. The jury refused to upset the decision which had been reached on 12 February. Not merely was the stigma even more firmly attached to Dilke's name, but the case against him had been strengthened. 'Charles', his wife wrote, '*was* terribly discouraged and depressed by Hannen's ruling [Sir James Hannen was the presiding judge] . . . but I told him he must not let it appear, and he *must* continue to wear a brave face however sick at heart.'

The imponderables of the case remain and will never be resolved. Dilke was confronted by a group of frustrated, unstable and unreliable women. Mrs Crawford was intelligent, young—only 23—but, at least in sexual matters, far from inexperienced. Why had she 'gunned' for Dilke in the sure knowledge that in making her confession to her husband she was hounding Dilke out of public life? She can hardly have been egged on by her mother, desirous of revenging herself as a discarded mistress, since she was barely on speaking terms with her. If, in fact, Virginia Crawford had been, if but very temporarily, Dilke's mistress, then the termination of the arrangement in July 1884, at the time that Pattison was known to be dying, could have evoked in her a desire for vengeance. It seems more probably, however, that it was her wish to protect her real lover, Captain Forster, that affords the most likely explanation of her action. Although she testified that her affair with Forster did not antedate 1884, there was clear evidence that it had been in being since 1881, and that on more than one occasion she had shared his favours with her sister, Helen (and not his favours alone) at a *maison de passe* at 9 Hill Street. Forster, who appears as a kind of Victorian Don Juan, was a professional army officer. Donald Crawford suspected correctly that he was his wife's lover. To divert attention Virginia named Dilke, and, in the view of some critics, transferred episodes in her affair with Forster to Dilke, including conceivably the 'threesome' in a bed. Her story, though presented with verve, was full of pitfalls. It seems inconceivable that in a house so replete with servants as was 76 Sloane Street that Mrs Crawford's comings and goings could have passed unnoticed. Moreover the plan she drew of the house was plainly fallacious. That she had committed adultery can hardly be doubted, but whether it was with Dilke was unclear. Yet in 1889 Cardinal Manning received her into the Roman Church. It seems again extraordinary that if she had then made a confession to the Cardinal that some form of contrition should not have required her to make amends to Dilke for the wrong she had perpetrated, if wrong it was. Throughout the crisis Manning remained friendly and sympathetic towards Dilke. In such a morass it is easy to lose one's way and to sink without reaching dry ground. For reasons which are obscure, Helen, who had shared lovers with her sister, quarrelled bitterly and gave evidence against her while her other sister, Maye Dilke, stood by Virginia, so severing her relations with her husband's family. Mrs Rogerson's role was as unclear. More immediately she had endeavoured to maintain friendly relations with all parties, more especially seeking to win the good opinion of the new Lady Dilke. She denied that she had any responsibility for bringing on the case and expressed the hope that she and Lady Dilke should be 'wholly friends'. She then experienced a nervous breakdown and only emerged from the nursing home shortly before the second trial in which she gave evidence in support of Mrs Crawford. 'If she had been beautiful and sane', Henry James observed, 'she would have been one of the world's great wicked women.'[28]

In spite of all this, Dilke's own position is not devoid of difficulty. He appeared shifty and that he had something to hide, even from his devoted wife, seems not improbable. His life had been, as he admitted, in his early days far from impeccable. It could well be that if Mrs Crawford had not been his mistress, there might have been other sordid episodes which he wished to screen from the public, even from the beloved Emilia, as she now wished to be called. What was curious was the state of Dilke's engagement diary which had been lacerated by snippets cut out from every page. His explanation that he had removed such engagements with scissors once they had been fulfilled appears wholly unconvincing. It was difficult not to feel that such deletions might have been intended to remove evidence of engagements with a person which he did not wish to record. Even more perplexing was the disappearance of Fanny Gray, the servant girl, with whom, it was alleged, he had shared a bed with Mrs Crawford. Her evidence could at least have put paid to that story, supposing it were untrue. Contrariwise had she been Dilke's mistress it could only have added fuel to the fire. But Fanny went underground and when she did eventually surface she remained mum; her silence had been bought, and if bought then most probably by Dilke. The case was strewn with red herrings none of which could be caught. What, for instance, passed between Mrs Crawford and Joseph Chamberlain when she called, presumably by appointment, at his house in 40 Princes Gardens, on 15 July 1885, *two* days before her confession to her husband? Chamberlain never mentioned the call to Dilke and later asserted that he had never actually seen Mrs Crawford as he was out of the house when she called, but this, on the evidence of the private detective employed by Crawford to tail his wife, seems most unlikely.

What stands out is Lady Dilke's devoted loyalty to her husband. 'I find', she wrote on 14 December 1885, 'that I want all my strength and patience to meet the REAL *facts* of our trouble and that it is but a hideous and useless burden to lay on my mind all the filth that vile imaginations conjure up and embroider on them. We are going straight on, striving to bring the truth and the whole truth before those who must judge.'[29] 'Courage and fortitude seem to me what I am decreed to need all my life.' She had never been more in need of it, even during the most critical period of her relationship with Mark. 'You always said', Charles Dilke told his wife, 'that that family would lead us to shame, you could not have guessed to what shame. I believe I shall have to let the Crawford suit at the last moment go without defence, on condition that nothing is said, because otherwise they not only *press* the adultery with the mother and also bring a charge of unnatural crime—Heaven save the mark—with the brother. This they have already abandoned as a lie and a mass of other charges supported by conspiracy and perjured evidence ... I believe your love can forgive even shame and exile. 76 [Sloane Street] must be burnt down after you have cleared the things from it.'[30] On this Lady Dilke commented some weeks later 'Do you remember his talking to you of the room which he kept locked and barred to his best thoughts and assocations, the room in which he was born, his mother's bedroom and now mine? *This* is the room on which Mrs Crawford fixed as the scene of some of her most horrible tales! Can you wonder that he said he would burn down the house so that I could never sleep there! I *insisted* on doing so, as the only wholesome way of meeting the impression which will fade in time, but which I see cropping up now and then in the pain of his face.'[31]

But the work of exorcising the evil spirits was not accomplished easily. Dilke was aware of critical glances in the House of Commons. If outwardly friendly, Gladstone's attitude was glacial. Dilke had narrowly retained his seat at Chelsea in November 1885, by 175 votes, only to lose by the same narrow margin, 176 votes, in the general election of 1886. Even if the slimness of the loss suggested that the voters were not unduly influenced by the current scandal, his political future was at best gloomy and at worst seemingly beyond reprieve.

In this deluge of misfortunes Lady Dilke stood firm as a rock. She thought it ridiculous to withdraw from politics. 'I am sure of my own nerve and sure that I can stand a long pull; all my combative instincts are aroused and I inherit a large supply of them ... I am ready to do anything which you think wise to be done—you may rely on my being ready and proud to co-operate with you in any way you may point out.'[32] She had to share with him the social ostracism which the scandal precipitated but she never faltered in her firmness, patience and courage.

The repercussions resounded for a long time. There seemed even a possibility that Dilke might find himself charged with perjury on oath, a charge that could certainly have been brought against Mrs Crawford; and he tinkered with the notion of living abroad to escape the stigma of prison, only ultimately to reject it. But as the threat receded, so he and his wife began to pick up the threads of their political and social life. Lady Dilke continued tenaciously to follow up any clues that would support her husband's innocence. The shadow cast over Dilke for some time stemmed any attempt to re-enter public life; but in July 1892 he was elected MP for the Forest of Dean, holding the seat until his death nearly twenty years later. Lady Dilke continued to read, study, and write, and was active in the movement for women's rights. With her husband she had achieved, if late in life, a perfectly harmonious union, each complementing the other. She died suddenly on Monday 24 October 1904, he, seven years later, in 1911.

In 1887 Hector Malot published a book *Vices français*, the title taken from Mrs Crawford's assertion that Dilke had taught her 'every French vice'.[c] The novel was not merely a thinly disguised account of the Dilke case, leaning heavily in favour of Sir Charles, but some of the sentences seemed to be copies in French translation of actual letters, suggesting that the author may well have had access to information which Lady Dilke supplied. An English translation *Josey* (Mrs Crawford appears in the novel as Josephine or Josey Macdonnel) was published, with Mrs Crawford in her riding-habit providing the illustrated frontispiece; but it seems not to have attracted much attention.

Mrs Crawford had undertaken some journalistic work for W. T. Stead while he was editor of the *Pall Mall Gazette*, but in 1889 she was received into the Roman Church and devoted the rest of her long life to religious and social work. She became chairman of St. Joan's Social and Political Alliance, and of St. Joseph's Home for Girl Mothers, was one of the founders of the Catholic Social Guild, a member of the Local Board of Guardians and the first Labour member of St. Marylebone borough council. She was a prolific author, writing on art and religion, *Studies in Foreign Literature*, a little book on Fra Angelico, another on Frederic Ozanam, and a description of Switzerland. Intelligent and later formidable, she never married again and died aged 85 on 19 October 1948, sixty-three years after the major event in her life to which she never afterwards seems to have

[c] May Laffan had edited Malot's popular novel *Sans famille*, translated as *No Relations* in 1880.

alluded. Her first husband, Donald Crawford who married again, in 1914, Lilian, the daughter of Lord Moncrieff, was prominent in the political and social life of Scotland, dying on New Year's Day 1919. Captain Forster married his rich girl, but whether he lived happily ever after might be doubted.

The other actors in the drama too faded from the scene. The Eustace Smiths, their moral integrity somewhat tainted, gave up their rich residence in 52 Prince's Gate to move, at least temporarily, to Algiers. The Stirkes, who must have been rivetted by Mrs Pattison's new role, were absorbed into their Yorkshire background from which their uncle had momentarily extracted them. Mary, with all her zest for life, died unmarried. To Mark's disgust, Jeannie had married Charles E. Newton Robinson, a barrister, on 9 April 1884. He was a Cambridge graduate, an enthusiastic yatchsman, and an expert fencer who was a member of the British épée team at the Olympic Games held at Athens in 1906. He collected engraved gems and drawings, wrote poetry, *Tintannabula, Viol of Love*, and *Ver Lyrae* as well as other works of minor literature, such as *Cruise of the Widgeon, Picturesque Rambles in Purbeck*, and *Alice in Plunderland*. he died in 1913 at the age of 60: they had no children. Her sister Rachel married the Reverend Gother Mann, the nephew of Mark's eldest sister, Eleanor.

Eleanor died in 1896, her husband, the Reverend Frederick William Mann, Rector of the 'Castel' in Guernsey, six years later. They had two children. Both married but they were childless, the last, Lady de Saumarez, dying in 1947. Frank Pattison, Mark's brother, died at the age of 78 on 16 September 1922. There were thus no direct living descendants of the Pattison family.

Meta lived on unmarried. In that last fateful year, 1884, she had embraced the single life that was to carry her through the next forty years. 'You mustn't think', she told Mark in his last illness, 'for a moment that I wish our friendship had been other than it has ... Whatever anyone may say or think, I am absolutely content ... I don't believe I should ever have loved anyone well enough to marry him. I've never had the faintest spark of feeling of that sort for anyone, though I have many true friends among men ... But friendship isn't marriage and I've no wish to lose the first by the second. Of course I don't want reminding that the life of an unmarried woman must be desolate and lonely, but it has many compensations and fewer risks than that of a married woman, and I long ago made up my mind which I'd choose. I did it with my eyes open and don't repent.'[33]

After Mark's death, Meta had thrown herself into her social work with greater determination than ever, self-absorbed to the point of nervous tension. 'Meta', W. Hunter told Courtenay Ilbert, referring evidently to Courtenay himself, 'like a certain other member of the family not unknown in India is simply killing herself by overwork ... doing her work by pure nerve force instead of by calm physical strength.' Eventually, in spite of Dean Bradley's disapproval, she sought, ironically not unlike Mrs Pattison, to escape from the damaging prison of the past by travelling to India to join her sister. It is not plain how long she stayed in India, but Jessie was writing on 19 April 1886 that 'Meta seems to be enjoying herself. It is fortunate that she likes riding about with young Hadow.' Was there on Jessie's part a secret hope that 'young Hadow' or some other young man might help Meta to forget Mark? But Hadow disappeared from the scene, accompanying a Miss Bogle, the governess, on an expedition to the Kangra valley. It would be, Jessie told Courtenay, 'a change for him and I don't know what on earth we would do with him here during the rains'. So much for young Hadow! Yet the possibility of romance did not entirely disappear. 'Meta', Courtenay told his wife two years later [15 June 1888] 'absolutely denied the truth of the report of her engagement and asked to whom she was supposed to be engaged. I hope she is really free from any entanglement of the kind.'

In this Indian summer, Meta apparently continued to enjoy herself. Then catastrophe struck, and she fell seriously ill. 'It was very hard to have her visit, which she was enjoying so much, marred by such an ugly catastrophe. It must make you very anxious till you hear news of her recovery.'[34] Jessie had in fact to return home in the autumn of 1886, leaving Meta to recuperate slowly. It seems likely that she stayed for part of the time with a friend of the Ilberts, Sir Charles Aitchison, Lieutenant-Governor of the Punjab. At any rate at the beginning of 1888, Lord Dufferin reassured Courtenay Ilbert that he had seen Meta recently at Ismail Khan and at Lahore, 'looking remarkably well and very becomingly dressed', an unusual tribute to one who was usually so neglectful of fashion. It was, however, a verdict in which Courtenay himself concurred. 'Meta looks extremely well and youthful and really pretty. Her short grey clustering locks have a very piquant effect. Perhaps this is what Helen [Ilbert] meant when she told me afterwards she didn't think Meta looked quite proper.'

Recover, however, Meta did, to settle into the bland monotony of a life that was spinsterish yet useful, perhaps with a slight note of artificial gaiety which bordered on the brittle. She became a sort of archetypal aunt. She continued to paint pretty little water colours and to play the piano. She flowed over with good will, but its excess led her over-embarrassed nephews and nieces to avoid her company. She continued to dress in a frumpish way without concessions to taste or fashion. In conversation she still used the abbreviations and expressions which belonged to her adolescence. She adapted her own life to thrift and even parsimony, the fruit of the penurious income she had had to live on after her father's death.

In her excellent novel, *The Invader*, published originally in 1907 but reprinted and revised in 1923, Margaret Woods, one of her closest friends, seems to have embodied some of her characteristics in her portrait of the student, Flora Timson. Flora is described as a 'sallow comic little face and small meagre figure ... set off by a garment which had in a remote past been somebody else's red velvet evening gown, trimmed with fur, and now with shortened sleeves and girt round the middle with a shining black leather belt, did duty as Tims' 'tea-gown.' 'Fashion!' she said, 'what does it matter whether you look the same as every fool in the street or not.' 'She was constantly discovering ... the existence of superb tailors who made dresses for two guineas and a half.' She used word like 'you rotter', 'old chap', 'old boy', 'poor old chappie', 'tommy rot'. She had elevated 'economy from a mere practice into a sport, and the feats of activity by which she pursued the cheapest haddock or head of celery to its lair, made her life as well furnished with thrills as that of any average sportsman.'[35]

If Flora Timson was mannish, clumsy and tactless, the portrait of Aunt Minnie in the novel *Three Daughters*, written by her niece, Olive Heseltine and published in 1930 under the pseudonym of Jane Dashwood, was not wholly dissimilar. 'Aunt Minnie, who was in every respect the exact antithesis of her only sister—small and

meagre, where Lady Pomfret was solid and ample, timid and propi-
tiating where Lady Pomfret was severe and commanding—Aunt
Minnie stood for Failure, Silliness, and the more extreme and
depressing of the Christian virtues, as opposed to Prosperity, Common Sense and a just and proper regard for the standards of the Civilized World. That in some legendary past their aunt had been the
victim of a devastating love affair, had behaved in a manner which
Lady Pomfret described as intensely foolish, and caused all her
friends and relations the greatest anxiety—even this record could not
invest Aunt Minnie's personality with pathos or romance. She
remained something slightly less than human—an irritating
mosquito-like presence, to be brushed away or dodged.' 'Aunt
Minnie's parsimony, obliged her to live under conditions which
Lady Pomfret [her sister, based on Olive's mother, Lady Ilbert]
described as "filth and squalor", sharing a house with four other
women in the dingy district of Notting Hill Square. Yet she kept a
number of aged persons regularly supplied with cocoa and carbolic
soap, subscribed generously to all good causes and tipped her nieces
handsomely every birthday and Christmas.' We find her rebuking
Daniel and Miranda to whom she has lent her bed-sitting room, 'a
crowd of wicker-work chairs, a little of wool work and two thin
cats', for not turning off the gas stove, 'so extrav.!' Her wedding
present to them was a cheque and a 'portable india-rubber bath'.
'You must'nt sit in it', she explained to her niece when presenting it
to them 'and be very careful in it, as it is so easily upset'. All in all,
Aunt 'Minnie' was an 'example of forlorn virginity, whose ignomini-
ous existence was a warning to every girl'.[36]

In an autobiographical sketch, *Lost Content*, privately printed in
1948, Olive Heseltine's portrait of her aunt was as unsympathetic.
Aunt Meta was a 'fragile, pretty, silly little creature ... born to be
petted or bullied'. 'Her presence resembled that of Alice through the
looking-glass's gnat ... Indifferent to her own comfort, a zealous and
indefatigable social worker, her protégés were as numerous as they
were ungrateful, and few good causes lacked her support. The parsimony which she had inherited from her father extended to the
curtailment of her syllables—'econ., extrav., imprac., imposs.' To
these eccentricities she added individual touches, such as going to
bed under an open umbrella, but her tactlessness was all her own.

"Surely *not* your colour, dearest!" she would gasp, wincing, as a debutante in a new dress entered the room. "Pity the cream is just on the turn" she would remind an anxious hostess, and when a diminutive warrior announced with simple dignity, 'Six foot of earth is all I ask," she quickly suggested, "Surely you mean five foot five.""[37]

At this distance of time it is difficult to ascertain how fair or unfair were these somewhat devastating judgements. Aunt Meta appeared to be a semi-comic figure, a person not to be taken too seriously, a fay creature in an adult world. Fussy and silly she may have been, but others remember her as a rosy-cheeked old lady with white hair, resolute, humane, and kind. Latterly she lived in a fairly capacious and comfortable flat at the Finchley Road end of Grove End Road, in a big block near the junction of the roads. She died in her seventieth year, twelve months younger than Mark, in February 1923.

She would have been pained by the impressions she created. Even with Mark she had always been slightly on the defensive, a stout, stalwart, even at times complacent, defender of her own views and life-style. What her nieces wrote about her was doubtless in many respects true. Only a silly, rather humourless girl, it might be thought, could have fallen in love with an elderly, crabbed, egotistical scholar. Yet that very act, or rather attitude, had had a redemptive quality. She had, if but momentarily, experienced in some degree the pleasure and happiness that love for another person provides. 'My only really happy time lasted just 2 months, rather a short allowance for a lifetime . . . I have lived, loved and been loved, and that is more than a good many people can say with truth.' Contemporaries condemned or sneered. Her sole affair seemed decked with more comedy than tragedy. Was it only a feeble, foolish unjustified romance? Fundamentally, surely, it had quality. It provided Meta with the spiritual resources that were to keep her going through the passing years. 'Not even death can alter the fact that you and I were friends for years, which fact I shall ponder with perplexed pride.' It had enriched, if fleetingly, an old and tortured spirit. 'You gave the heart of affection that warmed up again my chilled nature which had not known *love* for 5 years, and was craving it so terribly.' 'You made the joy and sweetness of my life and of my home . . . Every day brings me some fresh proof of your providence over me.' Normally the passion of love seems romantic when it concerns only the handsome and beautiful of both sexes, young in mind, body and spirit. But love's frontiers are never closed nor exclusive, in terms of either gender or appearance, or age or looks. Meta and Mark came tentatively within its territory. Like Mrs Crawford, Meta seems rarely in later life to have spoken of her lover; but she kept the letters that had passed between them and bequeathed them to Mark's friend and pupil, Theodore Althaus who in his turn gave them in 1927 to the Bodleian Library at Oxford, whence, a century after their short-lived friendship had ended, it seems fitting, as both of them would surely have wished, to reveal their contents to a wider public.

Notes and Sources

Unless otherwise stated references to manuscripts are to manuscripts in the Bodleian Library, Oxford, and all references to printed materials are to works published in London. The following works are abbreviated:

(i) V. H. H. Green, *The Commonwealth of Lincoln College, 1427-1977*, (Oxford, 1979), as *Commonwealth of Lincoln*.
(ii) John Sparrow, *Mark Pattison and the Idea of a University*, (Cambridge, 1967), as *Idea of a University*.
(iii) M. Pattison, *Memoirs* (1885), as *Memoirs*.

Chapter I

1. Augustus J. C. Hare, *The Story of My Life* (1896) I, 303-15, 332-5.
2. Letter in possession of Sir John Winnifirth.
3. Ibid.
4. Ibid.
5. *Story of My Life*, I, 390.
6. Jane Dashwood, *Three Daughters* (1930), p. 67.
7. Pattison MSS, 123, 25.5.82.
8. A. C. Benson, *Edwardian Excursions*, ed. David Newsome (1981), p. 12.
9. Dashwood, *Three Daughters*, p. 15.
10. Pattison MSS, 126, 15.4.84.
11. M. Francis, 'The Origins of Essays and Reviews: An Interpretation of Mark Pattison in the 1850s', *The Historical Journal*, (1974), 797-811; Ieuan Ellis, *Seven against Christ: a study of Essays and Reviews* (Leiden, 1980).
12. See *Memoirs*, pp. 271-300; V. H. H. Green, *Oxford Common Room* (1957), pp. 146-70; *Idea of a University*, pp. 98-104; *Commonwealth of Lincoln*, pp. 447-68.
13. *Memoirs*, pp. 42-60 and for the wine party, pp. 142-4.
14. For a fine discussion of his religious development: Fergal Nolan, 'A study of Mark Pattison's Religious Experience 1813-50' (D. Phil. thesis, Oxford, 1978).
15. For consideration of the differing views on this problem see *Commonwealth of Lincoln*, Appendix 9, 'Mark Pattison and Dr Casaubon', pp. 698–706.
16. A recent study is Betty Askwith, *Lady Dilke* (1969).
17. MSS, Pattison, 140, 16.11.85.
18. Ibid., 140, 11.1.70.
19. Ibid., 118, 12.10.80.
20. Mrs Humphry Ward, *A Writer's Recollections* (1918), pp. 102-3.
21. On the Crewe Trust: C. J. Stranks, *The Charities of Nathaniel Lord Crewe and Dr John Sharp 1721-1976* (Durham, 1976); *Commonwealth of Lincoln*, Appendix 8, 'Lord Crewe's Trust', pp. 688–97.
22. Pattison MSS, 118, n.d., 1875.
23. Ibid., 60, 9.8.75.
24. Ibid., 118, 9.8.75.
25. Ibid., 118, 14.12.75.
26. Ibid., 60, 20.1.76.
27. Ibid., 60, Thurs. n.d. 76.
28. Leon Edel, *Henry James The Conquest of London 1870-1883* (1962), p. 337.
29. Pattison MSS, 118, 9.11.76.

Chapter II

1. Pattison MSS, 119, 29.10.79.
2. On Max Müller see the recent study Nirad C. Chaudhuri, *Scholar Extraordinary, Max Müller* (1974).
3. Pattison MSS, 132, 4.11.79.
4. Ibid., 132, 17.11.79.
5. Ibid., 132, 22.1.80.
6. For Bywater see memoir by W. W. Jackson, *Ingram Bywater* (Oxford, 1917).
7. For Pattison's remark on Rhoda Broughton see Pattison MSS 132, 16.11.79.
8. Ibid., 132, 29.12.79.
9. Ibid., 132, 22.11.79.
10. *The Academy* xvi (6 Dec. 1879), 401.
11. Pattison MSS, 132, 6.12.79.
12. Ibid., 132, 23.12.79.
13. Ibid., 132, 13.1.80.
14. Ibid., 119, 17.2.80.
15. *Idea of a University* (Cambridge, 1967), p. 49.
16. Pattison MSS, 10.2.80.
17. Ibid., 118, 17.3.80.
18. Ibid., 132, 28.2.80.
19. Ibid., 124, 29.7.82.
20. Edel, *The Conquest of London*, p. 334.
21. W. Tuckwell, *Reminiscences of Oxford* (London, 1901), pp. 216–24.
22. S. Gwynn and G. Tuckwell, *Life of Sir Charles Dilke*, (London, 1917), 2 vols.
23. See *DNB*, 1951–60, p. 987.
24. Pattison MSS, 119, 3.3.80.
25. Ibid., 119, 23.3.80.
26. Ibid., 139, 23.3.80; 1.4.80.
27. Ibid., 119, 15.4.80.
28. Ibid., 119, 19.4.80.
29. Ibid., 119, 28.5.80.
30. Ibid., 119, 12.6.80.
31. Ibid., 119, 15.4.80.
32. Ibid., 119, 16.4.80.
33. Ibid., 119, 19.4.80.
34. Ibid., 121, 9.7.81.
35. Ibid., 121, 9.7.81.
36. Ibid., 119, 22.7.80.
37. Ibid., 119, 16.10.80.
38. Ibid., 121, 6.12.81.
39. Ibid., 119, 19,4.80.
40. Ibid., 119, 14.10.80.
41. Ibid., 119, 19.4.80.
42. Ibid., 121, 9.7.81.
43. Ibid., 119, 16.10.80.
44. Ibid., 119, 18.10.80.
45. Ibid., 119, 22.7.80.
46. Ibid., 141, 25.6.81.
47. Olive Heseltine, *Lost Content* (1948), p. 76.
48. Dashwood, *The Three Daughters*, p. 21.
49. Pattison MSS, 120, 2.2.81.
50. Ibid., 121, 22.5.81.
51. Ibid., 120, 6.2.81. Ibid., 120, 7.2.81.
52. Ibid., 120, 8.2.81.
53. Ibid., 120, 9.2.81.
54. Ibid., 121, 23.5.81.
55. Ibid., 119, 16.10.80.
56. Ibid., 119, 13.7.80.
57. Ibid., 119, 20.4.80.
58. Ibid., 119, 22.4.80.
59. Ibid., 119, 29.4.80.
60. Ibid., 119, 15.5.80.
61. Ibid., 119, 19.4.80.
62. Ibid., 119, 15.5.80.
63. *Saturday Review*, 17 April 1880, pp. 511–2.
64. Pattison MSS 119, 27.5.80; 'Colonel Colvill is icy and forbidding, not obnoxious'; 123, 12.1.82.
65. Ibid., 119, 27.5.80.
66. Ibid., 119, 2.6.80.
67. Ibid., 119, 12.6.80.
68. Ibid., 119, 4.7.80.
69. Ibid., 119, 18.7.80.
70. Ibid., 132, 1.11.80.
71. Ibid., 119, 22.7.80.
72. Ibid., 119, 22.7.80.
73. Ibid., 119, 18.7.80.
74. Ibid., 119, 7.9.80.
75. Ibid., 119, 23.7.80.
76. Ibid., 119, 22.7.80.
77. Ibid., 119, 31.8.80.
78. Ibid., 119, 13.7.80.
79. Ibid., 119, 18.7.80.
80. Ibid., 119, 13.7.80.
81. Ibid., 119, 13.7.80.
82. Ibid., 119, 18.7.80.
83. Ibid., 119, 22.7.80.

84. Ibid., 119, 1.8.80.
85. Ibid., 141 contains copies of letters which passed between Mark Pattison and Gertrude Tuckwell written between 17.1.79 and 13.3.83, the originals of which are in the British Museum (Add. MS 44886).
86. Ibid., 133, 12.6.80.
87. Ibid., 119, 1.8.80.
88. Ibid., 119, 7.8.80.
89. Ibid., 120, 23.1.81.
90. Ibid., 119, 7.8.80.
91. Ibid., 119, 29.8.80.
92. Ibid., 119, 28.8.80.
93. Ibid., 119, 29.8.80.
94. Ibid., 119, 28.8.80.
95. Ibid., 119, 12.9.80.
96. Ibid., 119, 10.9.80.
97. Ibid., 119, 12.9.80.
98. Ibid., 119, 14.9.80.
99. Ibid., 119, 19.9.80.
100. Ibid., 118, 23.8.80.
101. Ibid., 119, 15.9.80.
102. Ibid., 118, 23.8.80.
103. Ibid., 119, 24.9.80.
104. Ibid., 119, 5.10.80.
105. Ibid., 119, 21.9.80.
106. Ibid., 119, 28.9.80.
107. Ibid., 119, 2.10.80.
108. Ibid., 144, 31.5.81.
109. Ibid., 119, 5.10.80.
110. Ibid., 120, 4.2.81.
111. Ibid., 121, 1.4.81.
112. Ibid., 121, 9.4.81.
113. Ibid., 121, 14.5.81.
114. Ibid., 121, 16.5.81.
115. Ibid., 119, 14.10.80.
116. Ibid., 119, 14.10.80.
117. Ibid., 119, 18.10.80.
118. Ibid., 119, 15.9.80.
119. Ibid., 119, 26.10.80.
120. Ibid., 119, 8.10.80.
121. Ibid., 119, 27.9.80.
122. Ibid., 119, 28.9.80.
123. Ibid., 119, 5.10.80.
124. Ibid., 119, 9.10.80.
125. Ibid., 119, 15.10.80.
126. Ibid., 119, 16.10.80.
127. Ibid., 119, 28.10.80.
128. Ibid., 119, 28.10.80.
129. Ibid., 119, 31.10.80.
130. Ibid., 119, 31.10.80.
131. Ibid., 133, 1.11.80.
132. Ibid., 133, 22.12.80.
133. *Idea of a University* (Cambridge, 1967).
134. Pattison MSS 133, 11.11.80.
135. Ibid., 133, 24.11.80.
136. Ibid., 133, 13.12.80.
137. Ibid., 133; entries for 2.11.80, 20.11.80, 21.11.80.
138. Ibid., 133, 15/16.12.80. Walter Besant, *The French Humourists from the Twelfth to the Nineteenth Century* (1873).
139. Pattison MSS, 120, 19.2.81.
140. Ibid., 119, 1.12.80.
141. Ibid., 133, 8.12.80.
142. Ibid., 119, 1.12.80.
143. Ibid., 119, 1.12.80.
144. Ibid., 133, 22.11.80.
145. Ibid., 120, 23.1.81.
146. Ibid., 120, 26.1.81.
147. Ibid., 120, 28.1.81.
148. Ibid., 120, 2.2.81.
149. Ibid., 120, 5.2.81.
150. Ibid., 120, 28.1.81.
151. Ibid., 120, 1.2.81.
152. Ibid., 120, 2.2.81.
153. Ibid., 120, 4.2.81.
154. Ibid., 120, 8.1.81.
155. Ibid., 125, 22.11.83.
156. Ibid., 120, 29.1.81.
157. Ibid., 120, 2.6.81.
158. Ibid., 120, 9.2.81.
159. Ibid., 120, 10.2.81.
160. Ibid., 118, 21.11.80.
161. Ibid., 118, 20.12.80.
162. Ibid., 140, 2.12.80.
163. Ibid., 120, 13.1.81.
164. Ibid., 120, 30.1.81.

Chapter III

1. Pattison MSS, 120, 7.1.81; 9.1.81; 10.1.81; 13.1.81; 16.1.81; 18.1.81.
2. Ibid., 120, 7.1.81.
3. Ibid., 120, 5.1.81.
4. Ibid., 120, 11.1.81.
5. Ibid., 120, 5.2.81.
6. Ibid., 120, 7.2.81.
7. Ibid., 120, 28.1.81.

8. Ibid., 121, 17.4.81.
9. Ibid., 120, 13.1.81.
10. Ibid., 120, 2.2.81.
11. Ibid., 120, 1.2.81.
12. Ibid., 120, 27.1.81.
13. Ibid., 120, 26.1.81.
14. Ibid., 120, 27.1.81.
15. See DNB XIX, 1063–5.
16. Pattison MSS, 120, 13.1.81.
17. Ibid., 120, 4.2.81.
18. Ibid., 121, 30.4.81.
19. ibid., 120, 20.1.81.
20. Ibid., 120, 25.2.81.
21. Ibid., 120, 26.1.81.
22. Ibid., 120, 11.1.81.
23. Ibid., 120, 27.1.81.
24. Ibid., 120, 17.2.81.
25. Ibid., 120, 23.1.81.
26. Ibid., 120, 26.1.81.
27. Ibid., 120, 23.1.81.
28. Ibid., 120, 24.1.81.
29. Ibid., 120, 24.1.81.
30. Ibid., 120, 25.1.81.
31. Reprinted in the North American Review, CCXCIII (April 1881), pp. 320–31.
32. Pattison MSS, 121, 2.5.81.
33. Ibid., 120, 6.2.81.
34. Ibid., 120, 4.2.81.
35. Ibid., 120, 4.2.81.
36. Ibid., 120, 4.2.81 4.00 p.m.
37. Ibid., 120, 5.2.81.
38. Ibid., 120, 6.2.81.
39. Ibid., 118, 9.2.81.
40. Ibid., 118, 9.2.81.
41. Ibid., 121, 23.2.81.
42. Ibid., 120, 12.2.81.
43. Ibid., 120, 14.2.81.
44. Ibid., 120, 15.2.81.
45. Ibid., 120, 17.2.81.
46. Ibid., 120, 22.1.81.
47. Ibid., 120, 13.1.81.
48. Ibid., 120, 15.1.81.
49. Ibid., 120, 18.1.81.
50. Ibid., 120, 13.1.81.
51. Ibid., 120, 16.1.81.
52. Ibid., 120, 29.1.81.
53. Ibid., 120, 10.2.81.
54. Ibid., 120, 15.2.81.
55. Ibid., 120, 17.2.81.
56. Ibid., 120, 14.2.81.
57. Ibid., 120, 15.2.81.
58. Ibid., 120, 26.1.81.
59. Ibid., 120, 19.2.81.
60. Ibid., 121, 7.3.81.
61. Ibid., 120, 5.3.81.
62. Ibid., 121, 5.3.81.
63. Ibid., 120, 9.1.81.
64. Ibid., 121, 7.3.81.
65. Ibid., 121, 7.3.81.
66. Ibid., 118, 23.3.81.
67. Ibid., 121, 22.4.81.
68. Ibid., 120, 24.2.81.
69. Ibid., 120, 12.2.81.
70. Ibid., 120, 27.2.81.
71. Ibid., 121, 14.3.81.
72. Ibid., 133, 11.3.81.
73. Ibid., 121, n.d.4.81.
74. Ibid., 118, 23.3.81.
75. Ibid., 118, 27.3.81.
76. Ibid., 118, 30.3.81.
77. Ibid., 118, 30.3.81.
78. Ibid., 133, 5.3.81.
79. Ibid., 121, 5.3.81. Sat. p.m.
80. Ibid., 121, 5.3.81.
81. Ibid., 121, 5.3.81.
82. Ibid., 133, 8.3.81.
83. Ibid., 121, 10.3.81.
84. Ibid., 121, 10.3.81.
85. Ibid., 120, 3.3.81.
86. Ibid., 121, 21.3.81.
87. Ibid., 121, 17.3.81.
88. Ibid., 121, 17.4.81.
89. Ibid., 121, 17.4.81.
90. Ibid., 121, 23.3.81.
91. Ibid., 121, 24.3.81.
92. Ibid., 118, 30.3.81.
93. Ibid., 121, 23.4.81.
94. Ibid., 121, 22.4.81.
95. Ibid., 121, 23.4.81.
96. Ibid., 121, 28.3.81.
97. Ibid., 121, 1.4.81.
98. Ibid., 121, 6.4.81.
99. Ibid., 121, 9.4.81.
100. Ibid., 121, 8.4.81.
101. Ibid., 144, 14.4.81. Letter to Mrs W. Hertz.
102. Ibid., 121, 29.4.81.
103. Ibid., 121, 30.4.81.
104. Ibid., 121, 2.5.81.

105. Ibid., 121, 4.5.81.
106. Ibid., 121, 8.5.81.
107. Ibid., 121, 9.5.81.
108. Ibid., 121, 5.5.81.
109. Ibid., 121, 13.5.81.
110. Ibid., 121, 22.5.81.
111. Ibid., 121, 5.6.81.
112. Ibid., 121, 25.6.81.
113. Ibid., 121, 5.7.81.
114. Ibid., 121, 25.6.81.
115. On Jowett see G. Faber, *Jowett* (1957).
116. Pattison MSS, 121, 20.5.81.
117. Ibid., 121, 22.5.81.
118. Ibid., 121, 2.6.81.
119. Ibid., 121, 3.6.81.
120. Ibid., 121, 23.5.81.
121. Ibid., 121, 5.6.81.
122. Ibid., 121, 12.6.81.
123. Ibid., 121, 21.6.81.
124. Ibid., 121, 21.6.81.
125. Ibid., 144, 17.8.81. Letter to Mrs Hertz.
126. Ibid., 144, 25.6.81. Letter to Mrs Hertz.
127. Ibid., 121, 24.7.81.
128. Ibid., 144, 2.8.81. Letter to Mrs Hertz.
129. Ibid., 121, 24.7.81.
130. Ibid., 144, 12.8.81. Letter to Mrs Hertz.
131. Ibid., 144, 9.7.81. Letter to Mrs Hertz.
132. Ibid., 121, 29.7.81.
133. Ibid., 122, 21.8.81.
134. Ibid., 122, 20.8.81.
135. Ibid., 118, 30.3.81.
136. Ibid., 122, 21.8.81.
137. MS Bywater, 61, 21.8.81.
138. Pattison MSS, 122, 10.9.81.
139. Ibid., 10.9.81.
140. MS Bywater, 61, 17.9.81.
141. MS Bywater, 61, 18.9.81.
142. Pattison MSS, 133, 6.10.81.
143. Nouvelles Acquisitions françaises, Bibliothèque Nationale, Paris, letters of Lady Dilke to Eugene Müntz. 11305. 28.8.81. Quoted Askwith, *Lady Dilke*, p. 92.
144. Pattison MSS., 118, 29.9.81.
145. Ibid., 118, 29.9.81.
146. Ibid., 121, 29.5.81.
147. Ibid., 121, 20.5.81.
148. Ibid., 121, 26.5.81.
149. Ibid., 121, 12.6.81.
150. Ibid., 121, 18.6.81.
151. Ibid., 121, 21.6.81.
152. Ibid., 121, 27/29.6.81.
153. Ibid., 121, 24.7.81.
154. Ibid., 121, 10.9.81.
155. Ibid., 122, 12.9.81.
156. Ibid., 122, 9.7.81.
157. Ibid., 121, 11.8.81.
158. Ibid., 122, 20.8.81.
159. Ibid., 122, 22.8.81.
160. Ibid., 122, 31.8.81.
161. Ibid., 122, 4.9.81.
162. Ibid., 122, 10.9.81.
163. Ibid., 122, 10.9.81.
164. Ibid., 122, 27.9.81.
165. Ibid., 122, 21.9.81.
166. Ibid., 122, 23.9.81.
167. Ibid., 122, 10.10.81.
168. Ibid., 122, 31.10.81.
169. Ibid., 122, 23.11.81.
170. Ibid., 122, 5.11.81.
171. Ibid., 122, 27.11.81.
172. Ibid., 122, 11.11.81.
173. Ibid., 122, 11.11.81.
174. Ibid., 122, 5.12.81.
175. Ibid., 122, 15.11.81.
176. Ibid., 122, 15.11.81.
177. Ibid., 122, 6.12.81.
178. Ibid., 122, 15.11.81.
179. Ibid., 122, 14.12.81.
180. Ibid., 122, 19.11.81.
181. Ibid., 122, 14.12.81.
182. Ibid., 122, 26.11.81.
183. Ibid., 122, 23.12.81.
184. Ibid., 122, 25.12.81.
185. Ibid., 122, 17.11.81. See M. O. W. Oliphant, *Memoir of the Life of John Tulloch* (Edinburgh, 1888).
186. Pattison MS, 122, 14.12.81.
187. Ibid., 122, 17.12.81. On Victorian St. Andrews see R. G. Cant, *The University of St. Andrews* (Edinburgh, 1946), pp. 116–24; W. Knight, *Principal Shairp and his friends* Edinburgh (1888).
188. Pattison MSS, 122, 15.11.81.
189. A. C. Benson, *Edwardian Excursions*, p. 128.

190. Pattison MSS, 122, 19.11.81.
191. Ibid, 122, 26.11.81.
192. Ibid., 122, 5.12.81.
193. Ibid., 122, 17.12.81.
194. Ibid., 122, 18.12.81.
195. Ibid., 122, 14.12.81.
196. Ibid., 122, 26.11.81.
197. Ibid., 122, 5.12.81.
198. Ibid., 122, 9.11.81.
199. Ibid., 122, 6.11.81.
200. Ibid., 122, 27.11.81.
201. Ibid., 122, 4.11.81.
202. Ibid., 122, 6.11.81.
203. Ibid., 122, 8.11.81.
204. Ibid., 122, 5.12.81.
205. Ibid., 122, 11.2.81.
206. Ibid., 140, 7.11.81.
207. Ibid., 140, 23.11.81.
208. Ibid., 122, 5.12.81.
209. Ibid., 122, 23.12.81.
210. Ibid., 122, 25.12.81.
211. *Commonwealth of Lincoln*, pp. 499–503.
212. Pattison MSS, 122, 25.12.81.
213. Ibid., 122, 5.12.81.
214. Ibid., 122, 25.12.81.
215. Ibid., 122, 25.12.81.
216. Ibid., 122, 25.12.81.
217. Ibid., 122, 30.12.81.
218. Ibid., 122, 1.1.82.

Chapter IV

1. Pattison MSS, 123, 13.2.82.
2. Ibid., 123, 13.2.82.
3. Ibid., 123, 16.5.82.
4. Ibid., 123, 19.5.82.
5. Ibid., 123, 17.2.82.
6. Ibid., 123, 13.2.82.
7. Ibid., 123, 15.2.82.
8. Ibid., 123, 6.1.82.
9. Ibid., 123, 14.1.82.
10. Ibid., 118, 24.1.82.
11. Ibid., 118, 15.2.82.
12. Ibid., 118, 23.3.82.
13. Ibid., 118, 15.2.82.
14. Ibid., 123, 27.1.82.
15. Ibid., 123, 3.2.82.
16. Ibid., 123, 5.3.82.
17. Ibid., 123, 16.3.82.
18. Ibid., 123, 22.3.82.
19. Ibid., 123, 22.3.82.
20. Olive Heseltine, *Lost Content*, p. 95.
21. Pattison MSS, 124, 2.7.82.
22. Ibid., 124, 7.7.82.
23. Ibid., 124, 6.8.82.
24. Ibid., 123, 26.2.82.
25. Ibid., 123, 3.3.82.
26. Ibid., 123, 30.4.82.
27. Ibid., 122, 26.11.82.
28. Ibid., 123, 13.2.82.
29. Ibid., 123, 12.5.82.
30. Ibid., 123, 26.2.82.
31. Ibid., 123, 12.5.82.
32. Ibid., 123, 16.3.82.
33. Ibid., 133, 11.3.82.
34. Ibid., 133, 23.2.82.
35. Ibid., 123, 12.3.82.
36. Ibid., 123, 13.3.82.
37. Ibid., 123, 13.3.82.
38. Ibid., 123, 4.2.82.
39. Ibid., 123, 10.3.82.
40. Ibid., 123, 25.3.82.
41. L. Tollemache, *Recollections* (printed for private circulation, 1885; new edn. 1891).
42. Pattison MSS 123, 29.3.82.
43. Ibid., 123, 2.4.82.
44. Ibid., 123, 2.4.82.
45. Ibid., 123, 7.4.82.
46. Ibid., 123, 1.4.82.
47. Ibid., 123, 2.4.82.
48. Ibid., 123, 19.4.82.
49. Ibid., 123, 18.4.82.
50. Ibid., 123, 25.4.82.
51. Ibid., 123, 25.4.82.
52. Ibid., 123, 26.4.82.
53. Askwith, *Lady Dilke*, p. 223.
54. Pattison MSS 123, 17.5.82.
55. Ibid., 123, 19.5.82.
56. Ibid., 123, 12.6.82.
57. Ibid., 123, 12.6.82.
58. Ibid., 123, 15.6.82.
59. Ibid., 123, 16.6.82.
60. Ibid., 124, 21.6.82.
61. Ibid., 124, 28.6.82; *The Academy*, no. 530, 1 July 1882.
62. Pattison MSS, 124, 2.7.82.
63. Ibid., 124, 12.6.82.
64. Ibid., 124, 28.6.82.
65. Ibid., 124, 2.7.82.

66. Ibid., 124, 16.7.82.
67. Ibid., 124, 18.7.82.
68. Ibid., 124, 20.7.82.
69. Ibid., 124, 22.6.82.
70. Ibid., 124, 21.6.82.
71. Ibid., 124, 16.7.82.
72. Ibid., 124, 18.7.82.
73. Letters of July 13 and 21, 1882, from Jessie Ilbert to Courtenay Ilbert, quoted by kind permission of Mrs Mary Bennett.
74. Pattison MSS, 124, 22.6.82.
75. Ibid., 124, 2.7.82.
76. Ibid., 124, 11.7.82.
77. Ibid., 124, 24.6.82.
78. Ibid., 124, 28.6.82.
79. Ibid., 124, 7.7.82.
80. Ibid., 124, 24.6.82.
81. Ibid., 124, 12.7.82.
82. Ibid., 124, 29.7.82.
83. Ibid., 123, 11.2.82.
84. Ibid., 124, 10.8.82.
85. Ibid., 124, 13.8.82.
86. Ibid., 124, 21.8.82.
87. Ibid., 124, 1.9.82.
88. Ibid., 124, 5.9.82.
89. Ibid., 124, 16.9.82.
90. Ibid., 124, 19.9.82.
91. Ibid., 124, 21.9.82.
92. Ibid., 124, 28.9.82.
93. Ibid., 124, 1.10.82.
94. Ibid., 124, 1.10.82.
95. Ibid., 124, 2.9.82.
96. Ibid., 124, 29.9.82.
97. Ibid., 124, 15.10.82.
98. Ibid., 124, 15.10.82.
99. Ibid., 124, 29.10.82.
100. Ibid., 124, 13.10.82.
101. Ibid., 124, 17.19.82.
102. Ibid., 124, 25.10.82.
103. Ibid., 124, 5.11.82.
104. Ibid., 124, 15.11.82.
105. Ibid., 124, 18.11.82.
106. Ibid., 124, 19.11.82.
107. Ibid., 124, 18.11.82.
108. Ibid., 124, 5.11.82.
109. Ibid., 124, 5.11.82.
110. Ibid., 124, 19.11.82.
111. Ibid., 124, 20.11.82.
112. Ibid., 124, 20.11.82.
113. Ibid., 124, 22.11.82.
114. Ibid., 124, 23.11.82.

Chapter V

1. Pattison MSS, 134, 22.12.82.
2. Ibid., 134, 16.2.83.
3. Ibid., 134, 5.2.83.
4. Ibid., 134, 10.2.83.
5. Ibid., 134, 12.2.83.
6. Ibid., 124, 27.10.82.
7. Mrs H. Ward, *Robert Elsmere* (1888).
8. For the conflicting views see, *Commonwealth of Lincoln*, pp. 698–706.
9. Pattison MSS, 125, 20.11.83.
10. Ibid., 134, 30.4.83.
11. Ibid., 60, n.d. 1882.
12. Letter of Dean Bradley to Jessica Ilbert, 3.4.83, in the possession of Sir John Winnifrith.
13. Letter of Mrs Bull to Jessica Ilbert, 7.6.83, in the possession of Sir John Winnifrith.
14. Letter of Meta Bradley to Jessica Ilbert, 28.3.83, in the possession of Sir John Winnifrith.
15. Note in the possession of Sir John Winnifrith.
16. Letter of Dean Bradley to Jessica Ilbert, 18.5.83, in the possesion of Sir John Winnifrith.
17. Letter of Dean Bradley to Jessica Ilbert, 18.5.83, in the possession of Sir John Winnifrith.
18. Letter of Mrs Bull to Jessica Ilbert, 18.5.83, in the possession of Sir John Winnifrith.
19. Letter of Dean Bradley to Jessica Ilbert, 6.6.83, in the possession of Sir John Winnifrith.
20. Pattison MSS, 125, 15.6.83.
21. Ibid., 125, 14.6.83.
22. Ibid., 125, 15.6.83.
23. Ibid., 125, 9.4.83.
24. Ibid., 125, 9.4.83.
25. Ibid., 125, 16.4.83.
26. Ibid., 125, 28.4.83.
27. Ibid., 125, 26.5.83.
28. Ibid., 125, 28.4.83.

29. Ibid., 125, 10.5.83.
30. Ibid., 125, 25.4.83.
31. Ibid., 125, 28.4.83.
32. Ibid., 125, 3.5.83.
33. Ibid., 125, 25.5.83.
34. Ibid., 125, 25.5.83.
35. Ibid., 125, 27.5.83.
36. Ibid., 125, 3.5.83.
37. 'Tendencies of Religious Thought in England 1688–1750' in *Essays and Reviews*, ed. J. Parker, London, 1860; the other contributors were F. Temple, Rowland Williams, Baden Powell, H. B. Wilson, C. W. Goodwin and Benjamin Jowett.
38. Pattison MSS, 125, 3.5.83.
39. Ibid., 125, 5.5.83.
40. Ibid., 125, 7.5.83.
41. Ibid., 125, 4.6.83.
42. Ibid., 125, 4.6.83.
43. Ibid., 125, 14.6.83.
44. Ibid., 125, 26.6.83.
45. Ibid., 125, 28.6.83.
46. Ibid., 125, 5.7.83.
47. See Jo Manton's admirable biography, *Sister Dora*. (1971).
48. Pattison MSS, 125, 28.6.83.
49. Ibid., 125, 16.6.83.
50. Ibid., 125, 26.6.83.
51. Ibid., 125, 15.6.83.
52. Ibid., 125, 19.6.83.
53. On Mrs Pattison's relations with him see Betty Askwith, *Lady Dilke*, pp. 50, 94, 100.
54. Pattison MSS, 125, 26.6.83.
55. Ibid., 125, 1.7.83.
56. Ibid., 125, 8.7.83.
57. Ibid., 125, 15.7.83.
58. Ibid., 125, 26.6.83.
59. Ibid., 125, 5.7.83.
60. Ibid., 125, 22.8.83.
61. Ibid., 125, 23.8.83.
62. Ibid., 125, 26.8.83.
63. Ibid., 126, 1.9.83.
64. Ibid., 125, 5.9.83.
65. Ibid., 125, 18.9.83.
66. Ibid., 125, 26.9.83.
67. Ibid., 125, 2.8.83.
68. Ibid., 125, 3.8.83.
69. Ibid., 125, 24.8.83.
70. Ibid., 125, 3.9.83.
71. Ibid., 125, 26.9.83.
72. Ibid., 125, 26.9.83.
73. Ibid., 125, 29.9.83.
74. Ibid., 125, n.d.10.83.
75. Ibid., 125, 28.9.83.
76. Ibid., 125, 11.10.83.
77. Ibid., 125, 26.9.83.
78. Ibid., 125, 22.10.83.
79. Ibid., 125, 22.10.83.
80. Ibid., 134, 27.10.83.
81. Ibid., 125, 8.11.83.
82. Ibid., 134, 8.11.83.
83. Ibid., 125, 11.10.83.
84. Ibid., 125, 21.10.83.
85. Ibid., 125, 10.11.83.
86. Ibid., 125, 8.11.83.
87. Ibid., 125, 21.10.83.
88. Ibid., 125, 6.11.83.
89. Ibid., 125, 21.10.83.
90. Ibid., 125, 27.11.83.
91. Ibid., 125, 13.11.83.
92. Ibid., 118, 8.1.84.
93. Ibid., 125, 28.11.83.
94. Ibid., 125, 27.11.83.
95. Ibid., 125, 3.12.83.
96. Ibid., 144, 30.11.83.
97. Ibid., 134, 5.12.83.
98. Ibid., 144, 3.12.83.
99. Ibid., 125, 6.12.83.
100. Ibid., 134, 15.12.83.
101. Ibid., 125, 9.12.83.
102. Ibid., 125, 24.11.83.
103. Ibid., 125, 26.11.83.
104. Ibid., 125, 30.11.83.
105. Ibid., 125, 12.12.83.
106. Ibid., 125, 18.12.83.
107. Ibid., 125, 18.12.83.
108. Ibid., 125, 24.12.83.
109. Ibid., 125, 25.12.83.
110. Ibid., 125, 26.12.83.
111. Ibid., 125, 7.12.83.
112. Ibid., 125, 9.12.83.
113. Ibid., 125, 18.12.83.
114. Ibid., 125, 24.12.83.
115. Ibid., 125, 25.12.83.
116. Ibid., 125, 27.12.83.
117. Ibid., 125, 30.12.83.
118. Ibid., 125, 28.11.83.
119. Ibid., 125, 9.11.83.

120. Ibid., 125, 13.11.83.
121. Ibid., 127, 20.11.83.
122. Ibid., 127, 24.11.83.
123. Ibid., 125, 12.12.83.
124. Ibid., 125, 15.12.83.
125. Ibid., 125, 18.12.83.
126. Ibid., 125, 18.12.83.
127. Ibid., 125, 31.12.83.

Chapter VI

1. Pattison MSS, 126, 15.1.84.
2. Ibid., 126, 15.1.84.
3. Ibid., 126, 6.1.84.
4. Ibid., 126, 8.1.84.
5. Ibid., 126, 6.1.84.
6. Ibid., 126, 2.1.84. 6.1.84.
7. Ibid., 126, 11.1.84.
8. Ibid., 126, 19.1.84.
9. Ibid., 126, 21.1.84.
10. Ibid., 126, 25.1.84.
11. Ibid., 126, 28.1.84.
12. Ibid., 126, 2.2.84.
13. Ibid., 126, 9.2.84.
14. Ibid., 126, 2.1.84.
15. Ibid., 126, 2.1.84.
16. Ibid., 126, 8.1.84.
17. Ibid., 126, 15.1.84.
18. Ibid., 126, 8.1.84.
19. Ibid., 126, 28.1.84.
20. Ibid., 118, 26.1.84.
21. Ibid., 118, 1.2.84.
22. Ibid., 118, 8.1.84.
23. Ibid., 126, 22.2.84.
24. Ibid., 126, 3.3.84.
25. Ibid., 126, 20.2.84.
26. Ibid., 126, 22.2.84.
27. Ibid., 126, 29.2.84.
28. Ibid., 126, 1.4.84.
29. Ibid., 126, 3.6.84.
30. S. Gwynn, *Saints and Scholars*, (1929), p. 81.
31. Pattison MSS, 126, 11.4.84.
32. Ibid., 126, 15.4.84.
33. Ibid., 126, 26.4.84.
34. Ibid., 126, 29.4.84.
35. Letter from Dean Bradley to Jessica Ilbert in possession of Sir John Winnifrith, 6.6.84.

36. Papers in possession of Sir John Winnifrith.
37. Pattison MSS, 126, 1.6.84.
38. Ibid., 126, 29.5.84.
39. Ibid., 126, 18.2.84.
40. Ibid., 126, 24.2.84.
41. Ibid., 126, 3.3.84.
42. Ibid., 126, 2.2.84.
43. Ibid., 126, 20.4.84.
44. Askwith, *Lady Dilke*, p. 107; letter to Eugene Müntz, 13.5.84. Nouvelles Acquisitions francais Bibliothèque Nationale, Paris, 11305.
45. Pattison MSS, 126, 29.6.84.
46. Ibid., 126, 29.6.84.
47. Ibid., 134, 13.6.84.
48. Ibid., 118, 30.7.84.
49. Ibid., 118, 8.7.84.
50. Ibid., 118, 10.7.84.
51. Ibid., 118, 10.7.84.
52. Ibid., 118, 6.7.84.
53. Ibid., 118, 8.7.84.
54. Ibid., 118, 11.7.84.
55. Ibid., 118, 15.7.84.
56. Ibid., 118, 30.7.84.
57. Ibid., 112, 102–106 ff.
58. Ibid., 140, 21.7.84.
59. Ibid., 118, 26.7.84.
60. Ibid., 140, 30.7.84.
61. Ibid., 118, 26.7.84.

Chapter VII

1. Pattison MSS, 118, 2.8.84.
2. Ibid., 118, 2.8.84.
3. Bywater MSS, 58, 7.8.84.
4. Bywater MSS, 61, 4.8.84.
5. Lincoln College Order Book, 7 November 1929 'That after payment of any necessary expenses for the immediate repair of Mark Pattison's tomb at Harrogate the balance of Mrs Braithwaite Batty's benefaction for the purpose be invested, and that a Declaration be executed constituting a Trust for the carrying out of the donor's intention with regard to the future upkeep of the monument.' On 30 November 1929 the College agreed to apply the income from the invest-

ment to the upkeep of the tomb. In 1984 the tombstone was put in good order in accordance with the terms of the trust.

6. Pattison MSS, 140, 2.8.84; 118, 2.8.84.
7. Ibid., 140, 2.9.84.
8. Ibid., 118, 21.8.84.
9. Ibid., 118, 4.8.84.
10. Ibid., 118, 11.12.84.
11. Ibid., 118, 4.8.84.
12. Ibid., 118, 21.8.84.
13. Ibid., 118, 21.8.84.
14. *The Academy*, 9.8.84.
15. Bywater mentioned that Kegan Paul had originally expressed an interest in publishing the *Memoirs*. Pattison would have preferred Paul but had already agreed with Macmillans (Bywater MSS, 61, 30.12.83).
16. Pattison MSS, 140, 21.1.85.
17. *The Spectator*, 14 March, 1885.
18. *The Oxford Magazine*, 1885, 175–7.
19. *Macmillan's Magazine*, April 1885, 446–61.
20. Bywater MSS, 61, Aug. 1884.
21. Pattison MSS, 140, 13.4.85, to Gertrude Tuckwell.
22. There are very full accounts of the Dilke divorce case in Roy Jenkins, *Sir Charles Dilke*, (1958), pp. 215–370; and Askwith, *Lady Dilke*, pp. 137–76. Betty Askwith also wrote a novel founded on the case, *The Tangled Webb*, (1960).
23. Leon Edel, *Henry James The Middle Years 1884-1894*, (1963), p. 106.
24. Pattison MSS, 118, 10.9.85.
25. Ibid., 118, 27.9.85.
26. Ibid., 118, 4.10.85.
27. Jenkins, *Sir Charles Dilke*, p. 239.
28. Edel, *Henry James The Conquest of London, 1870-1883*, p. 335.
29. Pattison MSS, 118, 14.12.84.
30. Askwith, *Lady Dilke*, 23.1.86.
31. Ibid., 118, 23.1.86.
32. Askwith, *Lady Dilke*, p. 131.
33. Pattison MSS, 126, 3.6.84.
34. From information kindly supplied by Mrs Mary Bennett.
35. Margaret Woods, *The Invader*, (1907; reprinted & revised 1923), pp. 21, 37, 63, 151.
36. Jane Dashwood, *Three Daughters*, (1930), pp. 15–16, 46, 211, 270.
37. Olive Heseltine, *Lost Content*, (London, 1948; privately printed), pp. 75–6.

Index

Abbreviations used in the index:

MB   Meta Bradley
f.   fellow

MP   Mark Pattison
prof.   professor

James, Henry (*cont.*)
  Sir Charles Dilke 20 n, 21 n, 238; on Mrs
  Rogerson 238, 242
Jenkins, Roy, on the Dilke divorce case 240
Johnson, Mrs Arthur 84, 229
Jowett, Benjamin, master of Balliol Coll. xii,
  72, 74, 96, 109, 112, 163, 177, 181, 188; MP's
  relations with 96-7, 144, 183

Kensington, Fanny, friend of MP and MB xii,
  28, 29, 35, 39, 75, 109, 120, 131, 144, 183;
  writes to Mrs MP 64-5; stays with MP 58,
  59, 205; MP's opinion of 38, 85, 120
King, J. E., f. of Linc. Coll. 102
Knight, William, prof. at St. Andrews 114

Laffan, May, novelist xii, 57, 108, 245 n;
  friendship with MP 54-6, 167-8; visits to
  Oxford 84-6, 95; views on Dilke 55; acts as
  MP's intermediary 85, 165; MP's view of
  84-5, 118-19; MB's attitude towards 85, 95,
  108-9; marriage 180-1
Lake, George, solicitor 170
Lang, Andrew 56
Lankester, Fanny, MB meets 134
Lankester, Ray, MB meets 134, 136
Laseron, Mrs, friend of MB's mother 4, 5, 6
Lathbury, Mrs 130
Lawrence, Henry 110
Lee, Vernon (Violet Paget), MB meets 183
Leopold, Prince, friend of Mrs MP 182
Liddell, Mrs, wife of the Dean of Christ
  Church 60, 182
Lincoln College, Oxford: MP's relations with
  10-11, 122-4, 135, 136, 140-1, 158-9, 192,
  194; college meetings 23, 24, 56, 119-20,
  163, 194; undergraduates of 10-11, 57, 88,
  122; new statutes 25, 123, 124
Liverpool, MB visits 48-9
Lowe, Edward, former pupil of MP, meets
  him at Biarritz 137
Lowell, James Russell, MP meets 141
Lynn, Mrs, MP's landlady in London 176, 197

Macmillan, Frederick, MP meets 141
Malot, Hector, portrays Mrs Crawford in
  novel 245
Manning, Cardinal 242
Martin, Sir Theodore, at St Andrews 115-16
Matthews, Henry, lawyer, in Dilke divorce
  case 241
Meadows, Philippa, cousin of MP 148-9, 179
Merry, W. W., f. of Linc. Coll. 123, 135

Meyer, Paul, MP meets in Paris 68
Middlemarch, MP portrayed in 14, 15, 165
Milner, Alfred, friend of MB xii, 72, 204
Milton, John 24, 115, 118
Monro, D. B. 102
Monro, Hugh 112
Montefiore, Charlotte, friend of MP 27, 47,
  181
Montefiore, Claude, friend of MP 27 n, 141,
  180, 181
Montefiore, Leonard, friend of MP 72, 181,
  201
Moreau, Madame, housekeeper of Mrs MP
  18, 78, 129
Morison, J. C. 104, 135
Morley, John 6, 24, 72, 94 n, 104, 235, 240
Müller, Max 22, 60, 69, 163
Müntz, Eugene, correspondent of Mrs MP
  17, 103, 223, 225

National Health Society 134, 181
Newcome, Mrs, sister of Rhoda Broughton
  26, 56, 84, 86
Newman, Cardinal, relations with MP 12-13,
  149, 202, 227, 233; visits MP in his last ill-
  ness 212-15
Nicholls, H., MB stays with 48
Nicholls, Rose, MB friend of 48, 58, 60, 75, 76,
  130, 207
Nicholson, H. A., prof. at St. Andrews 115
Noel-Harvey, Walter, marries Miss Laffan
  180-1

Oriel College, Oxford 12, 203, 215
Ouida, MP reads novels by 27, 58, 60, 185-5,
  201
Owen, Sidney 60

Pall Mall Gazette 6, 72, 100, 240
Pater, Walter 23, 26, 56, 60
Pattison, Dora, sister of MP 179-80
Pattison, Eleanor, sister of MP 12, 246;
  Pattison dictates last letter to 228-9
Pattison, Fanny (Frances), sister of MP, MP's
  relations with xi, 41, 119, 154; at his death
  bed 226-7
Pattison, Frank, brother of MP, his relations
  with MP xi, 12, 30, 108, 149, 206, 226, 234,
  239, 246; goes on continental tour with MP
  184-7; attitude to MB 232-3
Pattison, Mrs Frank (Margaret) xi, 12, 30, 105,
  108, 147, 176, 206; relations with MP 105,
  186
Pattison, Jane, sister of MP xi, 154; visits MP
  148, 179